Spoken Dari

Mustafa A. Sayd

Spoken Dari

Mustafa A. Sayd

2010
DUNWOODY
PRESS

Spoken Dari

First Edition 2010
Second Impression 2013

All inquiries should be directed to:
Dunwoody Press
6525 Belcrest Road, Suite 460
Hyattsville, MD 20782, USA

ISBN: 978-1-931546-71-3
Library of Congress Control Number: 2009939162
Printed and bound in the United States of America

Table of Contents

Acknowledgments

Co-workers, consultants, and the administration have been very helpful with their advice and counseling during the process which resulted in this accomplishment, so I would like to take this opportunity to thank them.

I would like to thank my wife for finding me the job that resulted in the publication of this book. And I also would like to thank my brother for my many consultations with him, for his being a speaker for this reader, and for his proofreading the Dari text.

I am thankful to Tom Creamer, Director of the Language Research Center, McNeil Technologies, Inc, for giving me this opportunity and for his strong support.

The technical support staff, Aung Kyaw Oo, Mark Jeon, Alan Downing, and Alex Bonder, provided technical assistance in recording and digitizing the audio, formatting the book, and building a database. I am grateful for all their assistance.

I greatly appreciate Dr. R. David Zorc's help guiding me through the process of this project with his long experience in linguistics and his knowledge of practical and theoretical issues.

I would also like to acknowledge the work of the male and female speakers of this reader who wish to remain anonymous for their efforts. The time they spent providing these authentic voiced texts is greatly appreciated.

Finally, I would to like thank Dr. Elizabeth M. Bergman for her advice and assistance and Jack Jones, Rashad Ullah, Erin Gyomber and Carole Breakstone for their tremendous help in proofreading the English translations.

My appreciation to all of you.

Mustafa A. Sayd
Hyattsville, Maryland
January 2010

Introduction

Dari is one of the official languages of Afghanistan. Dari serves as the lingua franca in government and business since it is spoken by a majority of urban dwellers. It is also used in some regions of Afghanistan where other languages are spoken. Dari belongs to the Iranian branch of the Indo-European family of languages. Modern Dari began to develop in the 9th century. It is a continuation of the Khorasanian standard language, which had considerable Parthian and Middle Dari elements. It has a much simpler grammar than its ancestral forms. After the conquest by Arabs in the 7th century, Dari was written in Arabic script with only a few modifications. It has absorbed a vast Arabic vocabulary.

Dari is a dialect of Farsi (Parsi) spoken in Afghanistan, as are Farsi in Iran and Tajiki in Tajikistan. Over the centuries, the languages have been divided by politics and geography. These different names have been used throughout history but refer to the same language. Although the literary Farsi as used in Afghanistan and Iran differs little today, the spoken forms of the language vary considerably.

There are two theories regarding the origin of the word "Dari." One theory relates the origin of the word Dari to the word “dara” or "valley." Many accomplished language researchers admit that the language Dari or Farsi itself was born in Khorasan (the land between the Hindu Kush Mountains in central Afghanistan and the Amu River, consisting of the southern part of Turkmenistan including Marw (Mary), the eastern province of Iran), a mountainous land where people live in numerous valleys. Therefore, the name Dari came to refer to the language spoken by people of the valleys “dara” or in the valleys. The second theory posits that the word Dari comes from the word Darbar that means "court," courts of kings. This theory argues that this language was very respected and chosen for communication at the royal courts. Thus, it came to be known as the language of the courts or “darbari.” Later, the word “darbari” was shortened and evolved into Dari, which still has the same meaning as Darbari.

Afghanistan is divided geographically by high mountains and valleys, which created separate regions for different ethnic groups and many different languages. Ultimately, this separation also caused the Dari language to branch off into several dialects. In this book, I have included selections of Kabuli, Shamali (northern Kabul, also known as Kohdamanee) and Herati dialects of Dari.

About This Book

Inasmuch as the spoken form of Dari differs from the written forms, this book focuses exclusively on spoken Dari. The voice texts in this book are authentic and the speakers are having a normal conversation; they are not reading from a written text.

This book is intended for those who are familiar with written Dari and any elementary-level conversation manual or textbook. Focusing on listening to the voice texts is the key to learning the right pronunciation and differentiating between dialects. This book is divided into three parts. The first part is a brief outline of spoken Dari and a summary with examples of grammatical and systematic differences between spoken Dari and written Dari. The transliteration of examples used in this part is modeled on that used by the Center for Afghanistan Studies in Omaha, Nebraska for the *Dari-English Dictionary*. The main or second part of this book is made up of political, social, economic, educational, and cultural topics that enrich this book with a variety of spoken vocabularies. These topics are transcribed from audio recordings that were made by native language-speakers of Dari from the different Dari regions of Afghanistan. The transcription is written in the Arabic script. Transcriptions preserve the starts, stops, and slips of the tongue that occur in spontaneous speech. An English translation accompanies the transcription. Notes provide descriptive information about linguistic and cultural features of the topics and phrases that may not be clear to users of this book.

There are some things to note when using this book:

1. Brackets indicate the meaning of the prior word or what the speaker meant to say or when the speaker used an English word or phrase in the conversation.

2. The glossary consists of the Dari colloquial and Dari slang words that are not listed in the *Dari-English Dictionary*.

3. The transliteration used in this book was also developed by the Center for Afghanistan Studies in Omaha, Nebraska.

4. In spoken Dari, the word خو khu (OK) indicates rapport and are frequently used by speakers in this book. The meaning totally depends on the context and can include "OK," "Is that right?" "Good," "Alright," and "I hear you."

5. Ellipses ... at the end or in the middle of a sentence mean either that the words were cut off or that the speaker was mumbling (a meaningless sound).

The last part of this book is a glossary of words. It consists of the Dari colloquial and Dari slang words that are not listed in the *Dari-English Dictionary*, which was published by the Center for Afghanistan Studies, University of Nebraska at Omaha in 1993.

Modern Dari Alphabet

Name of Letter	Isolated	Equivalent
alif-mad	آ	aa
alif	ا	a i u
bay	ب	b
pay	پ	p
tay	ت	t
say	ث	s
jeem	ج	j
chay	چ	ch
hay	ح	h
khay	خ	kh
daal	د	d
zaal	ذ	z
ray	ر	r
zay	ز	z
zhay	ژ	zh
seen	س	s
sheen	ش	sh
swaat	ص	s
zwaat	ض	z
toy	ط	t
zoy	ظ	z
ain	ع	a
ghain	غ	gh
fay	ف	f
qaaf	ق	q
kaaf	ک	k
gaaf	گ	g
laam	ل	l
meem	م	m
noon	ن	n
waaw	و	1. w, 2. u, o, oo
hay	ه	1. h. a
hamza	ء	,
yaa	ی	1. y 2. ee ay

Dari Sounds

1. Consonants

Sounds	Dari Examples	English Equivalents	
/b/	baam	(roof)	bit
/p/	pul	(bridge)	part
/t/	tar	(wet)	teach
/j/	jann	(soul, dear)	jump
/ch/	chaay	(tea)	cheese
/kh/	khaana	(house)	loch (Scotch)
/d/	dil	(heart)	dear
/r/	roz	(day)	rose
/z/	zood	(quick)	zoo
/zh/	zharf	(deep)	measure
/s/	sar	(head)	sat
/sh/	shab	(night)	she
/gh/	gharb	(west)	Paris (French)
/f/	fardaa	(tomorrow)	foot
/q/	qalam	(pen)	qalam (Arabic)
/k/	kaar	(work)	keep
/g/	gap	(talk)	gate
/l/	lab	(lip)	lip
/m/	mard	(man)	man
/n/	naam	(name)	name
/w/	waalee	(governor)	well
/h/	hawaa	(air)	house
/y/	yak	(one)	yes

2. Vowels

Sounds	Dari Examples	English Equivalents	
/aa/	aab	(water)	ball
/a/	asp	(horse)	up
/i/	gil	(mud)	sit
/ay/	sayb	(apple)	pay
/ee/	peer	(old)	see
/u/	gul	(flower)	put
/o/	dost	(friend)	note
/oo/	pool	(money)	pool

3. Diphthongs

Sounds	Dari Examples	English Equivalents	
/aay/	paay	(foot)	my
/ai/	nai	(reed)	dates (British)
/aaw/	gaaw	(cow, ox)	gaaw (Dari)
/ow/	now	(new)	now
/oy/	joy	(brook)	hoy (today) (Spanish)
/ooy/	shooy	(husband)	cuy (guinea pig) (Spanish)

Diacritic Marks

ـَ	/a/	مَن	man	I
ـِ	/I/	دِل	dil	heart
ـُ	/u/	گُل	gul	flower
ـّ	for double consonant	اللّه	allah	God
اً	/-an/	يقيناً	yaqeenan	certainly

Calendar Table

Afghanistan			Gregorian
Hamal	حمل	(Aries the Ram)	March 21
Sowr	ثور	(Taurus the Bull)	April 21
Jowzaa	جوزا	(Gemini the Twins)	May 22
Sarataan	سرطان	(Cancer the Crab)	June 22
Asad	اسد	(Leo the Lion)	July 23
[1]Sumbula	سنبله	(Virgo the Virgin)	August 23
Meezan	میزان	(Libra the Balance)	September 23
Aqrab	عقرب	(Scorpio the Scorpion)	October 23
Qows	قوس	(Sagittarius the Archer)	November 22
Jadee	جدی	(Capricorn the Goat)	December 22
Dalwa	دلوَ	(Aquarius the Water Bearer)	January 21
Hoot	حوت	(Pisces the Fishes)	February 20

1 This word is written Sunbula, but it is pronounced Sumbula.

Symbols and Abbreviations

Italicized texts	Dari pronunciation
....	incomplete word or text
adj	adjective
adv	adverb
conj	conjunction
fut	future tense
n	noun
past	past tense
pl	plural
prep	preposition
pres	present tense
pro	pronoun
sing	singular
v	verb
h/s	he/she

Spoken Dari Versus Written

Written Dari	Spoken Dari	Translation

Verbs ending with the letter **dal (د)** drop the final consonant from the written form. For example:

maybaara**d** میبارد	maybaara میباره	it is raining
maykuna**d** میکُند	maykuna میکُنه	h/s is doing
maykhura**d** میخورد	maykhura میخوره	h/s is eating
maynosha**d** مینوشد	maynosha مینوشه	h/s is drinking

[2]bigeeraynd بگیریند bigeerayn بگیرین take! [imp.]

Verbs ending with **wad (ود)** is dropped.

maysha**wad** میشود	maysha میشه	it will happen/it will become
mayra**wad** میرود	mayra میره	h/s is going
bira**wayd** بروید	birayn (Kabuli) برین biray (Kohdamanee) بری	go! [imp. plur]
bira**w** بِرَو	buru بُرُ	go! [imp. sing]

In the following examples, the verbs are past continuous and the letter **ray (ر)** is dropped.

ka**r**d کَرد	kad کَد	h/s did
mayka**r**dam میکَردم	maykadam میکَدم	I was doing
mayka**r**dee میکَردی	maykadee میکَدی	you were doing
mayka**r**d میکَرد	maykad میکَد	he was doing

In most cases, the last consonant of a cluster at the end of a verb is dropped.

mayburdan**d** میبُردند	mayburdan میبُردن	they were carrying
maykhordan**d** میخوردند	maykhordan میخوردن	they were eating
maykhwaandan**d** میخواندند	maykhaandan میخاندن	they were reading

2 The letter bay (بِ) has a primary stress when used with verb forms in the imperative mood.

Written Dari	Spoken Dari	Translation

The word نشستن "sitting" in its various tenses has dramatically different forms between the written and spoken dialect. For example:

neshastan نشستن	shishtan شِشتَن	sitting
may**nesheenad** می‌نشیند	mayshena می شِنه	he/she will sit
neshast نشست	shisht شِشت	he/she sat

There are various sound changes in Dari:

1. Three syllables to two syllables
2. Change **dal** (د) to **tay**(ت)
3. Lose **ha/he** syllables
4. Final consonant lost or changes to the letter **noon** (ن).

For example:

be**dehayd** بدهید	be**tayn** (Kabuli) بتین	give!
	be**tay** (Kohdamanee) بتی	
may**dehayd** میدهید	may**tay** میتی	you will give
may**dehad** میدهد	may**ta** میته	h/s will give
may**dehand** میدهند	may**tan** میتن	they will give

For example:

mayra**wad** میرود	mayra میره	h/s will go
mayra**wand** میروند	mayran میرن	they will go
ma**n** من	ma مه	I
ee**n** این	ee ای	this
da**r** در	da دَ	in, at
ba**raay** برای	[3]ba به	for

---

[3] The word به meaning "to" in both written and spoken Dari, is also used in spoken Dari to replace برای "for"

Written Dari	Spoken Dari	Translation

Dari marks the definite direct object - **raa** (را). In spoken Dari "raa" becomes "a". For example:

gosht-**ash-raa** گوشت اش را	goshtisha گوشتِشه	its meat
qalam-**ash-raa** قلم اش را	qalamisha قلمِشه	his pen
kitaba-**ash-raa** کتاب اش را	kitabisha کتابِشه	his book
khana-**ash-raa** خانه اش را	khanisha خانشه	his house
haywaanaat**raa** حیوانات را	haywaanaata حیواناته	the animals

The **ay** (ای) is dropped from possessive pronouns. For example:

khaanee-**ay**shaan خانۀ ایشان	khaaneeshaan خانیشان	h/h or their house
qalamee-**ay**shaan قلمِ ایشان	qalameeshaan قلمشان	h/h or their pen
motaree-**ay**shaan موتر ایشان	motareeshaan موترِشان	h/h or their

In spoken Dari, the letter **hay** (ه) sound is usually eliminated in nouns that are pluralized with the suffix **haa** (ها). For example:

bacha-**haa** بچه ها	bachaa بچا	boys
ti.fil-**haa** طفلها	ti.flhaa طفلا	children
baagh-**haa** باغ ها	baaghaa باغا	gardens
maktab-**haa** مکتب ها	maktabaa مکتبا	schools
kaar-**haa** کارها	kaaraa کارا	works

Other noun changes:

bi**raadar** برادر	biyadar بیَدر	brother
khwaa**h**ar خواهر	khwaar خوار	sister
qal.a قلعه	qalaa قلا	palace, compound

Written Dari	Spoken Dari	Translation

In spoken Dari, the verb **ast** (است) "being" loses its last consonant. For example:

as**t** است	as اس	is
nays**t** نیست	nays نیس	is not
raadio **ast** رادیو است	raadios رادیوس	radio is

Selections

آمدن به امریکا[1]

احمد: سلامالیکم، خوب استی؟

جاوید: سلامالیک، چطور استی؟

احمد: بخیر استی؟

جاوید: خوب استی بخیر استی صحتت خوب اس؟

احمد: بخیر آمدین؟

جاوید: فضل خدا.

احمد: چطور بود درراه خو بتکلیف نشدین انشاء الله؟

جاوید: نی فضل خدا بالکل بسیار بخوبی به آرامی آمدم تکلیف نبود مصؤن بود راه آرام بود بسیار خوب بود.

احمد: خو... خو... بسیار خوب چه وخت رسیدین بخیر؟

جاوید: فقط تاریخ بیست و هفت دسمبر دوهزارویک رسیدم. اینجه بخیرده روز اس. ده روزه داینجه تیر کدُم.

احمد: خو.. خو..

جاوید: فضای بسیار خوب آرام بسیار خوب.

احمد: خو ..بسیار خوب آ... کلگی خوب بود فامیل همه گی خوب بود؟

---

[1] The speakers on this selection are Ahmad and Javid they attended high school in Afghanistan and Javid is a graduate of Kabul University and has a slight Kabuli accent and Ahmad speaks Kohdamani dialect of Dari.

Coming to America

Ahmad: May peace be up on you, are you well?

Javid: May peace be up on you, how are you?

Ahmad: Are you doing fine?

Javid: Are you doing fine? And how is your health?

Ahmad: Did you arrive safely?

Javid: By the grace of God, yes.

Ahmad: How was your trip? Did you have any trouble on the way here? God willing, you didn't.

Javid: No. By the grace of God, I arrived here without any trouble. And I had a safe trip.

Ahmad: OK, all right, very well. When did you arrive here?

Javid: I arrived here on December 21, 2001 exactly. It has been ten days. I have been here for ten days.

Ahmad: Good, good.

Javid: It is a very nice and pleasant environment here.

Ahmad: Very well, is everybody in the family well?

جاوید: همه گی خوب فضل خدا خوب اس. شما چطور استین خانه خیرت اس؟
احمد: فضل خدا شکر.
جاوید: دوستا دگه رفیقا همه خوب استن؟
احمد: آ، کلگی خوب استن شکر خوش شدیم از آمدن تان چوشمای ما روشن شد.
جاوید: بخیر باشین. کار و بار چطور اس. خوب اس؟ کارمیری کار داری نداری؟
احمد: آن، کاروبار خوب اس فضل خدا. کار میریم ومیایم. دگه از کار خو آدم هیچ نجات نداره.
جاوید: آن کار یک جز زنده گیس مجبور اس آدم کارکنه. کار که در زندگی نباشه. بیکاری خو... از یک طرف تنبلی آدمه خسته می سازه ، از طرف دگه زندگی پیش نمی ره. کار مجبور اس آدم کنه
احمد: بلی.
جاوید: د هر گوشی دنیا باشی.
احمد: چطو بود کاکایم شان خوب بودن؟
جاوید: آ فضل خدا خوب بودن صحتش خوب بود. همه گی دوستا اقارب کلگی خوب بودن. سلام می گفتن بر تان.
احمد: چطو بود مریضی کاکایم خوب بود؟

Javid: By the grace of God, everybody is well. How are you, and how is your family?

Ahmad: By the grace of God, fine and thank God.

Javid: Are your relatives and friends doing well?

Ahmad: Yes, thank God, everybody is fine. I am so glad that you came and I am so delighted to see you.

Javid: God bless you. How is your life and how is your work? Is it good? Do you go to work? Do you have a job or not?

Ahmad: Yes, by the grace of God, work and life are good. Yes, I work. It is impossible for someone not to work.

Javid: Of course, work is part of everyone's life. Everybody has to work. If you are jobless, you will be bored. On the other hand, life will not go on, so everybody has to work.

Ahmad: Yes.

Javid: No matter where in the world you are.

Ahmad: How is my uncle and the rest of the family?

Javid: By the grace of God, he is well and healthy. All friends and relatives were well and they said "Hello" to you.

Ahmad: How was my uncle's health?[2] Was he feeling better?

---

[2] In Dari, "How was my uncle's sickness?"

جاوید: آ، فضل خدا خوب اس صحتش خوب اس مریضی نداره تنا روی سفیدیس. د سن بالا د سن روی سفیدی آدم ضیف می شه دگه ضئیفی را داشت. فضل خدا مریضیش خوب اس زیر کنترول اس. بعضی تکلیفها داشت مثل تکلیف فشار اما زیر کنترول اس.

احمد: اوشتکا خوب بودن مکتب می رفت کلگی؟

جاوید: همه خوب اس فضل خدا کلش مکتب می رفت درس می خاندن.

احمد: رخصت نشدن د این وختا؟

جاوید: آ.. یکچند روز رخصتی زمستانی داشتن بر یک پانزده روز بعد از رخصتی خود باز به مکتب می رن. مکتب شان جریان داره.

احمد: اوضاع خوب بود از نگاه اوم...اقتصاد و چیزا؟

جاوید: اوضاع ... ما خو از پاکستان آمدیم اوضاع پاکستان از نگاه اقتصادی خوب اس. خوب منفعت زیاد گرفت از این کومکی که به اتحاد ضد تیروززم کرد. مگم اوضاع افغانستان بسیار خراب است. وضع اقتصادی شان بسیار خراب خراب اس.

احمد: خو ..خو بسیار خوب.[3]

جاوید: مردم نه خوراک داره، نه لباس داره، نه دوا داره، هیچ نوع امکاناتی نداره د زنده گی خود. مردم افغانستان اُمید است که بعد از ای خوب شوه.

احمد: خو بسیار خوب.

---

[3] In the background of this sentence, the listener is telling the speaker that he is listening; his is called a rapport marker or a phatic communion.

Javid: Yes, by the grace of God. His health is very good. He is not sick, only that he is just old. Being old, when age increases one becomes weak. So he was weak. By the grace of God his health is good and his sickness is under control. He had high blood pressure but it is under control.

Ahmad: How are the children? Are they in school?

Javid: By the grace of God, they are all in school and they are all studying.

Ahmad: Didn't they have a break recently?

Javid: Yes, they had a winter break for about fifteen days, but they are back in school now. School is in session.

Ahmad: How are the economic and other situations over there?

Javid: Situations... I came from Pakistan. Pakistan's economic situation was very good because the antiterrorism coalition countries have been helping Pakistan economically. But the safety and security situations in Afghanistan are very bad, the economic situation, too.

Ahmad: OK, very good.

Javid: People in Afghanistan don't have food, don't have clothes, don't have medicine and don't have anything to live on. But the people of Afghanistan have hopes that things will get better for them.

Ahmad: OK, very good.

Vocabulary

سلامالیکم *phrase religion colloquial* السلام علیکم *phrase* Islamic greeting (May peace be upon you)
استی *colloquial* هستی *v, pres* you are *v* being
چوطو *adv colloquial* چطور condition, how
صحتته *n colloquial* صحت تو، صحت شما *n+pron* your health
اس *colloquial* است *v, pres* is, to be
آمدین *colloquial* آمدید *past, pl* you came
خو *colloquial* خوب *adv* good, OK, well
نشدین *colloquial* نشدید *past, pl* you did not become, you did not get
وخت *colloquial* وقت *adv, n* time, period, moment *adv* early
اینجه *colloquial* اینجا *adv, n* here, this place
تیر *colloquial* گذشتاندن *adv, n* the act of passing, the act of crossing *v* staying
کلگی *colloquial* همه *prep* all, everyone
همه گی *colloquial* همه *prep* all, everyone
استین *colloquial* استتید *v, pl* you (pl) are
خانه *colloquial* فامیل *n* family *n* home, house
دوستها *colloquial* دوستا *n* friends, relatives
دگه *colloquial* دیگر *adj, adv* other, else *adv* then
رفیقا *colloquial* رفیقها *n,adj, pl* friends
استن *colloquial* استند *v, pl* they are
چشمای ما *colloquial* چشمهای ما *n, pl* our eyes
باشین *colloquial* باشید *v, pl* you stay, you are, may you be, may you remain
بار *colloquial* زندگی *n, sing* life *n* cargo, luggage
وختا *colloquial* وقتها *adv* recently *adv* times, sometimes
یکچندروز *colloquial* یک مدت، برای چند روز *adv* a few days, for awhile
میری *colloquial* میروید، میروی *v, pres, sing* you (sing) are going, you will go
میرم *colloquial* میروم *v, pres, pl* we are going, we will go
میایم *colloquial* میآیم *v, pres, pl* we are coming, we will come
نداره *colloquial* ندارد *v, sing* will not, does not have
کونه *colloquial* کند *v, sing* do, to do
نباشه *colloquial* نباشد *v, sing* not to be
آدمه *colloquial* آدم را *n, sing* to a person, to one's self, human, Adam, someone
سازه *colloquial* سازد *v, sing* to make, to turn into
نمی ره *colloquial* نمیرود *v, sing* would not go, will not go

د *colloquial* در *prep* in, at
گوشی *colloquial* گوشهٔ *n* part, corner
باشه *colloquial* باشد *v, sing* to be, is
بودن *colloquial* بودند *v, pl* they were
شان *colloquial* ایشان *pro* they
می گفتن *colloquial* می گفتند *past, pl* they would say, they said
برتان *colloquial* برای تان *prep* for you, to you
نداره *colloquial* ندارد *v, sing* does not have
تنا *colloquial* تنها *adj, adv, conj* only, just, alone
ضیف *colloquial* ضعیف *adj* weak
می شه *colloquial* می شود *v, fut* will become, will be done, will happen
ضیفی *colloquial* ضعیفی *adj, n* weakness
زیر *colloquial* تحت *prep* below, beneath, under
کنترول *colloquial English* تداوی *n* treatment, control
اوشتکا *colloquial* اطفال *n* children
کلّش *colloquial* کل ایشان *phrase* they all, all of them
می خَاند *colloquial* می خوانند *past, pl* they studied
وختا *colloquial* وقتها *adv* periods, times
یکچند روز *colloquial* یک مدت، برای چند روز *adv, phrase* a few days, for a while
می رَن *colloquial* می روند *v, fut* they go, they will go
داره *colloquial* دارد *v, sing* it is happening *v, sing* to have, he/she has
اوم *colloquial* *hesitation form* hesitation form
چیزا *colloquial* چیزها *n* things
تیرورزم *colloquial* عمل تیرورستی *n* terrorism
مگم *colloquial* مگر *conj* but, besides that
اقتصادی شام *colloquial* اقتصادی اش هم *phrase* also it is economical
ای *colloquial* این *adj, pro* this

مکتب ابتدائیه[4]

احمد: ما که مکتب می رفتیم ...آ.. وضع اقتصادی کمی خوب بود نسبت به وخت شما. اما در وخت ما مکتب ما سر نداشت و دیوال نداشت و چیزا. مچم که از شما چطور ..ام ... از شما بهتر بود دگه.

جاوید: از ما وقتی که مکتب می رفتیم د ابتدایه شامل شدیم مکتب ما شش صنف داشت و شش اتاق هر صنف در یک اتاق بود و خوش بختانه که در اُو وخت بر شاگردا چوکی هم بود میز هم بود در او صنفا یک دراز چوکی می گفتیم که دو نفر شاگرد پالوی هم می ششتن. یک میز پیشروی هر دوی شان بود خانی داشت که کتابای خوده مابینش می ماندن در روی سر میز کتاب و کتابچه را می ماندن نوشته می کردن می خاندن. مگر در وخت شما د مکتب میزوای چیزا نبود انی؟

احمد: د وخت ما نی چوکی بود بیدر، نی دگه بود. سر سنگ می ششتیم قرار درس می خاندیم. اُو رام که پیسه میپرتافتیم که بوریه بخریم او پیسه هم بس نمی کرد پیسه رام یا سر معلم می خورد. خو مخصد هیچ چیز نمی شد.

جاوید: در اُو وخت مکتب در منطقه شما که آمد ای... مکتب دگی در او نواهی در او نزدیکیها بود یا تنا اَمی مکتب بود ده اَموجه.

---

[4] The speakers on this selection are Ahmad and Javid they attended high school in Afghanistan and Javid is a graduate of Kabul University and has a slight Kabuli accent and Ahmad speaks Kohdamani dialect of Dari.

Elementary School

Ahmad: Back in the days when I went to school... Oh... the economic situation was better then when you went to school. But in my time, my school didn't have a roof or walls or anything. I don't know if yours was better off.

Javid: When I first started going to school, I attended elementary school. There were six classes and six classrooms in our school, so one room per class. Fortunately, there were chairs and desks for students at that time. There were benches which we called "long chairs." Two students sat next to each other on a "long chair." And there were desks with drawers; students kept their books in there, and students used the desk to read and write. But your school didn't have desks or anything like that, did it?

Ahmad: In my time there weren't chairs or anything else, my brother. We sat on rocks and studied. Also then, we raised money to buy reed mats, but there wasn't enough money; the school principal would keep some of the money. Anyway, we couldn't buy anything.

Javid: At the time when the school was established in your area, was there any other school close by.

احمد: نی، مکتب بوده اما دور بود بسیار. مکتب سرای خواجه بود، اما راهش بسیار دور بود به تکلیف می شدیم دگه. اُورام ام... خیر ببینه حاجی صاحب که مکتبه اَموجه آورده بود دگه.

جاوید: مکتب شما چند معلم داشت؟ ... از... مربوط دگه کدام مدیریت بود؟ مربوط کدام مکتب دگه شاخچه کدام مکتب دگه بود؟ یا چه ترتیب یا مکتببی بود که مربوط وزارت بودچه قسم پروگرامش؟

احمد: مکتب ما مربوط وزارت بود اما ابتدایه بود. باز د لیسه د میر بچه کوت می رفتیم.

Ahmad: No, there was a school but it was too far. It was the Saray Khwaja School, but it was too far and it was difficult for us (to get there). So, may Haji Sahib be blessed because he established a school there.

Javid: How many teachers were there at your school? … From ... was your school under another administration or a branch of another school or what? Or was the school part of the ministry, and how was its program?

Ahmad: Our school was part of the ministry but it was elementary. Then I went to Merbachakot High School.

Vocabulary

سر *colloquial* سقف *n* roof, top, ceiling
دیوال *colloquial* دیوار *n* wall
مچم *colloquial* مه چه میدانم *v, phrase* I don't know
او وخت *colloquial* آن وقت *adv* back then, that time
شاگردا *colloquial* شاگردها *n* students
پالوی *colloquial* پهلوی *prep* next to, beside
می ششت *colloquial* می نشست *v* would sit, used to sit
کتابای *colloquial* کتابهای *n* thier book, books
مابینش *colloquial* در بینش *prep* inside (n, pron), in
می ماندن *colloquial* می گذاشتند *v, pl* they put, they would put
اَنی *colloquial* یا نه *conj* isn't it?, or not?
بیدر *colloquial* برادر *n* brother, pal
ششتیم *colloquial* نشستیم *v* we used to sit
اورام *colloquial* آنرا هم *prep* then that, also that
پیسه *colloquial* پول، افغانی *n* currency, Afghani currency
می پرتافتیم *colloquial* جمع می کردیم، می انداختیم *v* we used to collect *v* we used to throw
بوریه *colloquial* بوریا *n* reed mat
می خورد (lit. used to eat) *colloquial* می دزدید *v* used to stell
مخصد *colloquial* مقصد *n* aim, goal, purpose
دگی *colloquial* دیگری *adv* other, another, the rest of
اَمی *colloquial* همین *adv* this one
اَموجه *colloquial* همان جای *adv* there, that place

دوران طُفولیت[5]

احمد: ما که خورد بودیم ام.. ام.. مه بودم و بیدر زادا[6]یم بود و بچای کاکایم کلان بود اما بودیم سه چار تا همرایش سات تیری می کدیم شما چطو، بیدرزاده و چیزایتان بود؟

جاوید: ما که خورد بودیم .. ام... بیدرزادایم نبود در او وخت بچای کاکا و دخترای کاکا و اینا بودن که با هم یکجا سا تیری می کدیم. چون که ما همراه کاکایم همراه با هم در یک قلا زندگی می کردیم. بچای کاکایم کسی که هم سن مه بود سید امین نام داشت بچه کاکایم بود د توپبازی(توپ دنده)[7] یکجای بودیم. دگه ما زنده گی ما خیلی بسیار پر محبت و دوستانه.

احمد: سر شماهم د خانه کار می کدن اَو چیزاره میا وردن؟

جاوید: بعض کار را د خانه می کدیم چون کار خانه خو در زنده گی اطرافی وزنده گی افغانستان تقسیم اس.

احمد: بلی، آن.

جاوید: کار کلان و سخته پدر می کنه، بعضی کارای یک قسمت خانه ره مادر می کنه، و یک قسمت کارای باقیمانده ره که کار خورد و ریزه اس او یک زره اَو بیار و یکمی نان بیآر و ای بیآر و باز کارای سر دستی ما میگویمشه. ایره سر طفلا و سر بچا و دخترای خورد می کُنَن.

احمد: خو خوب.

جاوید: باز کار دخترا مالوم اس که به نان آوردن و جارو کدن چیزا ... کار بچا ایس که یک زره حیواناته کمک می کنن، جابجا کدنش. به ای قسم کار تقسیم می شود.

---

5 The speakers on this selection are Ahmad and Javid they attended high school in Afghanistan and Javid is a graduate of Kabul University and has a slight Kabuli accent and Ahmad speaks Kohdamani dialect of Dari.

6 Nephews here, means sons of brothers.

7 A game similar to baseball that is played with a softer ball (like a tennis ball or a ball made of cloth). There are two bases in this game. Instead of tagging the runner, the runner could be hit with the ball. Instead of pitching the ball to the batter, the ball is gently lobbed in front of the batter from a close distance.

Childhood

Ahmad: When we were little, it was my nephews, my cousins, and I. My cousins were grown up at that time. There were the four of us who played and had fun together. What about you? Did you have any nephews to play with?

Javid: When we were little, there were no nephews at that time. But there were my uncle's sons and daughters and among my cousins, Sayed Amin was my age, we played toop-danda together. We had a lovely and friendly life.

Ahmad: Did they make you work at home too? Did they make you bring water and things like that to the house?

Javid: We did some work at home. Work is divided among family members in the Afghanistan countryside.

Ahmad: Yes, OK.

Javid: The father does the most difficult tasks. The mother does some of the work. They make the children, young boys and girls, do the rest of the work, the least difficult (tedious) ones like bringing water and bread to the house. We call it light work.

Ahmad: Good, good.

Javid: Then of course, girls' work is to help prepare food and sweep, these things. Boys help with feeding the domestic animals and bringing them to the barn. This way the work is divided.

احمد:	خو...خو.

جاوید:	د وخت شما هم تا جائی بود ای کارا ره شما هم می کدی.

احمد:	آن، ماهم دگه بعض کاره می کدیم اما ما تیر می کدیم خوده. می رفتیم یک جای دگه یا کلک بازی (دنده کلک)[8] میکردیم یا توپ بازی میکدیم. باز کاکایم میآمد که چه شَوَدی اُو بچا بیائی دگه. خوب بود دگه د وخت ما ساتیری هم بود کارهم بود.

جاوید:	در قسمت مکتب ما خو ... مکتبه می خاندیم اما اکثر وخت ساتیری وتفریح ما وخت زمستان بود.

احمد:	خو... خو

جاوید:	زمستان چون مکتبا رخصت می بود بر سه ماه آه.... بر... مکتب رخصت بود ما د خانه می بودیم از طرف صبح وچاشت دو وخت می رفتیم به مسجد درس می خاندیم باقی همی ساتیری و تفریح می کدیم بین هم. باز کمک همراه پدر خود می کدیم.

احمد:	آن همطُو بود از مام.

[8] A game of tip-cat played by children (in which a player using a stick taps a tip-cat on its end, and as it flies up, strikes it to drive it as far as possible).

Ahmad: Good, good.

Javid: Back in your day, did you do some kind of work?

Ahmad: Yes, we did some work; we also skipped work and then went to play the game of danda-klik and toop-danda. Then my uncle looked for us and shouted, "Where are you boys? Come to the house." It was good back then. We did some work and we had fun too.

Javid: Concerning school, we did go to school, but winter was the time for us to play and have fun.

Ahmad: Good, good.

Javid: Since we had a break from school in the winter for three months, we were home. At that time we studied in the mosque in the morning and in the afternoon. For the rest of the time we played and had fun, all of us together. We also helped our fathers with work.

Ahmad: Yes, ours was like that.

Vocabulary

ام *colloquial hesitation form* hesitation form
مه *colloquial* من *pro* I
بیدرزادایم *colloquial* برادرزاده هایم *n* my nephews (my brother's sons and daughters)
بچای *colloquial* بچه های *n* sons of
سات تیری *colloquial* ساعت تیری *n* playing, amusement, having a good time
چیزایتان *colloquial* چیزهای تان *n* your things
سخته *colloquial* سخت را *adj* the dificult one
اَو *colloquial* آب *n* water
سردستی *colloquial* کار آسان خانه *phrase* easy housework, light housework
میگویمشه *colloquial* آنرا یاد میکنیم *phrase* we call it
ایره *colloquial* اینرا *adv* this thing, this
سر *colloquial* توسط *adv* by, with *n* head
طفلا *colloquial* طفلها *n* children
مالوم *colloquial* معلوم *adj* known, visible, clear
کلک *colloquial* کلک *n* a game played with a short pice of wood (the size of a pen) and a bat

جغرافیه افغانستان[9]

قسمت اول

احمد: منطقی شمالی که شما استین، از نگاه جغرافیائی کدام شارای دگه طرف مثلاً جنوب وشمال وشرق و غرب اس.

جاوید: شمالی یک منطقی اس که میفامی شاید، که در قسمت شمال کابل واقیست ای یک دره ای بسیار طولانیس که طرف کوها احاطه شده و از ای کوها به قدر کافی د طول زمان مواد رسوبی آمده د منطقه آمده و ترسب کده ویک ساحه زراعتی بسیار خوب به میان آورده.

احمد: بلی.

جاوید: وهم از ای کوها آب بقدر کافی پائین می شه که ای منطقه از آب به انواع مختلف در بعض قسمت از دریا استفاده می کنن. کانال کشیدن در بعض مناطق به شکل کاریز[10] اس و در بعضی جاها به شکل چشمه زارها بیرون بر آمده.

احمد: کوهای اوندوکش طرف شمال افغانستان اس، یا؟

جاوید: کوه اندوکوش اصلاً یک سلسله کوهیست که از شرق... از شمال شرق افغانستان ای به جنوب غرب افغانستان رسیده. مگر در منطقه ما به طرف شمال شمالی واقیست که کوه تونل سالنگ[11] که سرک عمومی که ببین شمال و جنوب وصل کده از بین از اُو تیر میشه. منطقی شمالی که ما گفیم که ای شامل سه ولایت اس. یک قسمت ... چار و پنج ولسوالی از ای مربوط ولایت کابل اس باقیمانده یک ولایت پروان اس د ای منطقه و یکی هم ولایت کاپیساس. ای از لحاظ جغرافیائی ای منطقه تقریباً د مرکز افغانستان واقعس.

---

9 The speakers on this selection are Ahmad and Javid they attended high school in Afghanistan and Javid is a graduate of Kabul University and has a slight Kabuli accent and Ahmad speaks Kohdamani dialect of Dari.

10 Underground tunnels are dug to transport water, sometimes more than 2 mile long, collect water from the base of of mountains and delivers it to basins to provide water for irrigation and domestic use. These tunnels, called "karezes," have supplied a significant portion of the water for Afghanistan. The mounds result from numerous vertical shafts used to keep the water flowing.

11 It is also known as Salang Pass.

Geography of Afghanistan
Part One

Ahmad: Shamally (northern region of Kabul), where you are from, geographically which cities are located to the south, north, east, and west of it?

Javid: As you probably know, Shamally (northern region) is located north of Kabul. It is a long valley which is surrounded by mountains. After a long period of time the silt was washed down the mountains and was deposited in this region making this land suitable for farming.

Ahmad: Yes.

Javid: And also enough water comes down the mountains to irrigate this region. The water is used for multiple purposes. In some areas they have canals. In some areas it is kareez (subterranean irrigation). In some areas the water comes out of the ground as springs.

Ahmad: Are the Hindokush Mountains located in the north of Afghanistan? Or...

Javid: The Hindokush Mountains range from the northeast of Afghanistan to the southwest of Afghanistan, but they are located north of Shamally. The Salang Tunnel is in this mountain. This tunnel connects the road between north and south Afghanistan.There are three provinces in Shamally. There are four or five Kabul districts in the Shamally region in addition to Kapisa and Parwan provinces. Geographically, Shamally is located approximately in the middle of Afghanistan.

احمد: خو بسیار خوب.

جاوید: از لحاظ ....

احمد: در اطرافش کوهای دگه، کوه اوندوکش.

جاوید: بلی، از لحاظ دریا د آبای کافی مثل دریای سالنگ اس در اینجه دریای غوربند اس دریای پنجشیر اس. از ای سر چشمه می گیره از همی منطقه ای منطقه ره آبیاری می کُونه تیر می شه.

احمد: ای کوه بابا کدام طرف واقس؟

جاوید: کوه بابا در مرکز افغانستان اس که از شاخی کوه هندوکوش اس. از قسمت غرب شمالی واقست.

احمد: خو ... دقسمت غرب شمالی، طرف شرق چطور؟

جاوید: به طرف شرق شمالی کوهای به نام کوه صافیس او هم از سلسله کوهای هندوکش اس لاکن کوهای که ارتفایش کم اس آه... برف گیر نیست، سرد می باشه. برف و باران داره لاکن مثل سالنگ برف گیرو واچیز بلند نیست.

احمد: خو..خو..بسیار خوب.

Ahmad: Good, very good.

Javid: Concerning …

Ahmad: Around it are other mountains, the Hindokush Mountains.

Javid: Concerning the river, there is enough river water. For example, there are the Salang River, the Ghorband River, and the Panjshir River that originate here. They go through and irrigate this region.

Ahmad: In which direction is Baba Mountain?

Javid: Baba Mountain is located in the center of Afghanistan, west of Shamally. It is a branch of the Hindokush Mountains.

Ahmad: OK, to the west of Shamally. What about to the east?

Javid: To the east of Shamally there is a mountain called Safi. It is a range of the Hindokush Mountains but the altitude is not high. It is cold here but snow does not accumulate. It rains and snows here, but snow does not accumulate as it does on Salang Pass and it is not as high.

Ahmad: Good, good, very good.

Vocabulary

شمالی *colloquial* شمال *n* a region five miles north of the capital Kabul

منطقی *colloquial* منطقه ای *n* region, area

کاریز *colloquial* کاریز *n* underground tunnels dug to transport water, over 10 miles. Collected from the base of wetter mountains and delivered to drier basins to provide water for irrigation and domestic use. These tunnels, called Karaze, have supplied a significant portion of consumptive water in Afghanistan for many centuries. The mounds result from numerous vertical shafts used by workers to keep the water flowing.

اندوکش *colloquial* هندوکش *n* Hindu Kush the famous mountain range of Afghanistan

چار *colloquial* چهار *n* four

واقس *colloquial* واقع است *v* is located

ارتفایش *colloquial* ارتفاع اش *n* Its height

جغرافیه افغانستان

قسمت دوم[12]

احمد: اه... د افغانستان دگه شارای بزرگ بسیار اس، نی؟ کدام شارارا شما رفتین، دیدین؟

جاوید: افغانستان یک مملکتیست که نظر به دنیا بسیار پس مانده اس. لاکن شهرهای بزرگش مثل بعد از کابل هرات اس، قندهار اس، مزارشریف اس، جلال آباد اس، کندذ اس، ای شهرهای بزرگ اس. تو نرفتی د این شهرها د کدام یکیش؟

احمد: نی، مه نرفتیم ، خو، د کابل رفتیم. کابل دگه یک شار خوب مقبول بود و تعمیرهای کانکریتی داشت و سرک پخته و سینما و دگه و دگه داشت. مگم د اُو شارای چیز نرفتیم. شار مزار چطور اس؟ کابل واری اس یا ...؟

جاوید: شار مزار هم، آن... یکی از شارای بسیار خوب افغانستان اس، تعمیرات پخته داره سرک های پخته داره ویک ... تقریباً از یک طرف شهر بندریس که به آسیای میانه ارتباط داره از طرف دگه یک شهر اه... عایدات زراعتی منطقه در اُنجه خوب اس.

احمد: خودت گفتی که د اُنجه رفتیم ، کار کردیم نی؟

جاوید: بلی آن، مه د اُنجه د سرکها تقریباً چار ماه را د کار ستاژ خوده د سرک هیرتان کابل ... هیرتان و اه ... سرک هیرتان کار کردیم.

احمد: سرک هیرتان بین چیز اس ... بین روسیه ومزار؟

جاوید: بین اه... یک قسمت مزار. از مزار نا رسیده یکجابه نائب آباد می گویند ، بین از اُنجه و بین تِرمِز یک شهر ازبکستان اس.

احمد: خوخو...

جاوید: و در سرحد افغانستان را هیرتان میگویند، هَمُو شهر که بفاصلهٔ نَوَد کیلومتر یک سرک اس. سرک راه تجارتیس.

---

[12] The speakers on this selection are Ahmad and Javid they attended high school in Afghanistan and Javid is a graduate of Kabul University and has a slight Kabuli accent and Ahmad speaks Kohdamani dialect of Dari.

Geography of Afghanistan
Part Two

Ahmad: Are there large cities in Afghanistan? Which cities have you visited?

Javid: Afghanistan is left behind by the rest of the world, but the large cities are Kabul, Kandahar, Herat, Mazar-e-Sharif, Jalalabad, and Kunduz. These are large cities. Have you visited any of these cities?

Ahmad: No, I haven't visited any. I have only visited Kabul. Kabul was a beautiful city; it had concrete buildings, paved roads, and movie theaters and all those things. But I haven't visited the others. How is Mazar City? Is it like Kabul? Or...

Javid: Mazar City is also one of the most beautiful cities in Afghanistan. It has concrete buildings and paved roads. On the one hand, it is a border city for Central Asia; on the other hand, it has abundant agricultural produce.

Ahmad: You said that you have been there and worked. Or haven't you?

Javid: Yes, I worked there in my internship on the Hairatan Road, the road that connects Kabul and Hairatan.

Ahmad: Hairatan Road is between Mazar and Russia.

Javid: It goes along some part of Mazar and Naiebabad, just before you get to Mazar and Termez, a city in Uzbekistan.

Ahmad: Good, good.

Javid: They call the Afghan border Hairatan. The city has a 90-km-long road and this road is a trade road.

احمد: خوخو ...
جاوید: تو پاکستان خو رفتی نی؟
احمد: آن، پاکستان رفتیم.
جاوید: فقط اه...
احمد: مثل ....
جاوید: جلال آباد که بطرف پشاور سرک رفته هموطو از مزار بطرف ترمز و بطرف ازبکستان سرک بر آمده.
احمد: باز از مزار ایطرف بغلان هم خوب شار اس، میگویند من نه دیدیم دگه.
جاوید: از مزارکه ایطرف آدم میآمد، د ایبک میآمد، اُقَدَر شهر کلان نداره. شهر خورد اس. باز اه ... پلخمری میآیه. پلخمری شهرک خوبش اس. پخته خوب و تجارتی و حاصلات.
احمد: فابریکه و چیزاهم داره؟
جاوید: زراعتی وفابریکه و فابریکی نساجی داره، فابریکای مختلف ذغال سنگ داره، فابریکای مختلف داره. بغلان هم خوب فابریکی قند داره هم... بوره و قند تولید می کنه. حاصلات شان بسیار خوب اس د اُو منطقه. دگه شهرهایش ...
احمد: خو... دگه کدام شهرها اس د اُو منطقه؟
جاوید: شهر قندار ، از شهر قندار هم خوب شهر اس. لیکن یک قسمت شهر سابقه بود، متأسفانه که د این جنگها و د وخت تجاوز روس اُو از بین رفته. قسمت ...
احمد: میگن شهر قندار بسیار شار تاریخیس. آثار تاریخی بسیار زیاد اس د اُوجه؟
جاوید: د شار اُقَدَر آثارتاریخی نیس، بسیارکَم اس. آثار تاریخی زیاد در طرف مزار اس، که قلاه بلخ اس و قلاهای بسیار مهم اس.
د طرف قندار نی، د طرف نیمروز یک شار بسیار کلان و یکجای دگه اس بنام قلاه بُست میگن. د منطقهٔ سیستان افغانستان واقعس.

Ahmad: Good, good. ...

Javid: You went to Pakistan, didn't you?

Ahmad: Yes, I did go to Pakistan.

Javid: Only...

Ahmad: Like...

Javid: The road goes from Jalalabad to Peshawar, the same way this road goes from Mazar to Uzbekistan.

Ahmad: Coming this way from Mazar, people say Baghlan is a beautiful city; I haven't seen it.

Javid: Coming this way from Mazar, it is Aibak city, which is not a large city. It is a small city. Then farther this way it is the city of Pul-e-Khumri, which is a beautiful city with paved roads and concrete buildings. It is a trade city and has good produce.

Ahmad: Are there factories and things like this?

Javid: It is agricultural and has various factories, like Nasaji, a coal factory, and has other kinds of factories. Baghlan also has a factory, a sugar factory that produces granulated sugar and lump sugar. Production is good in that region. The other cities...

Ahmad: Good. Which other cities are there in that region?

Javid: Kandahar City. Kandahar City is also a beautiful city. A part of the city was ancient, but unfortunately it was destroyed during the recent war and during the Russian invasion.

Ahmad: People say that Kandahar is a very historic city and there are a lot of historical monuments.

Javid: There are not that many monuments in the city. There are a few. There are many historical monuments in the Mazar region, like Qala-e-Balkh and other famous Qala (palace, compound).

Not in the Kandahar area, but there is a very large one in the Nimrooz area.....(word cut off) In another area, it is called "Qala-e-Bust." It is located in Seestan, Afghanistan.

احمد: بسیار تاریخِیس چند هزار سال باشه همو قلاه بُست؟

جاوید: اُو قلاه بُستِ را من نمی فهمم ، تقریباً دوهزار سال قبل اُو ساخته شده.

احمد: اُو ... وی ...بسیار.

جاوید: خود قلاه چیزی نمانده تنها یک قسمت دروازیش مانده و باقی به مرور زمان جریان ریگ توسط باد د اُجه برده شده ، زیاد قسمت قلاه ره د زیر ریگ گور کرده.

احمد: خو خو...

جاوید: و هم جریان دریای هیلمند زیادتر ریگه د بالای منطقه هوار کرده. دگه شار قندار حاصلات زراعتیش بسیار خوب اس، میوه جات خوب داره.

احمد: میگن خوب اَنار داره قندار؟

جاوید: قندار اَنار بسیار خوب داره، انگور بسیار خوب داره، حاصلاتش بسیار خوب اس. میوه جات قندار. دگه شهر جلال آباد خوب اس.

احمد: این انارش د دگه جای ها هم میره. مثلاً دگه مملکتها.

جاوید: انار قندار بصورت عموم زیادتر د پاکستان تجارت ... صادر می شه. پاکستانی ها از او زیاد استفاده می کنن. چون وسایلی در افغانستان نیست که به دگی دنیا روان کنن اما پاکستان زیاد تر می خرد از او را.

احمد: آن، مه نرفتیم دگه مه تنها کابله دیدیم و همین منطقهٔ جلال آباده دیدیم. جلال آباد هم خوب اس، گرم اس. در زمستان مردم بسیار میره. اما او شارای دیگه را ندیدیم.

Vocabulary

رفتین *colloquial* رفته اید *v, pl* you have gone
دیدین *colloquial* دیده اید *v, pl* you have seen
پسمانده *colloquial* عقب مانده *adj* undeveloped, left behind
نرفتی *colloquial* نرفته ای *past* didn't you go? you didn't go
یکیش *colloquial* یکی، یکی ازآنها *adv* one of them
نرفتیم *colloquial* نرفته ام *past* I have not gone
واری *colloquial* مانند، مثل *prep* like, same as
اه *colloquial* *hesitation form* hesitation form

Ahmad: Is it very historical? How many thousands of years old is the Qala-e-Bust?

Javid: I don't know about Qala-e-Bust; it was built approximately two thousand years ago.

Ahmad: Oh… Okay… very…

Javid: There is nothing left of the Qala itself, only a part of the gate remains. Over a long period of time the sand that was blown by the wind has buried most of it.

Ahmad: Good, good.

Javid: And also the Helmand River deposits a lot of sand in that region. The agricultural production in Kandahar is very good. And it has delicious fruit.

Ahmad: They say that Kandahar has the best pomegranates.

Javid: Kandahar has very good pomegranates and grapes. And the fruit and other produce in Kandahar are very good, and then Jalalabad is a nice city.

Ahmad: Are pomegranates exported to other places, for example, to other countries?

Javid: Kandahar's pomegranates are almost totally exported to Pakistan. Pakistanis use them a lot. Since there is not a good method of transportation in Afghanistan to export to other countries, Pakistanis buy most of them.

Ahmad: Yes, I haven't gone. I have visited only Kabul and the Jalalabad region. Jalalabad is nice; it is warm there. People go there a lot in the winter. But I haven't seen the other cities.

نائب آباد *n* a district in northern Afghanistan

ترمز ترمز *n* the border between Afghanistan and Uzbekistan

همّو *colloquial* همان *adv* that, that very

هموطو *colloquial* همان طور *adj* like that, that way

بغلان *n* a province in northern Afghanistan

ایبک *n* the capital city of Samangan province

اُقَدَر *colloquial* آنقدر *adv* that much

خوبش *colloquial* قشنگ، زیبا، خوب *adj* beautiful, nice

قندار *colloquial* قندهار *n* Kandahar (one of Afghanistan's largest cities)

میگن *colloquial* میگویند *v, pl* it has been said, they say

اُو … وی *colloquial* *exclamations of surprise* exclamations of surprise

هوار *colloquial* هموار *adj, n* flat, level

خریداری

قسمت اول[13]

جاوید: خو ... د می منط ... شما که دطرف با... ضرورت زنده گی تانه میرفتی از بازار میخریدی چه قسم رفت و آمد داشتید چه قسم میگرفتید؟

احمد: از ما دگه دکانائیکه چیزای بسیار ضروری بود در همو قریه جات بود. دکانا ... اما چیزائیکه مثلاً لباس و بوت و مثلاً لوازم خانه و لوازم آشپزخانه و چیزا که بود اُو را از شار می خریدن. شار بسیار دور بود باید د موتر میرفتی تقریباً ازمنطقه ما آ.... نیم سات یا چل و پنج دقیقه دور بود.

جاوید: آ ... ای.... د زمان ما هم اینطور بود. ما هم در منطقی خود چیزهای مثل تار و سوزن وبعضی چیزهای عادی، رنگ و غیره را از دکانهای داخل قریه می گرفتیم. اما به خاطر بعضی چیزها مثل آرد و روغن و چای و بوره و نمک و اینطور چیزایکه ضروریات مصارف یومیه خانه است اینارا اکثراً از بازار محلی، بازاریکه به فاصلی دو سه کیلو متر از قریه ما دور بود از آنجه می آوردیم. اما چیزهای مهم را مثل ظروف و مثل لباس، مثلیکه خودت گفتی ایاره از شار کابل می خریدیم. شار کابل یک ذره فاصله داره هموطو گفتی نیم سات یا چل وپنج دقیقه د موتر آدم باید بره.
همچنان اما بعضی وخت یگانِ نفر مریض هم پیدا می شد در این نزدیکیهای ما داکتر نبود. ما می رفتیم. اَمُو ... اول د بازار نزدیک اگر اُنجه هم نمی بود. مریض مهم می بود د شار میرفتیم. باز از داکتر نوبت میگرفتیم، بر دو سات ، سه سات انتظار میکشیدیم تابه پیش داکتر نوبت می رسید و باز دواء بر ما می داد. باز نا وخت پس مریض را گرفته به خانه میآمدیم. اُنجه به ایطو ترتیبی که در دگه جایاس که به مریض رسیده گی می شه امبولانس اس، در منطقه ما امبولانس نبود. کسی امبولانس را نمی شناخت...ام.

احمد: آن ... آه ... مثلاً یک پَو چیز، بوره چند بود در وخت شما؟

جاوید: در وخت ما تقریباً یک پَو بوره را پنج افغانی میدادن.

احمد: چای ام .. چای چطو بود؟ چای ارزان بود یا قیمت؟

---

13 The speakers on this selection are Ahmad and Javid they attended high school in Afghanistan and Javid is a graduate of Kabul University and has a slight Kabuli accent and Ahmad speaks Kohdamani dialect of Dari.

Shopping
Part one

Javid: Well, in that [word cut off]... when you used to go toward Baza [word cut off]... How did you commute to the bazaar and buy your necessities?

Ahmad: The stores that were in the villages had the necessities. Stores...[cut off words]. But they used to go to the city to buy things like clothes, shoes, and kitchen supplies. The city was very far; you would have to go by vehicle. It was approximately half an hour to forty-five minutes away.

Javid: Yeah, it was like that in our time. Also in our region, we used to buy things like sewing needles, some ordinary things like ink from those stores in the village. But we used to buy necessities for the home, like flour, cooking oil, tea, sugar, salt and other things like that from the local bazaar in the district. The local bazaar was two or three kilometers away from our village.

But we used to buy important things like kitchen supplies and clothes from Kabul City, as you mentioned. Kabul City is a short distance away. Like you said, it would take you half an hour or fortyfive minutes travelling by vehicle.

Also, whenever somebody became ill, there wasn't a doctor nearby. Then we would go to the nearby bazaar. If the patient was critically ill, then we used to go to the doctor in the city. Then we used to take a number and wait two to three hours until it was our turn to see the doctor. Then the doctor used to give us a prescription. Then we would take the patient and get home late. It was like this there. But in other places they used to take care of the patients better because they had ambulances. In our region there was no ambulance. Nobody knew what an ambulance was.

Ahmad: Yes. For example, how much was one pound of sugar back in your day?

Javid: Back in my day, one pound of sugar was approximately 5.00 Afghani.

Ahmad: Also tea... what about tea? Was tea expensive or inexpensive?

جاوید: چای خوب بود ارزان بود، مگر چای چون از هند میآمد، از سیلون میآمد، نسبت به فعلاً ارزان بود اما..آه... نظر به اُو وخت. چای یکی از ضروریات ابتدائی زنده گی بود ایقدر[14] پیشرفته ضرورت نبود.

احمد: خوخو....

جاوید: د وخت شما آه... در[15] شهر عمومی که شما سودا می آوردی چیزها و چه قسم اُو را انتقال میدادی تا منطقه؟

احمد: آه .... سودا که می خریدیم آه .. ما خورد بودیم همراه پدرم میرفتم. باز مثلاً اگر بوت می خریدیم، باز می رفتیم د پای خود می کردیم بوته، کَت دکاندار جور میآمدیم و پیسه میدادیم دکاندار ره. و قیمت بوت اُو وخت اُوقَدَر قیمت نبود. بوتای بود که از خارج میآمد. بوت های لیلامی ما می گفتیم. دگه لباس هم، همچنان لباس لیلامی خوب، لباس خوب اکثراً از اوروپا میآمد. اوره که میخریدیم باز دگه د موتر کرائی می ششتیم. پس دموتر کرائی میآمدیم. آه... مثل سرویس و موتر های مینوبس وچیزها. آه.... دگه باز کسائیکه مثلاً لوازم خانه می خریدن بسیار زیاد می بود. باز اووا یک موتر لاری کرا میگرفتن. باز د موتر لاری می بوردنش.

جاوید: ما که لباس می گرفتیم، در وخت ما لباس به صورت عموم دو قسم بود. یکی مثل کرتی و بوت و ایطو چیز ها بود که هم د لیلامی پیدا می شد هم نواَش پیدا می شد. یکی لباس پوشیدن پیران و تنبان بود که اُو ره بصورت عموم تکه می خریدیم از بازار.

احمد: خو..

[14] The speaker meant that tea is not a necessity, but it is important.

[15] The speaker meant to say "from the city," not "in the city."

Javid: Tea was good, it was inexpensive. But tea was imported from India and Sri Lanka (Ceylon). Compared to now, it was inexpensive back then. Tea was a primary need; it wasn't that necessary.

Ahmad: Good, good. ...

Javid: Back in your days...[word cut off]. When you used to shop in the city, how did you transport the merchandise to your area?

Ahmad: Oh...when we used to shop oh... we were young. We used to go with my father. For example, if we bought shoes, then we wore the shoes and made a deal with the shopkeeper and paid him. The cost of shoes wasn't very high back then. Those shoes were imported from abroad. They were called used shoes.

Also clothes, good used clothes were imported from Europe. After shopping we used to take the bus to go home. For example the buses and minibuses and things... Oh... Also when people used to buy home furnishings, they used to rent a truck to transport them.

Javid: Back in our day when we used to buy clothes, there were two different ways. One if it was something like a jacket or shoes, it could be found as used or brandnew. Another, if it was a shirt and trousers, then we used to buy fabric from the bazaar.

Ahmad: Good.

جاوید: باز تکه را در خانه میآوردیم. در خانه مادرم یا خواهرما ایره می دوخت برما. باز اوره می پوشیدیم. دگه چیزهای داشتیم مثل قدیفه یا پتو ، که د گرد خود میگرفتیم بخاطر سردی. بالاپوش، کرتی، جمپر و چیزها را عموماً از لیلامیش مناسبتر بود.

چیز نَو هم پیدا می شد. خو .. قیمتش بسیار زیاد بود مردمِ اطراف قدرت خریدشه نداشت. یکتعداد مردم محدود ... مردم چیز نَو ره میَخریدن. دگه در قسمت خریداری بعضی چیزهای دگه، مثلیکه ظروف آشپز خانه و غیره آدم بخره ای چیزها مردم اکثراً.. از ظرف... د اول از ظروف محلی مثلیکه از گِل جورمی کردن. کلالی می گفتن اوره

احمد: بلی....

جاوید: گِل زرده و... اُو گِل بسیارِ صاف و نرم بود اُو را خمیر می کدن و باز جور میَکدن خُشک میشَد. باز اُوره در مابین داش می ماندن ، پخته می شد. مردم زیادتر از او استفاده میکرد. او هم آبِ یخه یخ نگه میکرد و گرمه گرم نگاه میکرد. زود زنگ نمی زدشه. تنها پاکَ و سُطره می شوشتن. از اُو استفاده میکردن.

Javid: Then we used to take the fabric home. At home either my mother or my sister used to sew it into a dress for us. Then we used to wear them. The other thing that we had were things like a woolen shawl or a cap. We used to wear them in the cold weather. Coat, jacket, jumper, things like this could be found used at a reasonable price.

New things could be found too. But they were expensive and people in the countryside could not afford to buy them. Only a few people used to buy new things. Another thing that people used to shop for was kitchen supplies. In the early days people used to make some clay pots. They used to call them kulali.

Ahmad: Yes. ...

Javid: From yellow clay and... It was very clean and soft clay. They made it from potter's clay, then it dried. Then they put it in the kiln to be baked. People mostly used to use that. That used to keep cold water cold and warm water warm. It would not rust easily. They only had to wash it clean. So they used to use that.

Vocabulary

آن *colloquial* خوب، بلی *adv, n* good, yes, OK

سات *colloquial* ساعت *adv* an hour *n* a watch

آ... ای *colloquial* *hesitation form* hesitation form

ایاره *colloquial* اینها را *pro* these, these things

پَو *colloquial* پاو *n* 0.985 pound

ایقدر *colloquial* اینقدر *adv* this much

کَت *colloquial* همراه *adv* with

می گرفتیم *colloquial* می خریدیم *past* we would buy *past* we would take

قدیفه *n* a kind of cloth sheet used by men in Afghanistan as and outer garment *n* bath towel

آب یخ *colloquial* آب سرد *n* cold water

نگَه *colloquial* نگاه *v* keeping *v* looking

زنگ نمی زدشه *colloquial* زنگ نمی زد آنرا *phrase* it would not rust

می شِشتن *colloquial* می شستند

خریداری

قسمت دوم[16]

احمد: د ای دکانائیکه پیش روی اه... خانه ویا دکانائیکه د قریه بود چه چیزا می فروختن اه...

جاوید: به صورت عموم د ای دکانا ضروریات بسیار ابتدائی زنده گی، مثل تیل خاک، دیزل، تار و زوزن، رنگ و بعضی دواهای بسیار عادی محلی، بعضی وقت اِینمی کلالی را زیاتر د اینجه می فروختن. یگان اندازه آرد کمی می فروختَن، چای وبوره می فروختن، یگان زره شرینی مثل گُر[17] و بوره و چاکلیت. اینطو چیزا ره می فروختن.

احمد: کلچه و کیک و چیزا چطو؟

جاوید: کیک و کلچه و چیزا رواج نبود. ای چیزا تنها د شارا بود. د اطراف اُقدر پیدا نمی شد.

احمد: د وخت ما که بود باز هم ... بر طفلها دگه کلچه داشتن و کیک داشتن. و یگان ساجق داشتن و اه... ای چیزا زیاد بود.

باز خصوصاً در روزهای عید که میشد باز ای دکانا خودشان جلیبی[18] جور میکردن و کلچه و کیک. هر کس ... اوشتوکا دگه پیسه میگرفت از کلانا، باز می رفتن اَموجه اه... ساجق و کلچه و کیک و چیزا میخریدن.

[16] The speakers on this selection are Ahmad and Javid they attended high school in Afghanistan and Javid is a graduate of Kabul University and has a slight Kabuli accent and Ahmad speaks Kohdamani dialect of Dari.

[17] The product of the first pressing of the juice of the sugar cane.

[18] Sweet dish in the form of a straw-like pastry fried in butter and covered with syrup.

Shopping
Part two

Ahmad: What did they sell in those stores that were located in front of the houses or the ones in the village?[19]

Javid: Generally, they used to sell something like kerosene, diesels, sewing needles and thread, ink, some ordinary medicine, and pottery in these stores. They also used to sell flour, pure cane sugar, tea, some sweets, raw or coarse sugar, candies, and things like these in these stores.

Ahmad: What about things like cookies and cakes?

Javid: Selling things like cookies and cakes was not a custom. These things were only in the cities. They were seldom found in the countryside.

Ahmad: They were in our time. They had cookies and cakes for children. They also had chewing gum, mostly things like these.

Especially in the Eid holidays, the shopkeepers used to bake cookies, cakes, and jelabi. Whenever the children received money from the adults, they used to go there and buy chewing gum, cookies, and cakes.

[19] Usually, the stores in villages are attached to houses.

جاوید: آ... ای چیزا کم کم بود مگر زیادتر کیک و کلچه و چیزا را از شار میآوردن. د اُنجه نبود. اه... همو چیزای ابتدائی اُجه بود. بصورت ... کیک و کلچه اه... در عموماً در کابل و در شهرهای دگی افغانستان ساخته می شد. اُو را عام مردم زیاتر خورده نمی تانست. تنها یَک تعداد مردم پیسه دار از اُو میخرید و میخوردن. و او رام در مراسم خصوصاً مثل عید مثل بعضی مراسم عروسی و مراسم شرینی خوری و در ایطو وختا از اُو استفاده می کردن. همیشه استفاده نمیکردن.

دگه بصورت عموم خوراک مردم همو نان گندم یا نان جواری بود، همراه شیر، همراه ماست، همراه دوغ. ای چیزا زیاتر مردم استفاده میکرد. دگه د قریه جات اه.... یگان قصابی می شد که مردم گاو و گوسفند را اُنجه حلال می کردن. به مردم گوشته می فروختن، مردم می خرید. ای ... یک اندازه غذا برحیوانات می فروختن. فرضاً جو بصورت عموم مردم بر حیوانات خود می خرید. در اُوجه پیدا می شد.

احمد: د ایچیز اه... گوشت بصورت ععموم تازه بود نی؟ باز گوشته خشک هم میکردن، گوشت خشک بسیار خوب. باز د زمستان می خوردن نی؟

جاوید: بلی، آن... در تابستان گوشتِ تازه میخریدن، گوشت گوسفند، کوشت گاو از پیش قصابا. اما زمستان چونَ اُنجه زیاد سرد بود، رفت و آمد از یکجای به جای دیگر مشکل بود، گوسفند هم زیاد پیدا نمی شد. هر کس دوسه گوسفنده می کُشت.گوشتشه قاق می کرد. باز اُو را قاقی میگفتن.

احمد: آن .. گوشت قاقَ...

جاوید: باز گوشت قاق .. باز پخته میکردن میخوردن.اُو را همراه حلیم می ماندن، حلیم را از دانه گندم جور میکردن.

احمد: بلی، ام .... د اُو دکانائیکه نزدیک سَر سرک عمومی بینِ کابل و پروان بود، د اُجه د وخت ما باز کوچی ها پنیر میآوردن. باز پنیر از اُوجه بسیار مشهور بود. مردم اِینا از شار میآمد، پنیر میخریدن همراه کشمش اه...

دگه ..اه...اه... میوه می فروختن. مثلاً یک چیزی بنام کنگینه می گفتن، که انگوره د بین دو پله گلی جور میکردن. و د بین از اُو می ماندن. وباز مردمیکه از شار میآمد اُو را مَیخرید. اُو بسیار خوب نگاه میشد. د زمستان انگور تازه بود بکلی مثلیکه نَو از تاک کنده باشیش.

Javid: Yes... they seldom had these things, but they used to bring cookies, cakes, and things like these from the city. They could not be found there. Those primary things and necessities could be found there. Generally ... cake and cookies used to be made in Kabul and other Afghan cities. Ordinary people could not afford to eat them. Only some rich people used to buy them and eat them. They used to serve them on special occasions like Eid and engagement parties and wedding parties. They didn't serve them always.

Generally, people used to eat bread or corn bread with milk, yogurt, and dogh (refreshing drink made of yogurt mixed with water and spices). Generally, people used to consume these things. Also they used to have slaughterhouses in the villages. They used to slaughter cows and sheep the Islamic way. They used to sell the meat to the people, and people used to buy. They also used to sell fodder for animals. For example, they used to buy barley for their animals. It could be found there.

Ahmad: In the things ...Generally, they used to sell fresh meat, didn't they? Also they would dry meat. Very good dried meat. Then they would eat it in the winter, wouldn't they?

Javid: Yes, yes, they used to buy fresh meat like beef or lamb from the butcher in the summertime. Since it is very cold there in the winter, travelling from one place to another was very difficult. Also there were not enough sheep. People used to slaughter two or three sheep, then dry their meat. Then they call it qhaaqhi (jerky).

Ahmad: Yes qhaaqhi.

Javid: Then they dried the meat...[word cut off] and then they cooked it and ate it. They used to make halleem (beef barley soup). They made halleem out of wheat grain.

Ahmad: Yes, Om...[word cut off] the stores that were located near the highway, which connects Kabul to Parwan, the Kuchi (nomad), used to bring cheese and sell it to those stores. The cheese that they sold there was very popular. People used to come from the city and buy cheese and raisins.

Oh...[word cut off] they used to sell fruit too. For example there was something called kangeena (container made of clay). It is two plates made of clay and they put grapes inside and seal them. People used to come from the city and buy them. The grapes were kept fresh in the wintertime just like you picked them from the vine.

جاوید: آ ... همی قسم د وخت ما هم هموطور بود. اه.. پنیر را از بصورت عموم مردم مالدار کوچی می ساختن میآوردن و میفروختن. دکاندارا کشمش هم از باغدارا میخریدن، به مردم می فروختن، مردم کشمش پنیر می گفت. بسیار به شوق میخوردن.
دگه همیطوریکه گفتی اه... ام... کشمش پنیر زوق زیاد مردم اس، خوب علاقه دارن مردم. دگه انگور خو د وطن ما هموطور اس. چون زمستان، غیر از اینکه د بین کنگینه نگاه کُنَن دگه وسیلهِ نگاه کردنش نیس. دگه قسم د هوا خشک میشه یا خراب میشه.

احمد: ام...

جاوید: د بین کنگینه دگه قید میشه هموطو نگاه میکردن. اه... فعلاً اُو گپانیس، آلا نگاه کرده نمیشه.

احمد: آلا خو کل چیز خراب شد، نی تاک ماند، و نی انگور ماند.

جاوید: همه چیز خراب شده.

احمد: هیچ چیز نشد. د وخت روسها بسیار زیادش از بین رفت، و فعلاً د وخت طالبا دردادن، از بین بردن. او چیز های سابق نمانده فعلاً دیگر.

Javid: Ah... It was in the same way in my time. Oh ...the Kuchi who had cattle used to bring cheese and sell it. Also the shopkeeper would buy raisins from the gardeners and sell them to the people. People used to call it keshmish-paneer (cheese and raisins). They enjoyed eating it.

Also as you said Ah...Om...(word cut off) people like keshmish-paneer. People are big fans of keshmish-paneer. Also the grapes from our region are like this. In the winter, the only storage to keep the grapes was kangeena not any other method. Otherwise the air would dry them out and rot the grapes.

Ahmad: Om...

Javid: It was enclosed inside the kangeena this way; it could be saved. Now it is not like that. You can't save it now.

Ahmad: Now everything is destroyed. There are no vines and there are no grapes.

Javid: Everything is destroyed.

Ahmad: Noting good happened. Most of them were destroyed during the Russian invasion and now the Taliban set them on fire, and destroyed them. It is not like the past now anymore.

Vocabulary

اینطو *adv colloquial* این قسم ، اینطور *adv* this way, like this

دکانا *n colloquial* دکانها *n, pl* stores, shops

اوشتوکا *n colloquial* طفلها ، اطفال *n, pl* children

کـلانا *n colloquial* ریش سـفـیـدان ، بزرگـواران ، بزرگـان *n, pl* elders, great men, great women, well respected old people or adults

عام مردم *n colloquial* مردم عام commn people, ordinary people, public

دگی *colloquial* باقیمانده دیگر، *adv* other, the rest of

اُو *colloquial* آن that, that thing

پیش *colloquial* نزد *adv* from

گوشتشه *colloquial* گوشت آنرا ، گوشتشرا *possessive phrase* its meat

کنگینه *n colloquial* کنگینه *n, sing* container made of clay to keep grapes fresh in the fall and winter

کنده باشیش *v colloquial* کنده باشد آنرا ، کنده باشد اش، *past* he/she has picked it

گپا *n colloquial* چیزها *n things, stories n* talks

ماند *colloquial* مانده *v* is left, remains

در دادن *v colloquial* به آتش کشیدند ، آتش زدند *v, pl, past* they burned them

ازدواج[20]

احمد: د منطقهٔ ما و شما عروسی هم اه.... د وختای سابق چه قسم رواج بود؟

جاوید: د سابق عروسی خو ایطو رواج بود که مردم، اول خو یک بچه و دختر یکی دیگر را هیچ نمی دیدند. اگر می دیدن هم د زمان طفولیت. باز وختی که می خواستن اُو دختره بگیرن، پدر و مادرش باید اُو پدر و مادر دختر را می شناخت پیش از اُو می رفتن.
باز مادرش خوارش اینا او دختر را می شناختن، می دیدن در مراسم عروسی، در فاتحه، در رفت و آمد فامیلی در غیره. یا از جملهٔ اقارب می بود که می شناختن. باز اول سه چار نفر زنا را روان میکردن که همین دخترکته به همین بچه ما بتی. ما خوش داریم که همی را بگریم. اگر پدر و مادر دختر راضی می بود باز کمی گپ نرم میزد برشان. اگر نی که راضی نمی بود کمی برشان تُند میگفت، نی نمیتم برو.
اگر راضی می بود باز کمی میگفت خو باش می بینیم چطور می شه. همی پدرش چه میگه، کاکایش چه میگه ، بیدرش چه میگه ، مامایش چه میگه ، فلانی ، بابیش چه می گه، بابه کلانش چه می گه. باز این بانه و هیله را می کردن. باز بچه والا که طلبگار بود باز می رفت سه چار روز باز میآمد. باز می رفت، بر پنج شش دفه که رفت و آمد کرده بود باز آنها اگر راضی می بودن.

احمد: خو ...

جاوید: می گفتن خو می تیم، خَی باز فلانه روز بیآید برایتان شرینی می تیم.

احمد: خو خو... باز ..اه ... از دختر صلاح میگرفتن اه... مادرِ دختر یا پدرِ دختر که چطوراس موافقه داری همراه از این بچهٔ فلانی؟ به اصطلاح .. یا... اه ... بدون مصلحت دختر اینا را می گفتن که بیائی که باز ما می تیم شرینی، می تیم یا نه؟

جاوید: اکثراً از دختر مادرش بعضی وخت یک پر سان می کرد. اما دختر ها هیچ ای چون د طور زنده گی بود که جرأت گفتن آن و یا نی را نداشتن. اکثراً خاموش می ماندن. اگر خاموش هم می ماندن علامهٔ رضاء بود.

---

[20] The speakers on this selection are Ahmad and Javid they attended high school in Afghanistan and Javid is a graduate of Kabul University and has a slight Kabuli accent and Ahmad speaks Kohdamani dialect of Dari.

Marriage

Ahmad: What was the marriage custom of our region in the past?

Javid: Marriage in the past was like this among the people first of all, the boy and the girl would not have seen each other. Even if they had seen each other, it would have been during their childhood. Then, when they want to marry a girl to their boy, the father and mother of the boy had to know the father and mother of the girl. Then they would go to their house.

Then, his mother or his sister would have known or seen the girl at a wedding party, funeral or during family visits, etc. Or she could have been one of their relatives so they knew her. First, they would send three or four women to their house for the proposal. They would say, "Give your daughter to our son; we would like to marry your daughter to our son." If the parents of the girl were interested they would have a pleasant conversation with them, but if they were not interested they would not speak nicely to them. They would say, "Go away; we don't want to give her to you."

If the parents of the girl were interested they would say, "OK, let's see what will happen. We want to know what her father will say, what her paternal uncle will say, what her brother will say, what her maternal uncle will say. Certain persons, what her grandfather will say, what her grandfather will say." They would make these excuses.Then the boy's side, the one asking, would visit the girl's parent for about four days and for five to six times. Then, if they were convinced.

Ahmad: OK...

Javid: then they would say, "OK, we will give her to you, then come on a certain day so we will give you the engagement sweets."

Ahmad: Good, good... then...oh ...would the girl's parents ask the girl for her opinion? For example, "What do you think, are you interested in marrying this boy?" Or without the girl's agreement they would tell them to come, "So we will give you the engagement sweets, or we won't."

Javid: Most mothers would ask their daughter's opinion. Since girls in that society don't have the courage to say yes or no, they would remain silent. When they were silent, that would be a sign of her interest.

احمد: بلی.

جاوید: در غیر از اُو دگه مادرش و پدرش خودش مصلحت دختر دیده به دل خود اُنموره می دادن به یک نفر. باز دگه دختر اه... نا راز هم می بود، می بود دگه خو... قبول میکردن اُنموره. پدر و مادرش داده بود. اُنمو هموره می گرفت دگه.

احمد: دگه هیچ اختیارات نداشت که بگوید که نی نمیگیرم و یا... :خو، وختی که پدر و مادر دختر موافقه میکردن و میگفتن (خو ما شرینی برتان می تیم) و بچه هم هتماً موافقییش می بود، یا پدر و مادر بچه هم از بچه هم پرسان نمی کرد، یک دختره میگرفتن برش؟

جاوید: بعضی مردم طوری بود که بچهٔ خود را زیادتر پرسان میکردن. خصوصاً که سن بچه زیاد می بود. اگر نی که خورد می بود پرسان هم نمی کردن می رفتن یکسی را برایش میگرفتن. بعد از اُو که باز پدرِ و مادرِ دختر راضی شده بود باز میگفت که د فلانه روز بیا برتان شرینی مِیتُم. باز ای چند نفر ریش سفید ها را گرفته میرفت.

باز یکذره شرینی، یکدانه قند د یک دستمال برشان میداد که ینه من دختر خوده به ای بچه از ای دادم. بعد از او یک چند وقتی که تیر میشد باز اه... بعضی مردم ایطور میکرد که شرایط می ماند ، میگفت که دختر خوده میتم به شرطیکه بیست هزار افغانی بتی.

احمد: خو[21] ..

جاوید: آن ... اُو میگفت که من... نه... مخو... بیست هزار پیسه زیاد اس دگه.

احمد: بیست هزار افغانی بچه خاطر؟

جاوید: بنام تویانه[22] میگرفتن.

---

[21] The speaker meant to say "is that right."

[22] The money given to the bride's family as the expense of the wedding cermony.

Ahmad: Yes.

Javid: Otherwise, her parents would go by their own opinion and marry her to somebody. Even if the girl wouldn't be happy, she would have to accept that, because her parents had married her off. And he would marry her.

Ahmad: Didn't they have any right to say, "No, I don't want to get married and/or....[23] OK, when the parents of the girl had agreed and would have said, "OK, we will give you the engagement sweets." And, would the boy have agreed too? Or, wouldn't the boy's parents ask the boy for his opinion? Or, they just married him off?

Javid: Some people would ask their son for his opinion, especially when the boy was older. Otherwise, they wouldn't even ask the boy, and they would marry him off to someone. When the parents of the girl have agreed, they would say, "Come on the certain day and we will give you the engagement sweets." Then, they, along with a few elderly men, would go there.

Then they would wrap some candy and lump sugar in a kerchief and give it to them, so that, "I married my daughter to their son." Later on passing this stage, some people would set a condition and say, "In order to marry my daughter off to your son, you have to give me twenty thousand Afghani."

Ahmad: OK.

Javid: Yes, he would say, "I ... no ...I don't... twenty thousand is too much."

Ahmad: What is the twenty thousand Afghani for?

Javid: In the name of toyana.

[23]The speaker meant to say "or what."

احمد: خو که خرچ و مصرف.

جاوید: خرچ و مصرف طوی شوه و یکی هم چون پدر و مادرش سر دختر خود زحمت... زحمت کشیده، خرچ کرده تا این سن رسانديش، که مصارف خوده پوره کنه. باز وختیکه ای دختر سطح. اه... ای وخت عروسی میشد باز هموطو یک جنجالکی پیدا میشد که اینقدر مواد بیآر که مه پخته کنم، به مردم عروسی خرچ بتم.

احمد: خو ...

جاوید: دختر والا می طلبیست. بچه والا می گفت اینقدر زیاد نفره چرا خرچ می تی، کم بتی. بالاَ خره یک چند نفر می ششت با هم دعوای شانرا حل می کرد. یک چیزی مواد برنج میخرید و روغن میخرید و چای و بوره میخرید و آرد می خرید و غیره چیزها برایش می داد.

و چقدر کالا بخرم برش، چقه کم بخرم و زیاد بخرم، ای دعوی می بود. ای دعوی که خلاص می شد. زودتر عروسی کنیم دیر عروسی کنیم. این مسائل را که حل می کردن، بعد از او باز مراسم عروسی را می گرفتن.

Ahmad: Right, for wedding expenditure.

Javid: To use it for the wedding expenditure, and one of the reasons, since the parents of the girl took care of her and spent money to raise her up to this age so they can get paid for their expenditures. At this stage of the marriage process there would also be an issue about, "Bring more groceries so I could cook and feed the guests."

Ahmad: All right.

Javid: The girl's side would ask for that. The boy would say, "Why would you feed this many people? Do less." Finally a few people would hold a meeting with them and solve their issues. He (the father of the groom) would give them (the parents of the bride) some groceries like, rice, cooking oil, tea, flour, sugar, etc.

"And how many clothes should I buy her? Should I buy less or more?" There would be this argument. After this argument was over, they would solve the issue like, "Should we do the wedding sooner or later?" Then they would do the wedding party.

Vocabulary

گپ نرم *colloquial* سخن نرم *adj* nicely speaking

گپ تند *colloquial* سخن سخت، تند گفتن، سخن تند *adj, n* rough talk

میگه *colloquial* میگوید *v* he/she says

بانه *colloquial* بهانه *n* false excuse

دفه *colloquial* دفعه، مرتبه *adv* degree, grade, periods of time

بچه والا *colloquial* فامیل بچه، فامیل شاه boy's family, groom's family

خی *colloquial* خوب، خیر *adj, adv* good, well *adv* wishing good luck

پرسان *colloquial* جویان، سوال *adj* questioning, inquisitive *n* question, inquiry

انموره *colloquial* همان را *adv, phrase* that thing, that object

بَرِش *phrase colloquial* برایش، برای او، بَرای آن *phrase* 1. for him/her/it *n* 2. its width

یَنَه *colloquial* اینک *adv* here it is.

توی *n colloquial Turkic* عروسی *n* wedding, wedding cermony

دختر والا *n colloquial* فامیل دختر، فامیل عروس *n* girl's family, bride's family

می طلبیست *v colloquial* می طلبید طلب میکرد would ask for, was asking for

چقه *phrase colloquial* چقدر، چه اندازه *adv, phrase* how much

حاصلات محلی[24]

احمد: حاصلات منطقه اکثراً در اُنجه چه بود اه... از ..اه... مثلاً مردم مصرف خوده از کجا پیدا می کرد؟ مصرف سالانه که بره بازار لباس بخره و مثلاً برای مکتب پیسه بته و همین مص... مصرف سالانه را از کجا میکردن؟ چه کار میکردن؟

جاوید: د وخت ما خو در محیط ما مکتبها از مردم پیسه نمیگرفت.

احمد: بلی...

جاوید: اُوجه مکتب حکومت ... از طرف حکومت بود و اُو هم بسیار کم بود. در کل ولسوالی یک مکتب بود.

احمد: بلی ...

جاوید: اما مردم عایداتش بصورت عموم مطلق از زراعت بود، دگه عایداتی نداشتن. حاصلات زراعتی منطقه ما درجه اول در اُو وخت حاصل گندم بود. بعد از او حاصل فروش آلو بخارا بود، بعد از اُو فروش انگور بود.
دگه مردم اول زمینهای خوده می کاشتن بسیار بشکل ابتدائی توسط قلبه، یکجوره گاو داشتن اُو قلبه میکردن و کُدام کود کیمیائی در اُو اولا نبوده از کود حیوانی استفاده میکردن. بعد از اُو گندمش را جمع میکردن، یکمقدارشه اگر کفایتشان میکرد خوب، اگر نمی کرد، جای.... از جای دگه از بازار یک اندازه را میخریدن. از کسی که زیاد می بود یک اندازیشه میفروخت.
دگه حاصل دوم منطقه ما آلو بخارا[25] بود. آلو بخارا درختایش زیاد تر در منطقه رواج داشت. مردم اُو را می شاندن اه.... وختیکه آلو بخارای از اُو پخته میشد جمع میکرد، پوست میکردن. باز اُو را در روی بوریا اَوار میکردن، خشک میشد، در بازار می فروختن، اُو را پِیسیشَه کالا میخریدن و به ضروریات باقیماندی خوراکی خود را مثل گوسفند میخریدن و روغن میخریدن و ایطو مصارف خوده از اُو پوره میکردن.

---

[24] The speakers on this selection are Ahmad and Javid they attended high school in Afghanistan and Javid is a graduate of Kabul University and has a slight Kabuli accent and Ahmad speaks Kohdamani dialect of Dari.

[25] This kind of plums originally grew in Bukhara, a city in Uzbekistan.

Local Products

Ahmad: What was the local product mostly in that region? Oh... from... Oh... for example, how would people earn their living? Where would they earn the money to buy clothes, for example, to pay for school and annual expenditures? And what kind of work would they do?

Javid: People in that society wouldn't pay for school at that time.

Ahmad: Yes.

Javid: Government school there... there was a government school. And there were only a few of them. There was only one school in the entire district.

Ahmad: Yes.

Javid: People earned their income by farming. They had no other sources of income. Wheat was the number one product of our region, then it was trade in plums and grapes.

Then, initially people would cultivate by plowing the field, like in ancient times; they would use a pair of plow oxen. There was no chemical fertilizer in the early days; they used to use animal manure. Then they would harvest the wheat. If they harvested enough wheat, it would be good. If they didn't, they would buy some from the market. If someone had extra, he/she would sell it.

Bukhara plums (this kind of plums originally grew in Bukhara, a city in Uzbekistan) was the number two product in our region. It used to be a custom for people in our region to have Bukhara plum trees. People used to grow them. Whenever the Bukhara plum was ripe, they would pick them and peel them, then lay them on a reed mat to be dried. Then they would sell them in the bazaar. They would buy clothes and other necessities, like sheep and cooking oil, with the money they had earned from selling plums. Also they would use it for other expenditures.

احمد: آه ...

جاوید: یک تعداد مردم انگور داشت. تاک انگوری که انگورشه میگرفت کشمش میکرد، می فروخت. بعداً باز این تغیر کرد. مردم زیادتر به طرف تاک رجوع کرد. خصوصاً وقتیکه سرکها جور شد. راه تجارت به کشورهای همسایه باز شد. مردم باز تاک شاندنه شروع کردن عوض گندم و آلوبخارا، آلوبخارا.. گرفتن تاک شاندن و حاصل تاکه انگوره تازه گرفتن به تجار فروختن و تجار اورا به بازارهای خارج فروخت. پیسهٔ خوب بدست آوردن.

احمد: بلی.

Ahmad: Oh…

Javid: Some people owned vineyards. They used to dry the grapes in the sun and sell them. Then it changed. Most of the people were interested in having vineyards, especially when paved routes were built and the trade roads were opened to neighboring countries.

Then people started growing vines instead of wheat and bukhara plums. They grew vines, then they sold the grapes to the merchant, and the merchant sold them to foreign markets. They made a good profit.

Ahmad: Yes.

Vocaulary

بِره *colloquial* بِرود *v* to go
اَوار *colloquial* هموار *n* flat, laying flat

میوه جات[26]

احمد: میوه هائیکه در آن منطقه در وقت ما بود اکثرش اه... درخت های پیوندی بود که مثلاً سیب بود و ناک بود و شفتالو بود و این چیزها بود. باز میآوردند پیوند میکردند. باز حاصلات بسیار خوب می داد.
در وقت شما همین کارها را میکردند؟ مثلاً پیوند یا از خارج تخم مواد چیز اه... خوبی که بود در آنجا میآوردند، در افغانستان اه... همان... میوه ها... میوه جات درختهائیکه بود آن را به... ترقی میدادند در آن منطقه؟

جاوید: در وقت ما میوه جات خو چیزهای مهم که در محیط پیدا می شد، همین انگور بود، سیب بود، ناک بود، شفتالو بود، گوردآلو بود، آلوبخارا بود، توت بود، شاه توت بود، توت بی دانه، و توت خنجانی، و این چیزها بود.
اه... بعداً باز بعضی میوه های دیگر هم خصوصاً همین میوه ها را چون به مرور زمان اینها جنسش خراب میشد. باز جنسهای خوبترش را میآوردند پیوند میکردند از جائیکه درخت تازه تر و خوبتر و حاصل خوب میداد.
اه... دیگر باز پسانها همین درخت سیب و شفتالو و ناک و چیزها را از بیرون آوردند. وزارت زراعت از بیرون آورد، نهالش را و تخمش را و باز نهالش را ...

---

[26] The speakers on this selection are Ahmad and Javid they attended high school in Afghanistan and Javid is a graduate of Kabul University and has a slight Kabuli accent and Ahmad speaks Kohdamani dialect of Dari.

Fruits

Ahmad: The fruit which were in that region in our time, most of them... were grafted trees, such as, for example, apples, and pears and peaches, and these things. They used to bring them and graft them. Then they would give very good harvests.

In your time, did would they do these things? For example, would they graft or bring the seed of some fruits from abroad to that region to improve the produce of those trees?

Javid: In our time, the fruits, the important things that were found in the region were grapes, apples, pears, peaches, kidney-plums, Bukhara plums, mulberries, king mulberries, seedless mulberries, and Khinjan mulberries, and these things.

Um... Later on, because over time the fruit's quality would worsen, they would bring [plants] of better quality from someplace where the trees were newer and better and were producing well and they would graft them on [to the roots of the old plants].

Um... Later on, they brought these apple, peach, and pear trees from abroad. The Ministry of Agriculture brought the saplings and seeds from abroad, then the saplings...

احمد: از ممالک های خارج.

جاوید: آن از... بنام سیب بیروتی میگفتند شفتالو و چیزها را.

احمد: از لبنان؟

جاوید: از لبنان آوردند و باز آن زیادتر رونق پیدا کرد و جنس بهترش بود. باز حاصلات از آن بسیار خوبش میشد. دیگر چیزهای که در محیط بود. دگر آنقدر زیاد شهرت نداشت. فرضاً در محیط منطقهٔ ما مالته و کیله و سنتره و چیزها نبود.

این چیزها عموماً از پاکستان میآمد یا در مناطق سرد(گرم)[27] مثل جلال آباد و اینجا ها پیدا می شد. دیگر میوه جات وطن، میوه جات وطن ما بصورت عموم میوه جات شرین بود. میوهٔ ترش نداشتیم.

احمد: خو...

جاوید: کلش شرین بود میوهٔ ترش بصورت عموم از مناطق سرد (گرم)[28] میآمد.

[27] The speaker meant to say "from warm regions."

[28] The speaker meant to say "they come from warm regions."

Ahmad: From foreign countries.

Javid: Yes, from... They used to call it Beiruti apple, also peaches and things.

Ahmad: From Lebanon.

Javid: They brought them from Lebanon and it became very popular and was better quality. Its harvest were very good. Other things that were in the region weren't that popular. For example, in our region, there weren't any oranges, bananas, tangerines, and things.

Usually these things were imported (lit. came) from Pakistan or they could be found in cold (sic) regions like Jalalabad or these places. Another thing is that the fruits from our region were generally sweet fruit. We didn't grow (lit. have) citrus fruit.

Ahmad: OK…

Javid: They were all sweet; generally the citrus fruits came from cold (sic) regions.

Vocabulary

گُردآلو *colloquial* آلو *n* plum

کُلَش *colloquial* همه اش تمام اش *adv, phrase* all of them

دکان و دکاندار[29]

احمد: در منطقهٔ شما دکان و دکانداری به چه قسم بود؟

جاوید: هان، در منطقهٔ ما دکانها، اول خود دکانها، بازار بصورت عموم از خامه جور شده. یعنی گِل را تر کردند و باز آن را دیوار کردند.
دکانها دومترِ در دومتر یا دومتر در سه متر، دروازه های چوبی دارد. اه...
دکانهای بسیار کلان کلان، مغازه ها نیست.

احمد: بلی...

جاوید: این همین دکانها موادِ غذائی می فروشند بعضی اِش... بعضی اِش البسه می فروشد. بعضی اِش ضَروریات باقی بصورت عموم ضروریات زنده گی را میفروشد. بعضی اِش قرطاسیه و مواد مکتب را میفروشد.
آنهائیکه مواد غذائی میفروشند یک مقدار مواد غذائی را از شهر میآورند، مثل چای، بوره، روغن، و یک مقدار دیگر را هم از خود منطقه از کسانیکه زیاد تولید میکند میفروشند یا میخرند.
مثل اه... یک مقدار روغن زرد، روغن دنبه، یا مسکه، یکمقدار فرضاً قُروت[30]، اه... یک اه... اندازه آرد، آردجواری و غیره چیزها را اگر مردم منطقه میفروشند آن را میآورند و در دکان خود باز آن را می فروشند به مردُم یکمقدار مواد.
فرضاً البسه را که دکانهائیکه البسه میفروشند، اینها میروند البسه را از شهر میآورند. در شهر البسه یا از خارج مملکت تهیه می شود مثل لباس جاپانی، تکهٔ جاپانی بسیار مشهور است در وطن ما بسیار مردُم میخرد.

---

[29] The speakers on this selection are Ahmad and Javid they attended high school in Afghanistan and Javid is a graduate of Kabul University and has a slight Kabuli accent and Ahmad speaks Kohdamani dialect of Dari.

[30] Dried sour milk preserved in the form of very hard pellets.

Shops and Shopkeepers

Ahmad: What were shops and shopkeeping like in your region?

Javid: Yes. The shops in our region... first, the shops themselves were generally made of unbaked bricks and clay. That is, they mixed clay and water (lit. they wet clay) and then built walls with it.

The shops are two by two meters or two by three meters. They have wooden doors. They are not big shops and they are not supermarkets.

Ahmad: Yes...

Javid: Some of these shops sell food. Some of these shops sell clothing. Some of them sell other necessities, generally basic necessities (lit. life necessities). Some of them sell office supplies and school supplies.

The ones who sell food would bring some of the food, like tea, sugar, and cooking oil, from the city. They would buy some locally, from people who produced a lot and sold [some], such as clarified butter, or sheep fat, or butter.

For example, some qorut (dried sour milk preserved in the form of very hard pellets), some flour, cornmeal and other things. If local people sell it, [shopkeepers] bring it to their shop and sell it to people.

They would sell clothes in the clothing store here. For shops that sell clothes, they would go and bring back clothes from the city. The clothes in the city are either from abroad, like Japanese clothes... Japanese fabric is very popular in our homeland and people buy a lot of it.

احمد: در آنجا این چیز نیست ،.. فابریکه ای که لباس بسازد، یا تکه جور کُند؟

جاوید: در افغانستان ... یک دو فابریکه ای بسیار ابتدائی است که لباس عادی تهیه میکرد. تکهٔ عادی مثل سان میگویم آن را. اه... آن تهیه میشود و باقی البسه که خوب است از خارج اکثراً میآید. باقی مواد ضروری هم از خارج میآید. مثل قرطاسیه در وطن ما هیچ تهیه نمی شود، کلش از خارج میآمد. قرطاسیهٔ مورد ضروریت مثل قلم، کاغذ، کتابچه، خطکش، و غیره چیز ها از خارج افغانستان تهیه میشود. باز در دکانها آمده می رود باز دکانها آن را میفروشند این ضروریات زنده گیست که مردم تهیه میکند.

Ahmad: Is there a thing… a factory to produce clothes, or to make fabric?

Javid: In Afghanistan... There are a couple of very basic factories that made ordinary clothes. Ordinary fabric, like the one we call san (a type of white woven cotton fabric). That is produced [there], but the rest of the clothes that are good mostly come from abroad. The rest of the necessities come from abroad, like office supplies, which are not produced in our country at all. They all are imported from abroad.

Office supplies that are necessary, like pens, paper, notebooks, rulers, and other things are imported from outside of Afghanistan. They keep coming in to the shops and the shops sell them. These are the basic necessities that people get.

Vocabulary

تکی *colloquial* تکه ای *n* fabric

زندگی اجتماعی[31]

احمد: در جائیکه شما زنده گی می کردید وضع اجتماعی فامیل ها چه قسم است؟ مثلاً اه ... کلان فامیل کی است؟ کلان فامیل چه مسئولیت دارد؟ خورد فامیل چه مسئولیت دارد؟ اه... این چیزها را اگر تشریح بدهید.

جاوید: اه ... در وطن ما فامیل ها یک بنیاد اصلی زنده گی مردم است. مردم، اه، شکل زندگی شان از فامیل شروع میشود. و بر فامیل بسیار اهمیت می دهند. در فامیل ها از قرنها به اه... به این طرف به همین یک شکل زنده گی دارند. کلان فامیل پدر یا پدر کلان است که او اه... تقریباً تمام زنده گی را تنظیم می کند.

باقیمانده قسمت کار خانه، داخل منزل فرضاً پختن، ششتن، دوختن، این چیزها به مادر تعلق دارد، مادر ترتیب و تنظیم می کند آن را.

اه ... درس خواندن، مکتب رفتن، مسجد رفتن، کارهای خورد و کوچکی که در خانه پیش میشود آن را بچه ها میکُنَند.

بعضی کارهای خورد و کوچک دیگر را دخترها میکنند. یکتعداد برادر های کلان و خواهرهای کلان آنها کارهای زیادتر در خانه میکنند. فرضاً مال داری داشته باشد کسی، آبداری در زمین و در باغ باشد.

---

31 The speakers on this selection are Ahmad and Javid they attended high school in Afghanistan and Javid is a graduate of Kabul University and has a slight Kabuli accent and Ahmad speaks Kohdamani dialect of Dari.

Social Life

Ahmad: Where you lived, what are social relationships (lit. condition) within families like? For example, who is the head of the family? What responsibilities does the head of the family have? What responsibilities do the younger members of the family have? If you would, could you explain these things?

Javid: Um... In our homeland, families are the basic foundation of people's lives. People's way of life originates in their family. People consider family very important. Families have lived this way for centuries.

The head of the family is the father or grandfather, who arranges just about all of [the family's] life.

The mother is in charge of the rest of the housework inside the home like cooking, washing, sewing, and things like that. The mother arranges that.

Studying, going to school, going to the mosque, small jobs that come up around the house, this is what boys do. Girls do some of the other small jobs.

Some of the grown-up brothers and sisters do the heavier work, for example, when someone raises cattle, or when the land or the orchard is irrigated.

اه... تهیهٔ بعضی ضروریات زنده گی. فرضاً از بازار میروند یک اندازه گوشت میاورند یا آرد و روغن چای و بوره این خریداری را بصورت عموم، درجه اول پدر می کند. اگر پدر روی سفید باشد باز برادر کلان. اینا میروند این مواد را از بازار تحیه میکُنَند.

اه ... حاصل زنده گی هم مشترک است در فامیل و خرچ هم ... در... بالای فامیل میشود مشترکاً از پول عاید فامیل خرچ میشود. همه گی میفهمند که ما چه باید بخوریم، چه باید بپوشیم. چون وضع اقتصادی فامیل برای شان معلوم است. و به همین ترتیب در یک فامیل کلانتر که چند نفر برادر های کلان باهم یکجا و فامیل شان یکجای است و آنها اولادها دارند و اینها هم اکثراً در وطن ما فامیل اه... زنده گی مشترک می داشته باشند.

عایدات خود را هر برادر میآورد در همان خانه بعد از آن عایدات کل شان مصرف میکُنَند. یکجوره لباس فرضاً یکنفر می رود .. اه ... از بازار فرضاً چندین متر تکه میخرد میآورد برای بچه ها تقسیم میکند باز هرکس مادر ها برای شان می دوزد.

احمد: بسیار خوب.

Um... the provision of basic necessities, for example, going to the bazaar and bringing back meat or flour or tea and sugar, primarily the father does this shopping.If the father is elderly, then the oldest brother [from among his children] goes and buys these things from the bazaar.

Income is shared within the family and the expenses that the family has are jointly paid from the family's income. Since they know the family's financial position, everyone [in the family] knows what they should eat and what they should wear. It is the same way in a larger family, where several grown-up brothers who have children live together. Usually families lived together in our homeland.

Each brother brings home his earnings. Then they all spend it.For a set of clothes, for example, one person goes and buys from the bazaar, for example, several meters of fabric, brings it back, and divides it among the children. Then everybody's mother sews it [into clothes] for them.

Ahmad: Very good.

Vocabulary

ششتن *colloquial* نشستن *v* sitting

جامعه[32]

احمد: زنده گی مردم وضع اجتماع به چه قسم در آنجا پیش میرود؟

جاوید: در آن وطنها شکل زنده گی شکل بسیار سابقه و قدیمیست تا اندازه ای با اه ... دین و مذهب مردم ارتباط دارد. و تا اندازه ای به عنعنات و رسوم همان منطقه ارتباط دارد. و بالای عنعنات و رسوم هم احکام مذهبی مسلط است. یعنی هیچ نوع عادات و رسومی در منطقه خارج از اه..... خلاف مذهب و خلاف دین بوده نمیتواند.

در منطقه زیاد تر نفر کلان یا روی سفیدِ منطقه یا ملک منطقه اینها زیادتر اختیار دارند مردم را نصیحت میکنند، مردَم را گپهای خوب میزنن کمک میکنند. و همچنان مردم یک زنده گی که باهم دیگر تعاون دارد همکاری دارد اه... فرضاً یک نفر فوت میکند در آنجا یک مرده خانه ای نیست، در آنجا امبولانسی نیست، در آنجا کدام گروپ کارگری نیست که برود برای از اینها قبر بکَند.

بلکه همین خود خویش و قوم و اقارب مردم محیط باهم جمع میشوند یکجا. یکتعدادش میرود قبر تهیه میکند. یکتعدادش میرود وسایل دیگری میآورد که اه.... جنازه را انتقال بدهد. یک اه... تعداد دیگرش مصروف میشود برای مردمیکه اینجا جمع میشود نان تهیه میکُنَند اه ...

---

[32] The speakers on this selection are Ahmad and Javid they attended high school in Afghanistan and Javid is a graduate of Kabul University and has a slight Kabuli accent and Ahmad speaks Kohdamani dialect of Dari.

Society

Ahmad: How do people's social lives develop?

Javid: The way of life in those regions is a very ancient way. To an extent it is connected to people's religion, and to an extent it is connected to the traditions of that region. Religious commandments have great influence over traditions. In other words, no custom in that region can be outside...contrary to religion.

In a region, the elder of a region or the leader of the region has the authority to advise people and tell people what the right thing to do is (lit. say good things) and help them. And also people have a life in which they help each other and cooperate with each other. For example, someone dies; there isn't a funeral home or an ambulance or a group of workers to go and dig a grave for them.

But the relatives (lit. maternal relatives and paternal relatives and relatives) and local people will get together themselves.Some of them go and prepare a grave, some of them go and bring something (lit. means) to carry the body, and some of them occupy themselves preparing food for the people who are gathered here.

به همین شکل یکی با دیگر همکاری میکُنَند، فرضاً در مراسم عروسی هم یکی با دیگر همکاری میکنند. در هوتل و رستوران اینطور چیزها نیست که مردم برود در آنجا مراسم عروسی خود را در محیط تهیه کند. بلکه بشکل اجتماعی مردم منطقه باهم خویش و قوم و اقارب و دوستها و رفقاء جمع میشوند، یک تعداد دیگ پختن را به عهده میگیرد، و یکتعداد تهیه مواد را به عهده می گیرد، یکتعداد لباس را ت...اه... هموار مکنند، فرش هموار میکنند، برای مردم جای ت... جور میکنند یکتعداد ظرفها را میشُویَد، یکتعداد آب میآورد.
این همین چیزها را کُل به کمک همدیگر تهیه کرده به کمک هم دیگر توزیع میکُنَند خودشان میخورند. مراسم خود را به پیش میبَرَند.

احمد: خو بسیار خوب.

جاوید: یعنی یک زنده گی اجتماعی که یکی بادیگر همکاریست پیش می برند.

احمد: بلی یعنی کُلگِی اه .. دست جمع یک کار را میکُنَند.

جاوید: بلی به دست جمعی با همدیگر همکاری میکُنَند.

This way everybody helps each other. For example they help each other at weddings too. There aren't hotels or restaurants in the region for people to go to and have their wedding. But, collectively, people of the region and relatives and friends get together. Some take responsibility for cooking dishes, some take responsibility for providing groceries, some lay out the clothes, set up the dining area (lit. spread the floor covering,) some wash the dishes, and some bring water.

Everyone helps each other in these things, and they serve the food (lit. distribute) with the help of each other and they themselves eat. They run their own event.

Ahmad: Good, very good.

Javid: In other words, it's a communal life in which everyone helps each other.

Ahmad: Yes. That means everyone does a job together.

Javid: Yes, they help each other together.

Vocabulary

میزنن *colloquial* میگویند، میزنند *v* they would say, they would tell

انتقال بته *colloquial* انتقال بدهد *phrase* to transport, to carry

واردات و صادرات افغانستان[33]

احمد: صادرات و واردات افغانستان چه قسم بود... در آنجا به مردم اه... محلی آن را بعهده داشتند یا آن تحت تسلط حکومت بود، یا حکومت بعهده داشت.

جاوید: صادرات و واردات در هر کشور یک ... یکی ازضروریات ، یکی از لوازم عمده یا اه ... کارهای عمدهٔ زندگیست. وطن ... افغانستان هم صادرات و واردات داشت. بصورت عموم صادراتش کم بود و وارداتش زیاد بود.

احمد: بلی.

جاوید: اه... صادرات افغانستان اول اه... پروگرامایش از طرف دولت تنظیم میشد.
باز مواد را تجارهای محلی به تجار عمومی میفروختند، تجار عمومی مواد را جمع کرده به خارج صادر میکرد. بطور مثال در وطن ما کشمش زیاد پیدا میشد، انگور زیاد پیدا میشد، سیب زیاد پیدا میشد، اه ... ناک زیاد پیدا میشد. اه ... پنبه سالهای قبل زیاد پیدا میشد. این پوست قره قول زیاد پیدا میشود، قالین زیاد پیدا میشود، پشم پیدا میشود، پسته پیدا میشود.
این مواد را تجار...اه... از...اه... ولسوالی ها و ولایات جمع کرده به مرکز به یگان تجار کلان، به شرکتها تهیه میکُنَند. شرکتها باز این را به همان کشورهای که از طرف دولت قرارداد صورت میگیرد بر آنها صادر میکند.
و در برابرش واردات افغانستان مطابق ضروریات محلی مردم، فرضاً ما آرد ضرورت داریم یا روغن ضرورت داریم، چای و بوره ضرورت داریم، البسه ضرورت داریم، موتر ضرورت داریم، این ضروریات را تجار نظر به قراردادتی که دولت قبلاً با دولتهای اه ... مقابل قراردادت کرده، این ضروریات خود را از آن محل خریداری میکُنَند.
و طبعاً پولی که این مواد را در آن خارج فروختند به آن کشور انتقال می دهند در برابرش پولیکه مواد را در داخل می فروشند این پول را میگیرند و به تجار و به مردمیکه مالش خریده شده بر از آن می دهند.

احمد: بلی بسیار خوب.

[33] The speakers on this selection are Ahmad and Javid they attended high school in Afghanistan and Javid is a graduate of Kabul University and has a slight Kabuli accent and Ahmad speaks Kohdamani dialect of Dari.

Imports and Exports of Afghanistan

Ahmad: How were the exports and imports in Afghanistan there... Were the local people in charge of it, or was it under the control of the government?

Javid: In every country, exports and imports are one of the necessities, one of the main necessities, or... the main activities of life. Homeland... Afghanistan also had exports and imports. Generally, they imported more goods than they exported (lit. its exports were few, its imports were many).

Ahmad: Yes.

Javid: Um… Exports of Afghanistan, first of all… um… the programs were organized by the government.

Then, the businessmen... the local businessmen would sell goods to the merchant. The merchant would collect all of the goods and export them abroad. For example, in our homeland there were a lot of raisins, grapes, apples, and pears. Um … there used to be a lot of cotton in past years. There are a lot of karakul skins, rugs. There is wool, pistachios.

The businessman gathers these goods from the districts and provinces and [takes them] to the provincial capital and sells them (lit. provides) to some large-scale businessmen, to companies. Then the companies would export them to countries that have a contract with the government.

And in return there are imports to Afghanistan according to the needs of the local people. For example, we need flour, or we need cooking oil, we need tea and sugar, we need clothes, and we need cars. The businessman buys from that area what he needs in view of contracts that the government has previously signed (lit. contracted) with other countries.

Naturally they transfer the money that they earned from selling goods abroad back to their country and give it to the people whose goods had been bought.

Ahmad: Yes, very good.

Vocabulary

دیگیش *colloquial* دیگراش، دیگرش *adv* the other one

مالیۀ افغانستان[34]

احمد: عایدات دولت چه طور بدست می آمد؟ این خود دولت فابریکه ها داشت یا ...... دولت سر مردم مالیه وضع میکرد. این جه ... به چه ترتیب بود؟

جاوید: همه دولت ها عایدات خود را از مردم خود بدست می آورند یکتعداد محدود کشورهاست که عایداتش از منابع طبیعی اش مثل کشورهائیکه تولید نفت شان بسیار زیاد است آنها اکثر عایداتشان از تولید نفت است. و لیکن در وطن ما عایدات بصورت عموم از مردم بدست میامد.

مردم بالای ... چند قسم مالیه داشت.

یکی مالیه بر دارایی مردم، کسی زمین دارد، خانه دارد، موتر دارد، پول نخت دارد، چه دارد ... چه دارد بالای از اینها دولت یک فیصدی مالیه وضع می کند که سال در سال آن مالیه را بر دولت می پردازن.

یک قسم مالیۀ دیگر مالیات بر عایدات است که عایدات مردم سالانه چه قدر از درک فروش انگور خود. از درک فروش اه... باقی فرضاً گندم خود، از درک فروش دیگر مواد خود چه قدر عایدات میکُنَند، بر از آن مالیه وضع میکند. که از آن هم مالیه جمع میکند.

یکمقدار عایدات خود را از منابع معدنی فرضاً لاجورد است، یا زمرد است، یا به سنگ رخام است، از این معادن چیزیکه فروش میکند دولت، اینها دارایی دولتیست. از این راه عایدات خود را تهیه میکند.

[34] The speakers on this selection are Ahmad and Javid they attended high school in Afghanistan and Javid is a graduate of Kabul University and has a slight Kabuli accent and Ahmad speaks Kohdamani dialect of Dari.

Taxes in Afghanistan

Ahmad: How was the government's income acquired? Did the government itself have factories? Or … did the government tax people? How did that work? (lit. How was this?)

Javid: All governments get their income from their people. There is a limited number of countries whose income is from their natural resources, such as countries which produce a lot of oil (lit. whose oil production is very great). Most of their income is from oil production. But in our country, the income generally came from the people.

There were a variety of taxes [imposed] on people.

One is a tax on people's assets. Someone who has land, a house, a car, cash, and has this [thing] and that [thing], the government imposes a tax of a percentage of it, which they pay to the government each year.

Another kind of tax is a tax on income. However much people's income annually... from selling their grapes, from selling their extra wheat, for example, from selling their other products, a tax is levied on however much income they make They collect tax from this, too. [It takes].

Some of its income from mined resources; for example, there is lapis lazuli or emeralds or marble.Whatever the government sells from these mines is the government's property. It gets its income in this way.

یکمقدار دیگرش مالیکه از خارج به داخل وطن وارد میشود این بالای از این یک تکس حکومت وضع کرده. آن میآید در گمرک و باز مامورین گمرک مطابق قیمتش...

احمد: تکس تجارتی؟

جاوید: تکس تجارتیست که از مال تجارتی تکس میگیرند. هم صادرات چیزیکه صادر میکُنَند از آن یکمقدار میگیرند و هم مالیکه وارد میشود در افغانستان از آن هم دولت تکس میگیرد. و اه... تقریباً هشتادوپنج فیصد بودیجه دولت افغانستان از تکس واردات و صادرات است.

باقی پانزده فیصد دیگرش از مالیهٔ زمین و منابع طبیعی افغانستان است. و چون وضع اقتصادی افغانستان بسیار خراب است، عایدات بسیار پایین است. به این لحاظ عایدات افغانستان یا دولت بسیار پایین می باشد.

Another portion of it, the government has imposed a tax on what is imported to the country from abroad. It comes to the customs office, and customs officials [would assess tax] based on its value.

Ahmad: Import/export tax.

Javid: It is import/export tax. They tax commercial goods. Both exports... they take an amount from things that are exported, and the government taxes goods that are imported to Afghanistan, too. Approximately eighty-five percent of the budget of the government of Afghanistan is from taxes on imports and exports. Um...

The other fifteen percent is from the land tax and Afghanistan's natural resources. And since Afghanistan's economic situation is very bad, and the income is very low, that is why income of Afghanistan or the government is very low.

Vocabulary

میتن *colloquial* میدهند *v they would give*

فصول و هوای افغانستان[35]

احمد: اه... در منطقۀ شما سه ماه برف میشود و سه ماه خوب گرمی می باشد و در تابستان و اه... در بهار و خزان هوا معتدل می باشد. و چقدر برف میشود در آن منطقه و چقدر سردی تا به چه اندازه میرسد؟

جاوید: هان، همینطوریکه گفتی افغانستان وطن ما خصوصاً منطقۀ ما همین چهار فصل را دارد.

احمد: بلی...

جاوید: فصل بهار و تابستان و خزان و زمستان. که زمستانش سرد است و برف باری دارد. برف باری سالهای قبل بسیار زیاد بود.
در این وقت ها بسیار کم شده بصورت عموم. باز هم سی سانتی۳۶، بیست سانتی، بیست و پنج سانتی برف در هر مرتبه می بارد. دو سه چهار مرتبه بعضی سالها برف زیاد ... تا حمل می ماند بعضی وقت ها در ماه حوت خلاص میشود.
این همین برف در آنجا یکی از ضروریات عمدۀ زنده گیست. در زمستان اگر برف نه شود، صدبار که باران هم شود ضروریات زراعتی سال آینده اش را ...سال بهار سال آینده را آن پوره کرده نمی تواند. وقتی که برف شد همین برف که کافی باشد در کوها ذخیره میشود و دریاها از همان سرچشمه میگیرد و اکثراً سال آینده اش سال پرفیض و با برکت می باشد. چون باران می... هم، در آن سال باز برف که زیاد باشد باران هم زیاد می باشد.

---

[35] The speakers on this selection are Ahmad and Javid they attended high school in Afghanistan and Javid is a graduate of Kabul University and has a slight Kabuli accent and Ahmad speaks Kohdamani dialect of Dari.

[36] = سانتی متر = centimeter, a unit of length equal to 0.3937 inch.

Seasons and Climate of Afghanistan

Ahmad: Um... In your region, it snows three months and it is very hot for three months in the summer and the weather is moderate in the spring and fall. How much does it snow in that area and how cold does it get there?

Javid: Yes, as you said, Afghanistan, our country, especially my region, has four seasons.

Ahmad: Yes.

Javid: The seasons of spring, summer, fall, and winter. Winter is cold and has snowfall. There used to be a lot of snowfall in past years.

Generally, it is greatly reduced nowadays. It snows thirty centimeters, twenty centimeters, twentyfive centimeters at a time, two or three or four times [a year.] Some years, lots of snow will stay on the ground until the month of Hamal. Sometimes it melts away in the month of Hoot.

This snow is one of the principal necessities of life there. If it doesn't snow in the winter, even if it rains a hundred times, it won't be able to fulfill the agricultural needs of the following year, of the spring year (sic) of the following year. When it snows, if this snow is sufficient, it is stored in the mountains. And it will become the source for rivers. And usually the following year will be a year of prosperous. Because rain in the same year... when it snows a lot, it will rain a lot too.

احمد: بلی....

جاوید: حاصلات زراعتی بسیار خوب میشود. مگر در بهار سال باران میشود بصورت عموم در ماه حمل و ثور. در ماه حمل بارانای زیاد میشود. در ماه ثور باران کم میشود. و این بارانها هم برای زراعت بسیار مفید است. برای تازه ساختن اشجار و اه... حاصلات زراعتی بسیار مفید واقع میشود.

احمد: شما قبلاً گفتید که در منطقهٔ شما چهار فصل است که بهار است و تابستان است و خزان است و زمستان است. کدام ماه ها مثلاً در این فصلها است؟ و اه... این ماه ها از کدام منجه گرفته شده؟

جاوید: فصل بهارسه... سه ماه ست، حمل، ثور، جوزا. فصل تابستان هم سه ماه ست اه... سرطان، اسد، سنبله. میزان، عقرب، قوس این فصل خزان است. جدی، دلوه، حوت این سه ماه ماهٔ زمستان است. و اینها بسیار در لسان دری بسیار سابقه دارد. اضافه تر از سه هزار سال قبل این ماه ها در این محیط منطقه رواج بود. و این اساسش به اساس گردش شمس است. به اساس قمری نیست.

احمد: بلی .. آفتاب.

جاوید: هان، آفتاب است. در حرکت آفتاب این ماه ها را تعین میکند.

احمد: خو.. از همان خاطراست که بسیار به طبیعت مطابقت دارد این ماه ها واین فصلها.

Ahmad: Yes.

Javid: Agricultural production will be very good. But when it rains in the spring of the year, generally in the months of Hamal and Sowr, it rains a lot in Hamal and it rains less in Sowr. And these rains are very beneficial for agriculture. It is beneficial for refreshing the trees and agricultural harvests. Oh… there will be good production from the farms.

Ahmad: You said earlier that there are four seasons in your region, which are spring, summer, fall, and winter. Which months, for example, are in these seasons, and um… where were these months taken from?

Javid: Spring season is three months: Hamal, Sowr, and Jowzaa.

Summer season is also three months, um… Sarataan, Asad, and Sumbula. Meezaan, Aqrab, and Qows, these are the fall season. Jadee, Dalwa, and Hoot, these three months are the months of winter. And they are have a long history in the Dari language.

These months have been in use in this environment and region for more than three thousand years. It is based on the rotation of the sun. It is not based on the moon.37 It's solar.

Ahmad: Yes… the sun.

Javid: Yes, it's the sun. The rotation of the sun determines these months.

Ahmad: OK… that's why these months and seasons correspond to nature very well.

[37] The Arabic calendar is lunar, but the Afghan calendar is solar.

جاوید: بلی هان، این ماه ها و فصلها بالکل مطابق دوران طبیعت، به همان شکل این هم دوران می کنند. فرضاً ما که بهار میگویم معنی از این است که حمل و ثور وجوزا شروع سال جدید است.
در این وقت زراعت هم نَو شروع میشود، درختها نَو گُل کردن را شروع میکُنَند نهال شانی در این وقت میشود، کار و بار زراعت در همین وقت شروع میشود. این را بنام شروع گرمی سال از زمستان خلاص میشود این همین بهار است. بهار معنی اش هم شروع همین سه فصل (ماه) است. بهار معنی اش ابتدای زنده گی را هم میگویند.

احمد: بلی بسیار خوب.

جاوید: و فصل تابستان آه ... فصل گرم است سه ماه شامل است که نام هایش را گرفتیم. دراین فصل حاصلات زراعتی بصورت عموم خود را پخته میکند.

Javid: Yes, indeed. These months and seasons completely correspond to the cycle of nature. These cycle in the same way. For example, when we say spring, that means Hamal, Sowr, and Jowzaa are the start of the new year.

Farming also gets started at this time. Trees start to bloom and the planting of saplings is done at this time. Farming work gets started at this time. This is called the start of warm weather and the end of winter, and this is spring. The meaning of spring is the beginning of these three seasons, and also the beginning of life is called "spring."

Ahmad: Yes, very good.

Javid: And summer season um… it is a warm season and it is three months long (lit. includes three months), which we have named. In this season, crops generally ripen.

Vocabulary

نخت *colloquial* نقد *n* cash

رخصتی ها[38]

احمد: اه... روزهای رخصتی اه... در یک هفته چند روز رخصتی میباشد؟ و درماه چند روز رخصتی میباشد؟ و در یک سال چه رخصتی میباشد؟ و در هفته کدام روزها رخصتی مردم میگیرد؟ و در آن روزهای رخصتی مردم عموماً چه میکُنَند؟

جاوید: اه... در وطن ما رخصتی در یک هفته روز جمعه است. روز جمعه بصورت عموم مردم اه... یکی کار عادی زراعتیست، یکی کارهای عمدهٔ زراعتی مردم نمی کنند.
فرضاً گِل کاری در این روز نمی کنند، نجاری در این روز نمیکنند. اه... این روز را روز رخصتی خود میگیرند.
مکاتب در این روز بسته میباشد، دفترهای دولتی در این روز بسته میباشد، دکانها بصورت عموم بسته میباشند. یگان دکان که ضروریات عادی مردم را تهیه کند. آن ..رو..رو.. میباشند باقی همه رخصت میباشند.
دیگر در یک هفته هفت روز است. مثلیکه گفتیم روز شنبه شروع میشود، یکشنبه، دوشنبه، سه شنبه، چارشنبه، پنج شنبه. پنج شنبه تا نصف روز کار میباشد نصف روز رخصتی میباشد، ادارات دولتی و بازار و غیره.
اما مردم بصورت عموم دهقانها در روز پنج شنبه هم کار خود را میکنند.

---

[38] The speakers on this selection are Ahmad and Javid they attended high school in Afghanistan and Javid is a graduate of Kabul University and has a slight Kabuli accent and Ahmad speaks Kohdamani dialect of Dari.

Holidays

Ahmad: Um... the holidays um... How many days are holidays in a week? And how many days are holidays in a month? And what holidays are there in a year? And what days do people take off as holidays during the week? And what do people generally do on those holidays?

Javid: Um... in our country, the day off in the week is Friday. Generally, people on Friday um... one thing is normal farm work; major work is another thing, people don't do it.

For example, they don't do construction on this day, they don't do carpentry on this day. Um... they take this day as their day off.

Schools are closed on this day, government offices are closed on this day, stores are generally closed on this day. Only a few stores provide ordinary everyday necessities for people; the rest are all closed.

There are seven days in a week. As I said, it (the week) starts with Saturday. Sunday, Monday, Tuesday, Wednesday, and Thursday. On Thursday, half the day is a workday (lit. there is work) and a half the day is a day off for government offices and bazaars and so forth.

But farmers generally work on Thursday.

احمد: ببخشید! هَمِین روز جمعه که گفتید روز جمعه ... اه... رخصتی مذهبیست یا این روز جمعه رخصتی از همان کولتور مردم همانطور تعین شده؟

جاوید: همین کولتور مردم اه... کولتور مردم جزء زنده گی مذهبیشان است.

احمد: بلی.

جاوید: باساس مذهب هم روز جمعه ... یعنی قید نیست که رخصت باشد. مگر مردم همین روز را چون روز بابرکت و برای عبادت خود تعین میکُنَند. این روز را روز رخصتی میگیرند و رخصتی است در این روز.

احمد: خو بسیار خوب.

جاوید: مردم در این روز فرضاً نماز جمعه میروند. جمع میشوند تعداد زیاد در مساجد یکجائی نماز میخوانند. فرضاً ملا برای شان تبلیغ میکند که کدام کار خوب است و کدام کار خراب است. کارهای خوب را بِکُنَند و کار خراب را نَکُنَند.

دیگر در سال بصورت عموم یکی نوروز رخصتیست، یکی دو عید رخصتیست، یکی روز استقلال وطن رخصتیست و روزهای جمعه در هر هفته رخصتیست.

احمد: بسیار خوب.

Ahmad: Excuse me. You mentioned About Friday, which you mentioned... Is Friday a religious holiday? Or was Friday selected as a holiday because of people's culture?

Javid: People's culture, um... The people's culture is part of their religious life.

Ahmad: Yes.

Javid: According to our religion, Friday… that is, it is not .... there is no restriction that it be a day off. But people, since this is a day of blessing and they choose this day for worship, they take this day as their day off and it's a day off. People chose this day as a holiday.

Ahmad: Good, very good.

Javid: On this day, many people get together and go to the mosque and pray the Friday prayer. On this day, people, for example, go to Friday prayer, a large number of people gather in mosques and pray together. For example, the mullah gives them guidance on what is right and what is wrong so that they would do good things and not do bad things.

Generally, in the year, Nawroz is a holiday, the two Eids are holidays, Independence Day is a holiday, and Fridays every week are holidays.

Ahmad: Very good.

Vocabulary

أمطو *colloquial* همان طور *adv, phrase like that, that way*
منجه *colloquial* منبَع *n* source

رادیو افغانستان

قسمت اول[39]

احمد: در افغانستان اه...اه... رادیو وتلویزیون و اه... نشراتی که می شد از طریق رادیو وتلویزیون کدام نشرات را میکردند و به چه قسم بود؟

جاوید: در افغانستان یکی پروگرام رادیو است و یکی پروگرام تلویزیون. پروگرام رادیو تقریباً در یکشبانه روز یازده ساعت نشرات دارد. از ساعت شش صبح شروع میکُنَند تا ساعت نُه صبح.

احمد: بلی.

جاوید: دراین نشرات خود اول قرآن کریم تلاوت میکردند بعد ترجمه وتفسیر از آن را میگفتند. بعد از آن باز پروگرامهای معلوماتی، تفریحی، اعلانات را نشر میکردند.

احمد: بلی.

جاوید: باز ساعت هفت بجهٔ صبح خبرهای داخلی و خارجی را میگفتند. از این خبرها بعضی قسمتهایش را شب گذشته هم گفته بودند و باز تکرار میکردند، بعضی خبرهای نو هم میگفتند.

احمد: بلی.

[39] The speakers on this selection are Ahmad and Javid they attended high school in Afghanistan and Javid is a graduate of Kabul University and has a slight Kabuli accent and Ahmad speaks Kohdamani dialect of Dari.

Radio Afghanistan
Part One

Ahmad: In Afghanistan...um...um...radio and television and the broadcasting that was done on radio and TV, what did they broadcast and how was it?

Javid: In Afghanistan, there is radio programming and television programming.

Radio programming is broadcast approximately eleven hours during a 24 hour day. They start at six o'clock in the morning [and broadcast] until nine o'clock in the morning.

Ahmad: Yes.

Javid: In these broadcasts of theirs, they would first read from the holy Koran, then they would give [lit. say] its translation and interpretation. Then they would broadcast educational, entertainment, and advertising programs.

Ahmad: Yes.

Javid: Then at seven o'clock in the morning, they would deliver [lit. say] domestic and foreign news. They had delivered some parts of this news the previous night too, and they would repeat [them] and also deliver some fresh news.

Ahmad: Yes.

جاوید: بعد از خبرها پیش گویی اوضاع ... اوضاع جوی بیست... بیست وچهارساعت گذشته و پیش گوئی اوضاع جوی بیست وچهارساعت اینده را میکردند. بعد از آن خبرها اعلانات تجارتی را میگفتند. اه... بعد از اه... از آن باز اه... ساعت تقریباً اه... اه... نُه بجه ختم میکردند.

اما تا آن وقت اینها اعلانهای فوتی را هم میگفتند بعضی وقت. اعلانهای فوتی در افغانستان چون تعداد کم رادیو را میشنید. تعداد کم از آن استفاده میکردند مشکل نبود...

باز پروگرام موسیقی بود در افغانستان در رادیو، خواندنهای پشتو وفارسی. بعد از اه... یک چند خواندن فارسی و پشتو اه... باز معلوماتهای مختلف برای مردم می دادند. فرضاً معلوماتای طبی، معلومات در مورد زراعت و دهقانی.

این معلوماتها ای یا بشکل مصاحبه با افراد فنی تهیه میشد. یا بشکل اه... دایلوگ ... دایلوگ بین دو نفر که به لهجۀ وطنی گپ میزدند، به لهجۀ محلی تا مردم از آن بفهمد و معلومات را به مردم میرساندند.

اه... بعضی وقت پروگرامهای فامیلی را که زنده گی در فامیلها چه قسم باید باشد، مردم چه قسم زنده گی کنند، این پروگرامها را نشر میکردند.

پروگرام دومش ساعت دوازدۀ ظهر شروع میشد و ساعت... تا ساعت دو بجه دوام میکرد.

پروگرام شام به همین ترتیب بود. یکذره مفصل تر بود. از ساعت چار الی ساعت یازدۀ شب باز بعداً تشریح می کنیم آن را هم.

Javid: After the news, they would give [lit. do] the weather forecast… forecast for twenty…the last twenty-four hours (sic) and the weather forecast for the next twenty-four hours. After those news, they would give the business news um… after that, then, approximately …um… um… nine o'clock they would end [the program].

But by then, they would have given the obituaries, sometimes. Obituaries in Afghanistan, since few [lit. a small number] would listen to the radio, few would use it [for obituaries]. It wasn't difficult.

There was a music program on the radio in Afghanistan. [There were] Pashto and Farsi songs. After a few Farsi and Pashto songs, then they would present [lit. give] various information for people, for example, medical information, and information about agriculture and farming.

This information would be provided either in the form of an interview with experts or in the form of a dialogue between two people. They would talk in colloquial accents (not formal Dari) so everyone in different regions could understand the information.

Um... Sometimes they [broadcast] programs about the family, about how family life [lit. life in families] should be, how people should live, they would broadcast programs like these programs.

Its second program would start at twelve o'clock noon and o'clock ... would continue until two o'clock.

The evening program was the same way (lit. in this very manner). It was a little bit more detailed. From four o'clock until eleven o'clock at night. I (lit. we) will explain that also later.

Vocabulary

بِفامه *colloquial* بفهمه *v* to understand, to know

رادیو افغانستان

قسمت دوم[40]

احمد: در رادیو افغانستان خواندنها را هم در پروگرامهایش می ماندند که مردم بشنوند. یا اه... در وقت... آن فرق دارد که در کدام وقت و زمان دیگر خواندن را می ماندند.
در وقت ظاهرشاه چطور بود؟ و در وقت طالبها؟

جاوید: هان، در رادیو افغانستان خواندنهای .. خواندنها و مو سیقی در دوره های مختلف، مختلف بود. فرضاً در زمان ظاهرشاه اول رادیو خواندنها داشت موسیقی داشت.
بصورت عموم موسیقی کلاسیک داشت، موسیقی محلی وفولکلورداشت. اما در زمان ...بعداً ... بعداً که در افغانستان آزادی و قانون اساسی و این مسائل آمد، باز خواندنهای زنها هم در رادیو افغانستان رواج شد.
اه ... زنها آمدند و در موسیقی سهم گرفتند.
بعداً در زمان داودخان باز موسیقی بیشتر شد، آزادی بیشتر دادند برایش. این دوام کرد، در زمان... در زمان حکومت خلقیها وتسلت روسها هم موسیقی را بسیار زیاد رونق دادند. دسته های مختلف موسیقی به میان آمد.
بعد از زمان خلقیها دوران حکومت مجاهدین هم موسیقی به همان شکل سابق زمان داودخان به پیش رفت.
در وقتیکه طالبها آمدند موسیقی را از رادیو و تلویزیون افغانستان از بین بردند. صرف برای خبرها، تبلیغات مذهبی و بعضی خواندنهای عادی که خود... خود... خوش خودشان میآمد همان را به نشر می سپردند و بس.
حالاَ فعلاً کهَ طالبها از بین رفته باز موسیقی در رادیو و تلویزیون افغانستان شروع شده.

---

[40] The speakers on this selection are Ahmad and Javid they attended high school in Afghanistan and Javid is a graduate of Kabul University and has a slight Kabuli accent and Ahmad speaks Kohdamani dialect of Dari.

Radio Afghanistan
Part Two

Ahmad: On Radio Afghanistan, did they put songs on its programs for people to listen to [lit. that people could listen]? Or um... at the time... does it depend on the time when they were airing the songs? [lit. does it make a difference at which time and period they were putting the songs?]

How was it in Zahir Shah's time? And in the time of the Taliban?

Javid: Yes, on Radio Afghanistan, songs... songs and music under different regimes (lit. reigns) were different. For example, during Zahir Shah's time, for the first time, radio had songs, had music.

Generally, it had classical music, had local and folk music. But at the time of... later, later when in Afghanistan freedom, a constitution, and these things (lit. matters) came, then women singing (lit. womens' songs) on the radio became common.

Um... then women came and participated in music.

Then in Daoud Khan's time, music increased. They gave it (music) more freedom. This continued during the time of... in the time of the Khalqi government and Russian rule, music was made to flourish. Different groups of musicians came into existence.

After the time of the Khalqis, during the Mujahedeen government, music kept going as it was before in Daud Khan's time.

When the Taliban came, they eliminated music from the radio and television of Afghanistan. Only news, religious propaganda, and some ordinary songs that they themselves liked, they allowed that to be broadcast, and that's all.

Now that the Taliban have been overthrown (lit. eliminated), music on the radio and television of Afghanistan has begun again.

احمد: در پروگرام رادیو در افغانستان چند ساعت بود؟ بیست وچهار ساعته بود یا یک وقت معین داشت؟

جاوید: اه... نشرات رادیو در افغانستان در دوره های مختلف مختلف بود. فرضاً در زمان اول، زمان ظاهرشاه از... ساعات محدود بود رادیو. فرضاً از ساعت شش تا هشت صبح بود. ساعت دوازده تا یک ظهر بود و از ساعت چهار تا ده شب.

بعداً زیاد شد در زمان حکومت داودخان حتی از ساعت شش صبح الی دوازدهٔ شب شد. بسیار دوام دار در سر هر ساعت خبرها داشتند.

بعداً اه... در زمان خلقیها هم همانطور زیاد دوام دار بود.

در زمان طالبها بسیار محدود شد. فعلاً پس دوباره زیاد شده.

احمد: کدام چیزها را میگفتند .... در رادیو مثلاً کدام پروگرامها را میگفت؟

جاوید: اه ... در رادیو اه... بصورت عموم پروگرامهای اه... اول شروع رادیو قرآن کریم تلاوت میکرد. بعد ازآن ترجمه و تفسیر، پروگرامهای موسیقی، معلومات علمی، معلومات زراعتی، خبرها، اعلانات.

اه... دیگر اه... بصورت عموم این همین مطالب را در رادیوی افغانستان نشر میکردند.

Ahmad: How many hours was radio programming in Afghanistan? Was it twenty-four hours or did it have a specified time?

Javid: Um... radio broadcasts in Afghanistan under different regimes were different. For example, in the first period, in the time of Zahir Shah, radio hours were limited. For example, it would be from six o'clock to eight in the morning, it would be from twelve o'clock to one in the afternoon, and from four o'clock to ten at night.

Then it increased, in the time of Daud Khan's government, it began to be all the way from six o'clock in the morning until twelve at night, it was prolonged. They had the news at the top of every hour.

Later, in the time of the Khalqis too, it was likewise very lengthy.

In the time of the Taliban it became very limited. Now, it has become extended once again.

Ahmad: What kind of things did they broadcast (lit. say) on the radio? For example, what kind of programs did they broadcast (lit. say)?

Javid: Um... on the radio... um... generally, programs...um... first, at the start of radio [programming] they would read from the holy Koran. After that, the translation and interpretation [of the Koran], music programs, scientific information agricultural information, the news, advertising...

Um... then, um... generally they broadcast these subjects on Afghanistan radio.

تلویزیون افغانستان[41]

احمد: وقتیکه من در افغانستان بودم در تلویزیون زیادتر پروگرامهای روسی را نشان میداد. مثلاً سریالهای روسی را و جنگهای... فلمهای جنگی و اه.. بعضی پروگرامهای... اه... کارتون که یک کرتون بود چه بود نامش همان کارتون؟ یادِ من رفته.

جاوید: من نمی فهمم کدام کارتون را می گویی.

احمد: یک کارتون بود یادِ من رفته. اوره آنها نشان می داد دیگر. اه... اه... پروگرامهای روسیَ زیادتر بود.
اما می گفتند که رادیو و تلویزیون همین استدیو وچیزهای کارهایش را جاپانی ها کرده بود در افغانستان.

جاوید: اه... تلویزیون در افغانستان بار اول در زمان داودخان به میان آمد. اُو از طرف خود افغانستان به کمک جرمنها ساخته شده بود.

احمد: خو...

جاوید: اه... استیشن. بعداً او انکشاف داده شد. وقتیکه تسلط روسها در افغانستان زیاد شد روابط شان قوی تر شد و حکومت افغانستان هم مجبوریت داشت از کمک های خارجی استفاده کند. روسها بیشتر کمک کردند تا بتوانند تبلیغات خود در افغانستان برسانند.

---

[41] The speakers on this selection are Ahmad and Javid they attended high school in Afghanistan and Javid is a graduate of Kabul University and has a slight Kabuli accent and Ahmad speaks Kohdamani dialect of Dari.

Afghan Television

Ahmad: When I was in Afghanistan, they mostly broadcast Russian TV programs on Afghan TV, for example, Russian miniseries, war movies war movies and, um... some cartoon movies. There was one cartoon. What was the name of that cartoon? I've forgotten.

Javid: I don't know what cartoon you're talking about.

Ahmad: There was a cartoon. I have forgotten. They (Afghan TV) used to show it. Um... Um... there were even more Russian programs.

It has been said that the Japanese did the technical work for the Afghan TV studio. Oh...

Javid: Um... the television station (lit. television) came into existence in Afghanistan for the first time in the time of Daud Khan. Afghans themselves, along with the help of the Germans, had built the Afghan TV station.

Ahmad: OK.

Javid: Oh...the station, later, it was improved. When the Russian influence in Afghanistan increased and relations [between the two countries] became stronger, the Afghan government had to use foreign help. The Russians helped more so they would be able to spread their propaganda in Afghanistan.

احمد: خی جاپانیها نبود؟

جاوید: جاپانیها نبودند، جاپانیها بعضی وسائله کمک میکردند. مثل کامره های ویدیوئی و کامره های عکاسی و وسایل تیپ کردن صدا و غیره وسایل را. اما اینکه فلمهای روسی را نشان می دادند سریالهایش را و بعضی کارتونها را، آن ره... بخاطر از این بود که خود افغانستان این چیزها را نداشت. بخاطر مصروف ساختن مردم مجبور بود یکتعداد را از بعضی جاها اه... مطالبه کنه.
در برابر مطالبهٔ حکومت تنها روسها بودند که جواب می دادند برای شان و همان چیزها را برایش تهیه میکردند و آن را هم برای... برای مردم نشر میکردند. به این خاطر از روسها زیاد نشرمیشد.

احمد: مردم چه فکر میکردند نَو که تلویزیون آمده بود چه می گفتند؟ خصوصاً مردم اطراف اه... برایشان یک چیز عجیب بود دیگر یا نی؟

جاوید: هم چیزِ عجیب بود برایشان، و هم بسیار خوش بودند.

احمد: خو ...

جاوید: خوش بودند که بار اول در افغانستان تلویزیون آمده و ما هرچیز را از خود.... به چشم و سر می بینیم، این برای بیدار ساختن اذهان مردم خیلی مفید بود.

Ahmad: So they weren't Japanese?

Javid: They weren't Japanese; the Japanese helped [us] with some equipment, for example, video cameras, and photo cameras, and sound recording equipment and other equipment. But that they used to show Russian movies and their miniseries and some cartoons, that was because Afghanistan didn't have these things itself.

To entertain people they had to get it (lit. some) from somewhere (lit. some places).

It was only the Russians who fulfilled the government's request and provided those things for it (the Afghan government), and they also broadcast [them] to people. That is why they would broadcast a lot [of programming] from Russians.

Ahmad: What did people think when television had just arrived? What did they say, especially people in the countryside? Um… It was a strange thing for them, wasn't it?

Javid: It was a strange thing for them, and also they were very happy.

Ahmad: OK.

Javid: They were happy because television had arrived in Afghanistan for the first time, and they could see things with their own eyes (lit. we see everything with the eyes in our head.) This was very useful for enlightening people (lit. awakening people's minds)

احمد: بلی، مردم هیچ تصور نمیکرد که اینطور یک چیزی باشد که عکس نفر را ببینند و ....

جاوید: در زمان بسیار قدیم اینطور فکر نمی کردند مگر پیش ازیکه تلویزیون بیآید تبلیغات تلویزیون در افغانستان زیاد آمده بود که کشور های همسایهٔ ما تلویزیون دارد، کشور های پیش رفتهٔ دنیا تلویزیون دارد. واینطور وسائل است که مردم از آن استفاده می کند.

مردم با نامش آشنا شده بود و خوش بودند، آرزو داشتند که اینطور چیزی در وطن بیآید.

احمد: بلی...اه... در تلویزیون پروگراهای خبرها را دیگر میگفت زیاد و مثلاً فلمها و چیزها را نشان می داد.

و در وخت ما خو همانطور بود. که من که در افغانستان بودم فلمهای روسی و چیزها را.

اه... بعد ازیکه اه... طالببها آمدند تلویزیون را بیخی قطع کردند یا....

جاوید: هان ... قبل از آن همانطورکه خودت گفتی همین پروگرامها بود. اما وقتیکه طالبها آمدند تلویزیون را بکلی بسته کردند. یک تعداد زیاد کستها وغیره را در دادند، سوختاندن، و استیشن را مطلق بند کردند، ازنشرات ماند.

اما وقتیکه باز طالبها از بین رفت، فعلاً حکومت دوباره آن را فعال ساخته.

Ahmad: Yes, people never imagined that there could be a thing such that you would see a person's picture and...

Javid: In very old times, they wouldn't have thought of it. But right before television was to come, people would talk about television (lit. lots of television propaganda had come to Afghanistan), that our neighboring countries have television, the developed countries of the world have television, and it is a device that people use.

People were familiar with its name and they were happy, they hoped and were happy that such a thing would come to the country.

Ahmad: Yes. Um... on television, they would show lots of news programs, and, for example, they would show movies and things.

It was like this in my (lit. our) time. When I was in Afghanistan, they would show Russian movies and things.

Um... after... um...the Taliban came, did they they cut off television [broadcasting] completely, or ...?

Javid: Yes, there were those programs before, as you said. But when the Taliban came, they totally shut down television. They set fire and burned a large number of cassettes, etc. They shut the station completely down and stopped broadcasting.

But now that the Taliban have been overthrown (lit. eliminated), the government has reopened it (lit. made it function again).

Vocabulary

مه *colloquial* من *pro* I, me

می گِی *colloquial* میگوئی *v* you are talking about

خبرا *colloquial* خبرها *n* the news

ره *colloquial* را postposition used after definite direct object

بیخی *colloquial* تماماً، بکُلی *adv* totally, completely *n* with the root

عسکری[42]

احمد: شما عسکری کردید در افغانستان؟ من خو از عسکری گریختم.

جاوید: نی در زمانیکه اه... اه... در افغانستان وقت عسکری ما آمد ما مخالف دولت بودیم. در عسکری نرفتیم در ضد دولت مبارزهٔ سیاسی می کردیم.

احمد: باید کُلگی عسکری کُند نی دوسال؟

جاوید: بلی در اَفغانستان سیستمِ عسکری جبریست. هرکس دوسال عسکری باید بکند که از سن هژده سالگی اِلی بیست یا نزده و بیست و یک... بیست... و بیست ودو ساله نفر باید عسکَری برود.

احمد: بلی هان از همان خاطر... اه... وقتیکه نوبت ما آمد در سن عسکری بودم، من خودم برآمدم از افغانستان باز در عسکری هم ...اه... چه چیزها را یاد می دادند؟ صحیح عسکر می شدند یا همانطور مخسد نامش عسکری بود؟

جاوید: اه... در افغانستان همان قسمیکه سویهٔ تعلیمی پائین است سطح زنده گی پائین است، سطح عسکریش هم پائین است.

مگر یکنفریکه در عسکری میرفت، عسکر بود از نظر به افراد عادی بسیار فرق داشت. یک دورهٔ تربیهٔ زنده گی بسیار مهم برای مردم افغانستان عسکری بود که دو سال عسکری می کردند. وقتیکه پس به وطن میآمدند یعنی یک آدمی که هوشیارتر، فهمیده تر می بود.

احمد: بلی هان در عسکری تنها اه... جنگ یادشان می داد یا مسائل اه... دینی و مسائل اجتماعی و چیزها را هم درس می دادشان؟

[42] The speakers on this selection are Ahmad and Javid they attended high school in Afghanistan and Javid is a graduate of Kabul University and has a slight Kabuli accent and Ahmad speaks Kohdamani dialect of Dari.

Military Service

Ahmad: Did you serve in the military in Afghanistan? I evaded military service.

Javid: No, when… um… um…. in Afghanistan, the time came for me to serve in the military, I was (lit. we were) anti-government and didn't go into the military. I was involved in anti-government political activity.

Ahmad: Doesn't everybody have to serve in the military for two years?

Javid: Yes, the military system in Afghanistan is compulsory.

Everyone has to do two years of military service from the age of eighteen to twenty, or nineteen to twentyone… twenty to twentytwo.

Ahmad: Yes, that is why, when my turn came, when I was military age, I left Afghanistan. In the military, um... what things did they teach? Did they become good soldiers? Or was the point that it was called military service?

Javid: In Afghanistan, just as the educational level is low and the standard of living is low, the standards of its military are also low.

But a person who served in the military, was a soldier was very different from civilians (lit. ordinary people). Serving in the military, which they did for two years, was a very important educational period of life for the people of Afghanistan. When they came back home, they were smarter and more intelligent people.

Ahmad: Yes, indeed, in the military, did they only teach them how to fight? Or did they teach them religious matters and social matters and things too?

جاوید: نی در عسکری درجه اول چیزیکه بود تعلیم و تربیهٔ عسکری بود.
احمد: بلی.
جاوید: اه ...و بعد از آن کوشش می کردند خصوصاً در زمان حکومت داود خان که عسکر را باسواد بسازند.
احمد: بلی.
جاوید: اما دیگر مسائله اه... حکومت سرشان تطبیق نمی کرد.
احمد: صاحب منصبها چطور بودند در افغانستان فهمیده بودند خوب صحیح، یا آنها هم همانطور مثل عسکر واری بودند؟
جاوید: نی صاحب منصبها خو مردم تحصیل یافته بود. بصورت عموم لیسانسه... بودند.
احمد: خو...
جاوید: اما سویهٔ عسکری نظر به سایر کشورها خصوصاً کشورهای پیش رفته عقب بود. ولی آنها صاحب منصب تحصیل یافته و فاکولته خوانده.. اه... در قسمت تعلیم و تربیهٔ افراد خود توجهٔ زیاد می کردند. مردم هوشیاری بودن.
احمد: بلی. باز عسکرها می گفتند در افغانستان که دو سال عسکری کردیم شینگرس[43] و کینگرس را نمی فهمم. یعنی تعلیم اِچیزه عسکری را.
جاوید: این خو بعضی گپهای بود که یگان نفر عسکر بخَاطریکه خود را بسیار کلان کار معرفی کند، پیش دیگرها خوده بسیار جسور معرفی کند این گپها را می زدند. اما به آن قسم نبود، عسکر را عسکر می ساختند. به همآن پروگرامی که داشت حکومت مطابق از آن او را عسکر می ساخت.
احمد: بلی هان.

[43] Most military terms in Afghanistan are from the Pashtoo language, therefore the words شینگرس and کینگرس are Pashtoo and they mean “right turn” and “left turn.”

Javid: No, in the military, the thing that was first priority was military training.

Ahmad: Yes.

Javid: After that, they would try, especially in the time of Daud Khan's government, to make the soldiers (lit. the soldier) literate.

Ahmad: Yes

Javid: But the government didn't train them in other matters.

Ahmad: How were military officers in Afghanistan? Were they very intelligent? Or were they like soldiers?

Javid: No, military officers were educated people. Generally, they were college graduates.

Ahmad: Good.

Javid: But the level of the military was underdeveloped compared to other countries, especially developed countries.

But they, the educated and college-graduate officers- paid close attention to (lit. in the area of) the training of their men. They were smart people.

Ahmad: Yes. Soldiers in Afghanistan would say, "We've served in the military for two years, and I don't know right face and left face," meaning military training and stuff.

Javid: That was just talk; some soldiers would say those things to make themselves look like (lit. present themselves) big shots to others and to make themselves look bold. That is why they would say that. But that's not how it was. They would make a soldier a soldier. And they would be trained according to the government's military training program

Ahmad: Yes indeed

Vocabulary

هوشار *colloquial* هوشیار *adj* smart, intelligent
شینگرس *colloquial pashtoo* شی گرز *n* right turn (military term), right face
کینگرس *colloquial* pashtoo کینگرز *n* left turn (military term), left face

عسکری در زمان انقلاب[44]

احمد: من فکر می کنم که در افغانستان مسئلهٔ عسکری پیش از انقلاب ضد روسها خوب منظم بود اه... بعد ازاین که انقلاب ضد روسها شروع شد، ضد کمونستها وروسها باز یک قسم گدوبدی آمد و اه... این... این به چی ترتیب اه اه...نتیجه اش چه قسم شد؟

جاوید: عسکری در افغانستان طبعاً در زمان حکومتهای شاهی و در زمان حکومت جمهوری داود خان منظم بود، اه ... بادسپلین بود. عسکر را تربیه می کردند. همه افراد ملت مجبور بودند که عسکری می رفتند، اِلی یک چند قوم محدود که در قسمت جنوب افغانستان بودند و نزدیک به خَاندان شاهی بود آنها به عسکری نمی رفت دیگر مردم همه به عسکری می رفت.

احمد: آنها هیچ عسکری نمی کردند؟

جاوید: هیچ عسکری نمی کردند. به نام از این که ما پاچاهی را برای نادر خان گرفتیم به عسکری نمی رفتند آنها.

احمد: این خو یک ظلم بود سر مردم بیچاره ای دیگر عسکری می کرد و سر از آنها نی؟

---

[44] The speakers on this selection are Ahmad and Javid they attended high school in Afghanistan and Javid is a graduate of Kabul University and has a slight Kabuli accent and Ahmad speaks Kohdamani dialect of Dari.

Military during Revolution

Ahmad: I think that the military in Afghanistan was very organized before the anti-Russian revolution. Um…after the anti-Russian revolution started, the anti-Communist and anti-Russian revolution, a kind of unrest came to the country.

How was this... What was its result?

Javid: Naturally, the military in Afghanistan under the royal governments and under Daud Khan's republic was organized um… and was disciplined. They would train the soldiers.

All citizens had to serve in the military except for a few tribes that were in the southern part of Afghanistan and were related to the royal family. (lit. from the same tribe) They didn't serve in the military but everybody else served in the military.

Ahmad: They didn't serve in the military at all?

Javid: They didn't serve in the military at all. They didn't serve in the military because they said "We helped King Nader take over the kingdom." That is why they don't serve in the military.

Ahmad: That was discrimination, wasn't it? They made the other poor people serve in the military and didn't make them.

جاوید: هان، بلی همین ظلم را میکردند حکومتها. اه... این عسکری به این شکل دوام داد. و وقتیکه کمونستها در افغانستان آمدند وعسکرروسی داخل افغانستان شد تعداد زیاد مردم از عسکری فرار کرد. به جای ازاین که به عسکری بروند به گروپهای مخالف دولت پیوستند و ضد کمونستها جنگ را شروع کردند، تا این که کمونستها سقوط کردند و باز حکومت مجاهدین آمد.

با آمدن حکومت مجاهدین قوای عسکری مکمل از هم پاشید. زیرا کمونستها در آن قوای عسکری بودند وصرف کمونستها بودند. می خواستن به این خاطر حکومت مجاهدین و آن قوای عسکری را مکمل منحل کرد. به جایش گروپهای مختلف را به میان آورد.

آن گروپها بین خود جور نامدند. بالآخره آن قوای عسکری هم عسکر نشدند. گروپهای مختلف بود تا طالبها آمدند.

احمد: چطور بود بین مجاهدین ضد روس آنها هم عین قانون عسکری را تطبیق می کردند یا ان را به کدام قسم دیگری همین عسکری خود را پیش می بردند.

جاوید: نی گروپهای مجاهدین خو داوطلب بود هرکسی که دلش می شد و در ضد روس بجنگه و مقاومت کند آنها هم میآمدند به گروپها پیوست می شدند. در آن جنگهای گریلائی بود آنها عسکر نبودند.

در زمان حکومت شان، حکومت مجاهدین هم عسکری به میآن نیامد. بالآخره طالبها آمدند،

طالبها هم عسکر یک تعداد[45]... در زمان حکومت مجاهدین چیزی بود که صاحب منصبهای عسکری باقی ماندند در قطعات و در تشکیلات دولت باقی ماندند.

اما در زمان طالبها همان صاحب منصبها را هم کُلّه را از عسکری رخصت کردند، به جایش... به جای هر کار یک طالب را مقرر کردند. فعلاً که طالبها از بین رفته دوباره می خواهند اُردو را در افغانستان بسازند.

[45] The speaker meant to say that the Taliban also didn't have a military.

Javid: Yes, governments carried out this kind of injustice. Um… the military service continued like this.

When the Communists came to power in Afghanistan and the Russian military entered Afghanistan, a large number of people deserted from the military. Instead of serving in the military, people joined anti-government groups and started fighting against the Communists until the Communists fell. Then the Mujahedeen government came.

With the coming of the Mujahedeen government, the military completely dispersed because Communists, and only Communists, were in that military. Because of this, the Mujahedeen government completely dissolved the military, and in its place created different groups.

Those groups couldn't come to agreement. Ultimately, the military even ceased to be a military (lit. became not a military).

There were various groups until the Taliban came to power.

Ahmad: What was it like among the anti-Russian Mujahedeen? Did they also follow the same military regulations? Or did they run their military in another way?

Javid: No, Mujahedeen groups were volunteer; whoever wanted to fight and resist the Russians, they would come and join the groups. They were guerilla fighters not soldiers.

During their government, the government of the Mujahedeen, a military wasn't created. Ultimately, the Taliban came to power.

The Taliban also some had military... During the Mujahedeen there was a thing where military officers stayed (lit. remained) in military units and governmental institutions.

But under the Taliban, they dismissed all of those officers from the military and replaced each one of them with a Talib. Now that the Taliban have been overthrown (lit. eliminated), they want to build the military again.

Vocabulary

گدوبدی *colloquial* نا آرامی، برهم خوردن *adj, n* unrest, instability
اُنا *colloquial* آنها *pro* they
گریلائی *colloquial English* پارتیزان، چریکی *adj, n* guerilla
بیارن *colloquial* بیاورند

حکومت[46]

احمد: اه... اه... دولت افغانستان در وقت ظاهر شاه و داود خان اه... نسبت به وقتی که مجاهدین کابل را گرفتند ونسبت به وقت طالبها بسیار فرق داشت نی؟

جاوید: هان، دولت در افغانستان اه... از سه صد سال تقریباً قبل که دولته بنام افغانستان تشکیل شده توسط احمدشاه بابا. و دولت های افغانستان کلش سیستم شاهی بود.

احمد: بلی.

جاوید: در این سیستم های شاهی بصورت عموم خاندان سدوزئی حکومت می کردند اه... پادشاهی میراثی بود بین اولادهای از یک پادشاه به پسرش می ماند. اه... تا زمان ظاهر شاه این به همین شکل دوام کرد.
متأسفانه که در همین ظرف سه صد سالیکه شاهی در افغانستان بود اینها حکومتهای بود که صرف کار برای همان فامیل خود و به دوام تسلط خود می کردند.
وقتی داود خان توانست حکومت شاهی را از بین ببرد در جایش حکومت جمهوری به میان بیاورد، این قدرت تقریباً به مردم داده شد.

احمد: داود خان هم خو از خاندان شاهی بود نی؟

---

[46] The speakers on this selection are Ahmad and Javid they attended high school in Afghanistan and Javid is a graduate of Kabul University and has a slight Kabuli accent and Ahmad speaks Kohdamani dialect of Dari.

Government

Ahmad: Um... um... the government in Afghanistan in the time of Zahir Shah and Daud Khan was much different from the time after the Mujahideen had taken Kabul and from the time of the Taliban, wasn't it?

Javid: Yes, the government in Afghanistan, um... From approximately three hundred years ago, when a government by the name of Afghanistan was established by Ahmad Shah Baba, and all the governments of Afghanistan were monarchies.

Ahmad: Yes.

Javid: In these monarchies, generally the Sadozai and clan ruled.... It was a hereditary kingship between the children of... it passed from a king to his son. It continued like that through Zahir Shah's time.

Unfortunately, during the three hundred years that there was monarchy in Afghanistan, they were governments that worked only for the sake of their own family and the continuation of their authority.

When Daud Khan was able to end the monarchy government and replace it with a republican government (lit. bring a republican government into being in its place), power was almost totally given to the people.

Ahmad: Daud Khan was from the royal family also, wasn't he?

جاوید: بلی داود خان پسر کاکای ظاهر شاه بود وهم شوهر همشیره اش. اه... اما فکری داشت که باید در افغانستان یک حکومت جمهوری باشد. ازاین شکل موجوده باید افغانستان کشیده شود.

احمد: پیش از... پیش از این سه صد سالیکه گفتید که افغانستان نامش افغانستان بود، پیش از آن چه بود نام افغانستان؟

جاوید: در دوره های مختلف نامهای مختلف داشت. فرصاً زیاد کسها خراسان می گفتند و از قسمت های مختلف... نامهای مختلف داشت در افغانستان.
اما بعد ازاین که احمدشاه بابا همین ساحۀ محدوده را .... محدوده را به میان آورد این را بنام افغانستان نام گذاشت.

احمد: خو... داودخان خَی یک انسان بسیار روشن فکر بود به اصطلاح می خواست که حکومت مردمی داشته باشد، نه حکومت خاندانی وشاهی.

جاوید: بلی، هان داودخان آدم روشن فکربود تحصیل یافته بود. او می خواست که در افغانستان یک حکومت جمهوری باشد که به مردم خدمت کند. و در دوران تقریباً پنج سال دوران حکومت خود اه... برای آبادی افغانستان بسیار پلانها و پروگرامها وضع کرد.
بسیار سروی کرد. و کوشش میکرد که افغانستان از این وضع موجوده اش... از آن وضع موجودۀ آن وقت خلاص شود.

احمد: خو بسیار خوب.

Javid: Yes, Daud Khan was Zahir Shah's cousin and also his sister's husband. Um... but he thought that there should be a republican government in Afghanistan and that Afghanistan should be taken out of its present condition.

Ahmad: Before the three hundred years ago you mentioned, when Afghanistan was called Afghanistan... before that, what was Afghanistan called?

Javid: In different eras, it had different names. For example, many people called it (lit. said) Khurasan. Different parts of Afghanistan had different names.

But after Ahmad Shah Baba established this area with boundaries, he named it Afghanistan.

Ahmad: OK... so Daud Khan was a very enlightened person. For example, he wanted to have a democracy (lit. government of the people,) not a monarchy (lit. government of the clan and Shah).

Javid: Yes, Daud Khan was an enlightened person. He was educated. He wanted there to be a republican government in Afghanistan to serve the people. During the period of approximately five years, the period of his government, he introduced many plans and programs and conducted a lot of studies to build Afghanistan.

He did a lot of research. He tried to free Afghanistan from its current condition... from the current condition at the time.

Ahmad: Good, good. Very good.

Vocabulary

سروی *English n* survey

حکومت کمونستی[47]

احمد: بعد ازاینکه حکومت را کمونستها از داودخان گرفتند و داود خان را کشتند همراه فامیل و چیزهایش. اه... کمونستها... اه... حکومتشان یک حکومت دست نشاندهٔ روسها بود.
این کل کارهایشان از طرف روسها این چیزمی شد اه...ترتیب و اه... باصطلاح کنترول می شد.

جاوید: اه... کمونستها در افغانستان حکومت را گرفتند اه... فقط یک کودتای خونین عسکری کردند که حکومت را گرفتند و چون در افغانستان سیستم های احزاب قبلی وجود نداشت...

احمد: بلی.

جاوید: کمونستها یک تعداد مردم بسیار اوباش و بی سواد و کم تحصیل و در عین زمان بسیار عقده دار بودند.

احمد: خصوصاً خلقیهایش.

جاوید: خصوصاً خلقی و پرچمی هردویش بسیار مردم باعقده بودند در برابر کسهائیکه تحصیل کردهٔ خوب است در برابر سرمایه دارها، در برابر کسهائیکه زنده گی مرفع دارد بسیار عقده داشتند.
اینها وقتیکه حکومت را گرفتند اه... توسط کودتای خونین خود. طرز پیشبرد حکومت را نمی فهمیدند، فوری روسها همراه شان کمک را شروع کرد. یک تعداد زیاد مشاورین روان کرد برای از اینها به افغانستان.

[47] The speakers on this selection are Ahmad and Javid they attended high school in Afghanistan and Javid is a graduate of Kabul University and has a slight Kabuli accent and Ahmad speaks Kohdamani dialect of Dari.

The Communist Government

Ahmad: After the Communists seized the government from Daud Khan and killed Daud Khan and his family and stuff and so forth, the Communist government was a Russian puppet government.

Everything they did (lit. all their work) was organized and, in other words, controlled by the Russians.

Javid: Um… the Communists took over the government in Afghanistan. Um... they carried out a bloody military coup d'etat and took over the government. And since political parties (lit. party systems) hadn't existed in Afghanistan before, that time,

Ahmad: OK...

Javid: the Communists were some very vulgar, illiterate, and uneducated people, and at the same time, they were very vengeful.

Ahmad: Especially the Khalqis among them.

Javid: Especially Khalqis and Parchamis, both of them. They were people who really bore a grudge against those who were well-educated, against the rich, and against the upper class (lit. those who have a comfortable life), they really had a grudge.

When they took over the government through their bloody coup d'etat, they did not know how to run a government. The Russians started helping them immediately. They sent many advisors to Afghanistan for them.

این مشاورین در همه شعبات در همه مقامها وجود داشت. فرضاً رئیس جمهور یک دو سه مشاور داشت. صدراعظم مشاور داشت، هر وزارت مشاور داشت، هر قطعهٔ عسکری مشاور داشت به اصطلاح در فرقه پنج شش نفر اه... مشاور بود.

باز در سطح غند هم بود باز در کندک هم بود. هر جا مشاورین بود.

در فابریکه هم مشاور بود، در دستگاه اداری هم، در قضا، در پولیس، در هرجا مشاورین روسی بودند که باز اینها را رهنمائی و هدایت میکردند. و اینها مطابق مشورهٔ مشاورین روسی پیش می رفتند.

احمد: همانطور بود که در اول گفتیند که اینها اه... یک عقده داشتند ضد خاندان شاهی و یا کسهائیکه اه... پول دار و زمین دار و جای دار بود. از همان خاطر زمینهای مردم را می گرفت برای خلقیها و پرچمیها خود توزیع می کرد. یا کدام سیستم کمونستی همین قسم بود؟

جاوید: اه ... هر دوشکل داشت از یکطرف این مردم بسیار با عقده بودند در برابر این ... دیگرها و ازطرف دیگر سیستم کمونستی همین قسم را میخواهد که سرمایه دار نباشد، زمیندار نباشد همه چیز ملی باشد.

اینها کوشش می کردند که همه چیز را طوری بسازند که به حکومت تعلق بگیرد و سیستم کمونیستی در افغانستان مروج شود به این خاطر.

احمد: بلی.

These advisors were in every office and in every post. For example, the president had like, two or three advisors. The prime minister had an advisor. Every ministry had an advisor. Every military unit had an advisor. For example, there were five or six advisors in a military division.

They were also at the regimental level, in the battalion too. There were advisors everywhere.

There were advisors in factories, in administrative offices in the judiciary, in the police department. Russian advisors were everywhere to guide and instruct them. They would manage all their work according to the advice of the Russian advisors.

Ahmad: Was it as you said at first, that they had a grudge against the royal clan and those who were wealthy or landowners or property owners? Was this why they took people's land and distributed it to their own Khalqis and Parchamis? Or was the Communist system like that?

Javid: Um… it was both ways. On one hand, these people were very resentful of others, and on the other hand the Communist system wants there not to be wealthy people, not to be landowners, wants everything to be nationalized.

They were trying to make everything so that it would belong to the government, and so that the Communist system would come to be in general use in Afghanistan, that's why.

Ahmad: Yes.

Vocabulary

کنترول *colloquial English* تسلط *n* control, supervision
بگره *colloquial* بگیرد *prep* to happen, to become *v* to take

خانه ها در قریه جات[48]

احمد: مردم اطراف، قریه جات اه... در خانه های... اکثرش در خانه های گِلی اه ... زنده گی میکرد که آنها را خودشان جورمیکرد.
اه... فکر می کنم بسیار مشکل بود خانه جور کردن در آنجا یا برایشان بسیار قیمت تمام می شد که... که خشت پخته و چیزها جور می کردند؟

جاوید: در اطراف افغانستان خو بصورت عموم خانه ها گِلیست. از خشت پخته هیچ کس جور کرده نمی تواند.
اول ازاینکه خشت پخته پیدا نمی شود اه... برای پخته کردن خشت پخته مواد سوخت بسیار کاراست که در افغانستان کم است. مواد سوخت نداریم از اه... از این خاطر.
و دوم سمنت در افغانستان پیدا نمی شود، بسیار کم پیدا می شود.
مردم خانه های خود را بصورت عموم از گل جور می کُنند. همان گل زمین خود را می کَنند سر از آن آب می اندازند بازَ آن را کَت پای خود یا کَت پای حیوانات خود لگد می کُنند، لگد می کُنند تا خوب آب وگَل مخلوط شود.
خوب مخلوط که شد و آن یک قسم خاصیت اینطور لاسدار را پیدا کند که کش شود، زود نشکند، شکنن نباشد. باز آن را منظم همراه دست خود یکی را بالای دیگر میگذارند آن را دیوار جور می کُنند.
دیوارهم بصورت عموم در مناطقیکه خاکش مَت زیاد دارد دیوار از آن از یک منزل بالا استاد نمی شود اه... و درجائیکه خاکش مَت ندارد اه... گلی (که) با رِیگ گَد است، گلی همراه جغل و رِیگ مخلوط می باشد. آن مقاومتَش زیاد می باشد.
باز آن تا دو منزل هم است، حتی سه منزل هم است از این چیز استفاده می کُنند.

48 The speakers on this selection are Ahmad and Javid they attended high school in Afghanistan and Javid is a graduate of Kabul University and has a slight Kabuli accent and Ahmad speaks Kohdamani dialect of Dari.

Houses in the Villages

Ahmad: People of the countryside and the villages um... in houses... most of them lived in clay houses that they would build themselves.

Um... I think that building a house was very difficult over there... or that it was very expensive for them to build with baked brick and stuff?

Javid: Generally the houses are made of clay in the countryside of Afghanistan. Nobody can build them from baked bricks.

First of all, baked bricks aren't found, um... for baking baked brick lots of fuel is needed, of which there is little in Afghanistan. We don't have fuel. That's why.

And the second [reason is that] cement is not not found in Afghanistan. Very little is found

Generally, people build their houses from clay. They dig up mud from their land, pour water on it, then they stomp it under their feet or under the feet of their animals (lit. they step on it and step on it with their feet or the feet of their animals) until the mud and water are mixed really well. When it is mixed very well, it gets a kind of elastic characteristic so it would stretch and not break easily (lit. quickly). So it should not be breakable. Then methodically they put them by hand one on top of another and make them into a wall.

Generally walls in areas where the soil has a lot of loam, the walls made of this won't stand higher than one floor. Um... in a place where the soil doesn't have loam um... the mud is mixed with sand, the clay that has gravel and sand with it, is strong. This would have stronger resistance.

Then they use that to build two or even three-story houses.

احمد: این تهداب و این چیز را، خانه ها را اه... از خ...سنگ می گیرند یا از همان گِل چیز جور می کُنند گِلیکه لگد می کُنند یا گِلیکه پخته می کُنند؟

جاوید: تهداب خانه ها در بعَضی مناطق فرق دارَد.

در مناطقیکه به این چیز نزدیک است. اه... در سطح آب زیرزمینی نزدیک است آنجا تهداب خانه را بصورت عموم از سنگ جور می کُنند.

اما مناطقیکه سطح آب زیرزمینی دور است، نم ندارد تهدابش را از همین گِل پخته می کُنند.

احمد: خو بسیار خوب.

Ahmad: Do they build the foundations and stuff of houses, um… from stone or from the mud... mud that they stomp on or mud that they bake into bricks?

Javid: The foundation of houses vary from area to area.

In areas where the level of ground water is close to the surface, they build the foundation of houses from stone.

But in areas where the ground water level is lower from the surface and it doesn't have moisture, they build the foundation from mixed clay.

Ahmad: OK, very good.

Vocabulary

شاره *colloquial* شارد *v* worn away
قندوز *colloquial* کُندُز *n* a province in northern Afghanistan
دستک *n* round beam, girder (used in roofing)
سرش *colloquial* بالای آن *adv* over it, on top of it
دبل *colloquial English* ضخیم *adj* thick, double

تربیه حیوانات در مزارع[49]

احمد: در افغانستان در اطراف افغانستان خصوصاً در قریه جات و اه.. منطقه های زراعتی مردم بسیار به مالداری علاقه دارد و بسیار کارشان میشد از طریق مالداری و مثلاً گاو و گوسفند و اه... خر و چیزها را نگاه می کُنند.
اه... نگاه کردن از این دیگر اه... بسیار جنجال می خواهد نی؟

جاوید: بلی در افغانستان خو سیستم مالداری بصورت عموم در همین اطراف است.
باز هرکس از خود مالداری دارد و دو سیستم مالداریست.
یکی سیستمی است مردم رمه های گوسفند را نگاه می کُنند. مثل رمه های گوسفند قره قول رمه های گوسفند بخاطر شیر و گوشتش، که این زیادتر در شمال افغانستان رواج دارد.

احمد: آن رمه های کوچی را میگوید یا دیگر چیز؟

جاوید: نی از مردم کوچی نی، از مردم محل درشمال افغانستان.

احمد: خو...

جاوید: یکی رمه هایست که مردم کوچی هم دارند آنها هم می داشته باشند که در بسیار جای افغانستان می گردانند. باز میآورند می فروشند.

---

49 The speakers on this selection are Ahmad and Javid they attended high school in Afghanistan and Javid is a graduate of Kabul University and has a slight Kabuli accent and Ahmad speaks Kohdamani dialect of Dari.

Raising Animals on Farms

Ahmad: In Afghanistan, in the countryside of Afghanistan, especially in villages and farming areas, people like to raise livestock. They benefit a lot from raising livestock and, for example, they keep cows, sheep, and donkeys and stuff.

Um... keeping these is a lot of trouble, isn't it?

Javid: Yes, in Afghanistan, generally livestock is raised in the countryside. Then everybody raises his own livestock. There are two ways to raise livestock.

One way in which people keep flocks of sheep, like flocks of karakul sheep, and flocks of sheep for their milk and meat, which is widespread mostly in the north of Afghanistan.

Ahmad: Are you talking about the flocks of the nomads or something else?

Javid: No, not of the nomads, of the local people in the north of Afghanistan.

Ahmad: OK.

Javid: There are also the flocks that the nomads have. They have them too and they shepherd them all over Afghanistan for grazing. Then they bring them and sell them.

احمد: بلی.

جاوید: دیگر سیستم اه... مالداری در قریه جات است که هر فامیلیکه یک چیز زمین دارد بر... به زراعت مصروف است بخاطر مصارف خود و بخاطر تهیۀ روغن و شیر برای شان، او یک یا دو دانه گاو شیری نگاه می کُند یا بز نگاه می کُند.

بخاطر انتقال مال خود از یکجا بجای دیگر یگان خر یا اسپ نگاه می کُند.

بخاطر مصارف زمستان خود یکی دوتا، سه تا گوسفند نگاه می کُنند.

این مالداری به... در اکثر نقاط افغانستان رواج است. فرضاً باز ... این مردم این مال خود را در یک جائی نگاه می کُنند. خانه ... اتاق برایش جور می کُنند چون زمستانهای افغانستان سرد است.

احمد: در تبیله خانه.

جاوید: آن را بنام تبیله میگویند. باز اینها را در داخل از آن نگاه می کُنند. برایش کاه را در.... کاه گندم را، قسمت پایینش میده می کُنند. بنام کاه سفید.

احمد: بلی.

جاوید: یگان ذره سبزه را در تابستان جمع می کُنند خشک می کُنند. یک قش... قسمتش را با هم تاب میدهند آن را بیده میگویند. اینها را باهم جمع می کُنند در اتاقهای به نام کاهدان جمع می کُنند. زمستان آن را مصرف می کُنند سرشان.

و درتابستان از همان سبزیجاتیکه در محیط مثل شفتل و رشقه وغیره چیزهایکه است از آن برایشان میدهند.

اه... یک قسمت مصارف عمدۀ زنده گی اطراف را همین گاو و گوسفند و بز برایشان تأمین می کُند.

Ahmad: Yes.

Javid: Another way of, um…raising livestock, in the villages is that each family that has a whatchamacallit of (lit. thing) land... is occupied with farming, for its own expenses and for providing oil and milk for themselves, they keep one or two milk cows or they keep a goat.

For transporting their goods from one area to another they keep a donkey or a horse.

For fresh meat in the winter, they keep two or three sheep.

Raising livestock is a custom all over (lit. in most places of) Afghanistan. For example... These people keep their livestock in a place. They build a room for them because Afghanistan's winters are cold.

Ahmad: In the stable.

Javid: They call it tawila. They would keep them inside that. They feed them straw, straw from wheat. They crush the lower part of the wheat, called straw (lit. white hay or straw).

Ahmad: Yes.

Javid: They collect some green clover in the summer and dry it. A part of it they twist together and they call that bayda. Now they collect it, collect it in rooms called kahdan, and use this for them in the winter.

In the summer, they feed (lit. give) them from the greenery that is found in the region, like clover or alfalfa, etc.

Um… these cows, sheep, and goats provide for some the basic (lit. main) needs of life in the countryside.

احمد: از شیر و ماست و مسکه و چیزهایش استفاده می کنند.

جاوید: استفاده می کُنند. بلی هان.

احمد: مردم قدرت از این را ندارد که برود شیر بخرد و یا ماست بخرد. همان یک گاو که دارد یا یک گوسفندی که دارد همآن طفلهای خود را شیر هم میدهد و ماست هم میدهد و اه... همه تهیه از همان می شود.

جاوید: بلی آن همان برایشان زنده گیشان را اه... خوب است ضروریات اول زنده گیشان را پوره می کُند.

Ahmad: They use their milk, yogurt, and butter and stuff.

Javid: They use them, yes.

Ahmad: People can't afford to (lit. don't have the ability to) go and buy milk or buy yogurt. Those cows or sheep that people have would provide them and their children with milk and yogurt.

Javid: Yes, that provides for their life...um... It is good, it fulfills the primary needs of their life.

Vocabulary

گَو *colloquial* گاو *n* cow, bull, ox
ماس *colloquial* ماست *n* yogurt

حکومتهای محلی افغانستان[50]

احمد: اه... در قریه جات، در اطراف همین مردم چه قسم سیستم کنترولش، کِی کلان قریه بود یا منطقه بود یا از طرف حکومت اِینها کدام نماینده داشتَند یا این خودشان کدام نفر را انتخاب می کردند.
این چه قسم ادارات محلی در آنجا پیش میرفت؟

جاوید: افغانستان خو اه... از لحاظ ادارات به دوصد و شانزده ولسوالی تقسیم شده بود که یک ادارۀ محلی را کوچکترین ادارۀ محلی را در افغانستان بنام ولسوالی می گفتند.

احمد: خو...

جاوید: و از آن پائینتر البته یکی دیگر هم علاقه داری بود که آنقدر زیاد مشهور نبود. ولسوالی مشهور بود. این ولسوالیها از خود یک ولسوال داشت، کلان منطقه بود از طرف حکومت مرکزی تعین می شد.
یک قاضی داشت که اُمور قضائی ومشکلات قضائی مردم را حل میکرد.
یکنفر مامور پولیس داشت که مسائل... اه... جرم و جنحه و غیره را بررسی میکرد. یک نفر مامور مالیه داشت که مالیۀ از... اه... عایدات مردم جمع می کرد.
اه... یک نفر دیگر هم به اصطلاح مامور تعلیم و تربیه داشت اُمور تعلیم و تربیه را پیش می بُرد. یکنفر امور شفاخانه ها را پیش می بُرد.
اه... اینها فقط در مرکز ولسوالی بودند و شاخچه های از اینها دربین قریه جات نبود هر ولسوالی ممکن سی، چهل، پنجاه قریه داشت. اه... ادارۀ محلی در بین قریه نماینده گی نداشت.

---

[50] The speakers on this selection are Ahmad and Javid they attended high school in Afghanistan and Javid is a graduate of Kabul University and has a slight Kabuli accent and Ahmad speaks Kohdamani dialect of Dari.

Local Governments in Afghanistan

Ahmad: Um... in villages and the countryside, what was the system for exercising authority over (lit. controlling) people? Who was the head of the village or region? Or did they have a representative from the government, or did they choose a representative from among themselves?

How did local administration run?

Javid: As for administration, Afghanistan was divided into 216 districts. They called a local administration, the smallest local administration in Afghanistan, a district.

Ahmad: OK.

Javid: And lower than that, of course, there was also the sub-district, which wasn't that common.

The district was common. A district (lit. these districts) had a district governor, who was the head of the region. He was appointed by the central government.

There was a district judge who would resolve people's and judicial problems. There was a district police chief who would investigate criminal matters and etc. There was a district finance officer who would collect taxes on people's incomes.

There was also another person, for example, an education officer who would manage educational affairs. One person would manage the hospital affairs.

They were only in the district center; they didn't have any branches, there were none in the villages. Each district had maybe thirty, forty, or fifty villages. The local administration didn't have a representative in the villages

احمد: باز این...

جاوید: در داخل قریه جات مردم خودشان.

احمد: ای َملک وَملِک داری و این چیزها چطور بود؟

جاوید: حالا تَشریح می کنم نِی.

احمد: خو...

جاوید: این حالِی مردم در قریه جات بخاطر تنظیم اُمور خود اه... از... از...َملک داشتند َملک یعنی نمایندۀ یک قوم یا یک ولسوالی در نزد حکومت. و اَین همچنان نما... کلان همان قوم هم بود. همین َملک وقتیکه بین چند نفر جنجالی بمیان می آمد، دعوای بمیان میآمد، مشَکلی بمیان میآمد یا کدام خدمتی بمیان میآمد باز حل شود...

احمد: باز پیش َملِک می رفتند.

جاوید: باز پیش ... اول روی سفید های خود همان قوم باهم کوشش میکردند حل شود. در غیر از آن پیش ملک میرفتند.

باز ملک بین شان مشکل شان را کوشش می کرد که حل کند یا توسط چند نفر روی سفید را تعین میکرد که آن مشکل را حل کُند. یعنی مشکلات مردم محل در محل ...به... از طریق خودشان یا از طریق ملک حل می شد. حتی مشکلات مردم در محل توسط ملک به حکومت میرسید.

احمد: این... این ملکها از طرف حکومت معاش هم داشتند یا همانطور اه... بخاطر خدمت مردم معاش و چیزها نمی گرفتند؟

جاوید: نی ملکها مامور رسمی دولت نبود، معاش نمی گرفت، زنده گی شخصی خود را پیش می بُرد. اه... صرف برای خدمت مردم، نمایندۀ مردم در نزد حکومت بود.

احمد: خو بسیار خوب.

Ahmad: Then this…

Javid: Within the villages, people themselves...

Ahmad: How did the head of the village and these things work (lit. how were they)?

Javid: I'm explaining it now, aren't I?

Ahmad: OK.

Javid: And now people in the villages had a (malik) chieftain for arranging their affairs. He, this leader was also the head of the tribe. Whenever a conflict among people arose, a lawsuit arose, a problem arose, or some kind of issue arose to be resolved...

Ahmad: They would go to the head of the village.

Javid: Then to… first, the elders of that tribe itself would try together among themselves to resolve it. Otherwise, they would go to malik (the head of the village.)

Then the malik would try to mediate to resolve their problem (lit. resolve their problem among them). Or he would ask a few elder men to resolve their problem. It means that local people's problems were resolved locally by the people themselves or by the malik. The problems of people in the local area would even reach the government through the malik.

Ahmad: Did the maliks have a salary from the government, or did they not accept a salary since they were serving the people?

Javid: No, maliks were not government officials. They did not get a salary. They took care of their own livelihood. They were the representatives of the people to the government only for the sake of serving.

Ahmad: Good, very good.

Vocabulary

دُگام *colloquial* دیگر هم *phrase* and also, in addition to that *adv* more
جُنحه *colloquial* جنایی *adj* criminal
اِنالی *colloquial* الآن، حالا *adv* now, now that
آلی *colloquial* فعلاً، حالا *adv* right now, now

حمل و نقل[51]

احمد: در افغانستان مسئلهٔ حمل و نقل اه... اول خو مثلاً در قریه جات یک مواد را که از یکجای به دیگر جای می بَرَند توسط مرکب یا اسپ استفاده می کنند. باز جاهای دور اه... از موتر لاری وموترهای بس وچیزها استفاده می کُنند. این سیستم ترانسپورت در افغانستان اه... بسیار اه... پیشرفته نبود نی؟ بسیار همانطور مثلاً یک... مثل جهان سوم به اصطلاح.

جاوید: بلی افغانستان چون یک مملکت عقب مانده است، سیستم ترانسپورت در افغانستان سه سیستم است.
یکی درجه اول سیستم ترانسپورت موتر است که مواد زیاد به فاصلهٔ دُور اه... به قیمت کمتر توسط موتر انتقال می شود.

احمد: بلی..

جاوید: و این بهترین سیستم ترانسپورت فعلاً در افغانستان همین است.
سیستم دوم از این توسط حیوانات است یا توسط انسانهاست که به پای پیاده در بعضی مناطق چون موتر رفته نمی تواند این مردم توسط حیوان یا در پشت خود مال را گرفته انتقال میدهند.

احمد: خصوصاً در جایهایکه سرک نیست.

جاوید: بلی هان جاییکه موتر رفته نمی تواند، سرک نیست، مناطق کوهیست یا قریه جات است در اینطور جایها.
و سیستم سوم از آن سیستم طیاره است که البته انتقال مواد، بعضاً مواد تجارتی از کشورهای خارجی به افغانستان میآید. یا از مرکز افغانستان به بعضی شهرهای افغانستان انتقال می کُند. این سیستم ترانسپورت هوایست که آنقدر زیاد پیشرفته در افغانستان نیست.

---

[51] The speakers on this selection are Ahmad and Javid they attended high school in Afghanistan and Javid is a graduate of Kabul University and has a slight Kabuli accent and Ahmad speaks Kohdamani dialect of Dari.

Transportation

Ahmad: In Afghanistan, the issue of transportation.... um... first, for example, in villages, they transport things from one place to another place by donkey or horse. For distant places, they use trucks or buses. The transportation system in Afghanistan wasn't very advanced, was it? It was like in third world countries, for example.

Javid: Yes, since Afghanistan is an underdeveloped country, the transportation system in Afghanistan is three systems.

First, vehicles are the number one system of transportation. A lot of things can be transported a long way for lower cost by vehicle.

Ahmad: Yes.

Javid: And this is the best transportation system in Afghanistan at present.

The second system of these is by animal or by humans, who in some places, since a vehicle can't go there, these people transport things on foot by animal or on their backs.

Ahmad: Especially in places where there are no roads.

Javid: Yes, in places where a vehicle can't go, there are no roads, where it is mountainous terrain, or in villages or in places like these.

And the third system of these is the system of aircraft.Of course, sometimes goods come from foreign countries into Afghanistan or they transport them from the central city of Afghanistan to some cities of Afghanistan. This transportation system is by air, which is not that advanced in Afghanistan.

احمد: هان. همان سیستم هوائی هم خراب شد.

جاوید: اما دو سیستم دیگری که در... دو سیستم دیگری که در دنیا رواج است، یکی سیستم بحریست و دیگر سیستم ریل است متأسفانه ریل هم در افغانستان نیست و سیستم بحری هم در افغانستان نداریم.

احمد: بحر نداریم دیگر.

جاوید: بحر هم نداریم دریای کلان هم نداریم که از آن بر... برای انتقال مواد استفاده کنیم.

اه... دیگر در افغانستان تنها از این همین سیستم... اما در افغانستان سرک، دو سرک عمده داریم.

یکی سرکی است که از تورغندی به هرات، از هرات به قندهار، از قندهار آمده به سپین بولدک سرحد پاکستان وصل شده.

و سرک دومش از هیرتان آمده به مزار باز به کابل جلال آباد تورخم در سرحد باز در سرحد پاکستان برآمده.

احمد: این سرکها را هم روسها به خاطر اش... اشغال افغانستان جور کرده بود.

جاوید: بلی در همان وقت روسها همانطور یک پروگرام داشتند. همین سرکها را ساختند مردم افغانستان از آن استفاده می کنند.

و یک سیستم دیگری است که این دو سرک را باهم وصل می کند که از کابل إلی قندهار ساخته شده آن سرک مفید است.

این سیستم ... مجموعاً سیستم ترانسپورت افغانستان این همین چیز است.

Ahmad: Yes, even that air system has been destroyed.

Javid: The two other systems that are common in the [rest of] the world are sea and railway systems. Unfortunately, there is not railway system and we don't have a sea system, either.

Ahmad: We don't have a sea, anyway.

Javid: We don't have a sea and we don't have large rivers either to use for transportation.

Um... we only have these systems in Afghanistan...But as far as roads in Afghanistan, we have two main highways.

One is the highway that goes from Turghundi to Herat, then from Herat to Kandahar and then from Kandahar to Spinboldak, and connects to the Pakistan border.

And the second highway goes from Hairatan and comes to Mazar, then to Kabul and Jalalabad and Torkham, and also comes out at the Pakistan border.

Ahmad: The Russians built these highways also for the occupation of Afghanistan.

Javid: Yes, the Russians had that kind of a plan back then. They built those roads [but] the Afghan people use them.

There is another system [road] that joins these two highways together, which was built from Kabul to Kandahar. That road is useful.

This as a whole is the system of transportation in Afghanistan.

Vocabulary

مى بَرَن *colloquial* میدهند انتقال، می برند *v* they would transport, they would carry
همیس *colloquial* این است، همین است *v* this is it, this is
متَن *colloquial* میدهند *v* they would give
تورغندی *n the border checkpoint between Afghanistan and Turkmenistan*
سپین بولدک *pash n* a border checkpoint between Afghanistan and Pakistan
سیستم *colloquial English* منظومه، شیوه *adj, n* system

تعلیم و تربیه در وقت طالبان[52]

احمد: در وقتیکه طالبها در افغانستان سر قدرت رسیدند من خوب، در آنجا نبودم، میشنیدم که بسیار در همین حصهٔ تعلیم و تربیه توجه زیاد نمی کردند. همان تعلیم و تربیهٔ افغانستان بیخی اه.... به خرابی مواجه شده بود. شما نزدیک بودید دیگر، شما خبر دارید که چه قسم ...؟

جاوید: بلی تعلیم و تربیه در زمان طالبها بسیار خراب بود.
طالبها از روزیکه در افغانستان به... به میان آمدند تا روزیکه از بین رفتند تعلیم و تربیهٔ اصلی را در افغانستان تقریباً از بین بُردند..
آنها تمامِ مکاتب دخترها را مطلق بسته کردند. یک... تقریباً نصف نفوس افغانستان از تعلیم و تربیهٔ محروم ساختند، در قسمت بچه ها که باید تعلیم می کردند. تعلیم و تربیهٔ ساینس را بسیار ضعیف ساختند تقریباً از بین بُردند.
تعلیم و تربیهٔ اجتماعیات را تقریباً ضعیف ساختند از بین بُردند. چیزی را که آنها زیاد ساختند بسیار کوشش کردند که مسائل ملائی را، اه... مسائل تعلیم و تربیهٔ دینی را در درس مکاتب شامل بسازند که این بسیار زیاد وضع تعلیم و تربیه را خراب ساخت. یعنی هر شاگرد مکتب مجبور بود مثل یک طالب درس بخواند.

احمد: بلی.

[52] The speakers on this selection are Ahmad and Javid they attended high school in Afghanistan and Javid is a graduate of Kabul University and has a slight Kabuli accent and Ahmad speaks Kohdamani dialect of Dari.

Education under the Taliban

Ahmad: When the Taliban came to power in Afghanistan, I wasn't there.

I heard that in the area of education, they didn't pay much attention. Education in Afghanistan totally… was faced with destruction. You were closer and you know how it was.

Javid: Yes, education under the Taliban was very bad.

The Taliban, from the day that they came into being in Afghanistan until the day they were overthrown, they almost eliminated the foundations of education in Afghanistan.

They completely closed all girls' schools. They deprived approximately half of the population of Afghanistan of education. They didn't ban education for boys. They made the science education very weak; they almost eliminated it.

They made social studies education weak, eliminated it. One thing that they increased, they tried hard to insert "mullah subjects," religious education subjects into school curriculum, which ruined the educational system (lit. state of education). That means that every school student had to study like a Talib.

Ahmad: Yes.

جاوید: همچنان در سطح ... حتی در سطح پوهنتون اول تعداد زیاد استاذهای پوهنتون بنام نامطلوب گفته از افغانستان کش... از تعلیم ... از پوهنتون خارج ... این چیز کردند منفک کردند باز آنها از افغانستان بر آمدند.

اه...دوم سر شاگردها همین فشار آوردند، شاگردها باید ریش بماند، و شاگردها باید دستار بپوشد، پیراهن و تنبان بپوشد ، دریشی نپوشد، و باید پاک و ستره نباشد. و همین کلش باید عربی بخواند و کلش باید درس دینی بخواند.

همین شکلی را به میان آوردند که درسهای ساینسی و اجتماعیات تقریباً به سقوط مواجه شد وگفته می توانیم که در زمان طالبها یک دورهٔ قهقرائی را تعلیم و تربیهٔ افغانستان می پیمود مثلیکه مسائل اقتصادی مسائل اجتماعی هم همین دوره را پیمودن. تعلیم وتربیهٔ افغانستان هم تقریباً به سقوط مواجه شد.

احمد: حالی در اسلام خو نگفته که درس نخوان، ساینس نخوان. در اسلام خو بسیار مردم را تشجیع کرده برای درس خواندنِ ساینس یاد گرفتنِ علم مثلاً کاینات و این چیزها.

اینها خوب، بسیار کور مغز بودند یا بسیار پس مانده مردم بودند.

جاوید: اصلاً طالبها اینها از علم دین هم خبر نداشتند.

احمد: بلی.

جاوید: صرف تظاهر می کردند به دین.

احمد: بلی.

جاوید: در واقعاً اینها مردم بسیار جاهل بودند نه از دین می فهمیدند، نه از دنیا و به ...

همین عمل شان باعث خرابی افغانستان هم شد و باعث خرابی خودشان هم و باعث خرابی دین هم.

Javid: Also at the level of... even at the college level, first they called a large number of professors undesirable and [threw them out] of Afghanistan...out of academia...they fired them from college. Then they (the professors) left Afghanistan.

Second, they began to pressure this pressure to bear on students."Students must grow beards, students must wear turbans, must wear the perahan and tonban, must not wear suits, and must not be clean and not dress nicely.They all must study Arabic and they all must study religion.

They created a situation in which science and social sciences lessons almost vanished. And we can say that under the Taliban, education in Afghanistan went through a dark age. Just as economic issues and social issues went through this period, education in Afghanistan also were almost faced with destruction.

Ahmad: It doesn't say in Islam, "Don't study; don't study science." Islam encourages people to study science, to learn, for example, astronomy and things.

They were such dumb and backward people.

Javid: In reality, the Taliban didn't even have any knowledge about the religion (of Islam).

Ahmad: Yes.

Javid: They just pretended to be religious.

Ahmad: Yes.

Javid: In reality, they were very ignorant people. They didn't know anything either about religion or about the world.

Their actions ruined Afghanistan, themselves, and also the religion (of Islam).

Vocabulary

اُووا *colloquial* آنها *pro* they
اِییا *colloquial* اینها *pro* these

سفر به افغانستان در وقت اشغال شوروی[53]

جاوید: اه... همین خودت هم در زمان جهاد در زمانیکه روسها در افغانستان آمدند یکسال رفتی به داخل افغانستان یک مدتی.

احمد: بلی.

جاوید: من در آن وقت کوشش میکردم چون خورد بودی که باز داخل افغانستان نَروی که خدا ناخاسته برایت کدام خطر پیش نشود.
تو قصۀ هَمان سفرت را بکن سفرت چطور بود؟
خوب بود به داخل افغانستان.
به مشکلات گرفتار نشدی؟ کدام خطر برایت مواجه نشد؟ چطور بود سفرت؟

احمد: والله ... سفر خوب بود اه... خودت خو بسیار کوشش کردی که نَروی. اما آدم جوان که باشد باز از خطر و چیزها حس نمی کند میگوید بُرو جنگ است. دیگر یکی شوق جهاد بود، یکی شوق از این بود که ضد روسها آدم می جنگد. یکی دیگر این بود که در وطن بسیار وقت شده نرفته بودم و اه... کاکایم شان و بوبویم اینها را ندیده بودم.
باز گفتم می روم کَتِ بچه ها گَپ زدم و پاره چنار هم رفتم. تا پاره چنار هم که رفتم خودت احوالِ راهی کردی که نَروی. گفتم نی نمیروم، باز کَتِ بچه ها یکجای شدم و رفتم.
در همان روزهای اول یکذره مشکلات بود. در همین... اه... یکجای تریمنگل می گوید که از آنجا آدم بالامیشد، طرف جاجی می رود و در آن منطقه ها کوهای بسیار بلند بود یعنی پیاده گشتی.
باز یک، دو، سه روز که رفتیم بعد از آن باز رفتن ما عادی شد و باز در منطقه های اه... نزدیک پکتیا که رسیدیم در آنجا یکذره مشکلات نان و چیزها بود. جای نبود دیگر. هر جائیکه می رفتیم مقصد اه... در یک مسجد..... اگر مسجد می بود مسجد، اگر مسجد نمی بود در بیرون یکجای مقصد خود را میانداختیم.
و پیش ما مثلاً تفنگ و کلاشنکوف و تفنگچه و چیزها هم بود و اه... گفتۀ یگان تا همان (در خرجین ما وزنش زیاد بود دیگر) رفتیم آن طرف...

---

[53] The speakers on this selection are Ahmad and Javid they attended high school in Afghanistan and Javid is a graduate of Kabul University and has a slight Kabuli accent and Ahmad speaks Kohdamani dialect of Dari.

Trip to Afghanistan during the Soviet Occupation

Javid: Oh... You went to Afghanistan for a while one year in the time of jihad, when the Russians came to Afghanistan.

Ahmad: Yes.

Javid: At the time, because you were young (lit. little), I was trying to keep you from going to Afghanistan so you wouldn't be in danger, God forbid.

Tell me the story of your trip. How was your trip? Was it good?

Did you have any problems in Afghanistan? Were you in any danger? How was your trip?

Ahmad: Oh God...the trip was good...you tried very hard to keep me from going (lit. that you not go), but when you are young (lit. a person is young,) you don't feel danger and things. They say, "Let's go. It's just a war."

For one, [I had] a desire for holy war; for another, I had a desire to fight the Russians.

Another thing was that it had been a long time since I had been home... I hadn't seen my dad and mom and the rest [of the family].

Then I said I'm going to go. I talked to the guys, and I went to Parachinar. Even though I went to Parachinar, you sent me a message not to go. I said, "No, I won't go." Then I joined the guys and I went.

It was difficult on the first few days. In... there was a place called Tri Mangal which we had to climb. It goes toward Jaji. The mountains were very high there. That means walking on foot.

Then after we had hiked for two or three days, after that, we got used to walking. Then, when we got close to Paktia (lit. reached the regions near Paktia), we had some problems with food and things like that. There was nowhere [to stay]. Wherever we went, I mean...in a mosque. If there was a mosque, then in a mosque, if there wasn't a mosque, then someplace outside... meaning we'd crash down there.

And we had, for example, rifles and Kalashnikovs and handguns and things with us. And oh ...As they say "Our saddlebag was heavy" and we went.

جاوید: خو باز در این سفر یکه کردی در منطقهٔ سروبی از سرک پخته تیر می شدی پوستهای روس بود بسیار به عذاب نشدید.

احمد: هان بسیار بعذاب شدیم.

از این طرف خو آرام بود. از طرف پاکستان که می رفتیم تنها در منطقهٔ جگدلک که دشت است درخت و چیزها نیست که آدم خود را ستروااخفاء کند. در آن منطقه یکی دشت است. یکی خو مشکلات از این بود که آب یافت نمی شد. همان آبیکه کَت خود داشتیم نزدیک به خلاصی بود... دیگر آن منطق... مردم از آن منطقه رفته بود چون که آنجا بمبارد میکرد. و روسها تانکهایش می رفت و اه... تحت کنترول... هوای... چیز.... طیاره های روسی بود در آن منطقه مردمش بیخی برآمده بود.

آن بسیار دیگر مشکل بود، چرا نان و آب و چیزها نبود.

یک چیز دیگر این بود که آن منطقه را طیاره ازطرف روز میدید، ستر و اخفاء نداشت.

دیگر از آن خاطر بود که بسیار به مشکلات در همان منطقه مواجه شدیم.

Javid: On the trip that you took, in the Sorobi area when you were crossing the paved road there were Russian military posts. Did you run into any trouble? (lit. Did you suffer much?)

Ahmad: Yes, a lot, we suffered a lot.

It was quiet on the way there, when we were on the way there from Pakistan, only in the Jagdalag area which is a desert. There are no trees and things to camouflage yourself.

In that area, for one, it's a desert and for another, the problem was that there was no water to be found. The water that we had with us was almost gone. For another thing, that area…the people had left the area because they would bomb there, and the Russian tanks would go there… and um… the Russian airforce controlled it. The people of the area had completely left.

That was a big problem. Because there was no food, water, or things like that.

Another thing was that the area could be seen from an airplane during the day; there was no cover.

That is why we faced difficulties there.

Vocabulary

خودتام *colloquial* خودت هم *phrase* also you, and you also
نَشَه *colloquial* نشود *v* would not happen *v* should not happen
میگُ *colloquial* میگوید *v* he/she would say
می رُم *colloquial* می روم *v* I will go, I would go
کَت *colloquial* همراه، با *adv* with
رائی *colloquial* روان *n* sending
نان *colloquial* غذا *n* food *n* bread
پوستای *colloquial English* پوسته های، مرکزهای *n* military posts, military bases
یاف *colloquial* یافت، دریاب *n* finding, obtaining

لباس ملی[54]

احمد: در افغانستان در هر منطقه دیگر مردم رواج علیحده داشت.
که در یک منطقه مردم کلاه قره قولی می پوشید و در یک منطقه مردم لنگی می پوشید و در یک منطقهٔ دیگر مردم کلاه تاقن می گفتند از آن می پوشید و در یک منطقه چپَن می پوشید و بالاپوش و این چیزها.
در هر جای دیگر مختلف رواج همان منطقه بود به اصطلاح یک اه... کل افغانستان خو یکقسم لباس نمی پوشید.

جاوید: اه... بلی هان در افغانستان بعضی قسمتها اه... در بعضی قسمتها یعنی قسمتهای افغانستان لباسهای انسان فرق داشت اما یک چیز عمومیت داشت در کل افغانستان که آن عبارت از پیراهن و تنبان است.

احمد: خو.

جاوید: پیرانن تنبان همه مردم افغانستان می پوشیدند. الا مامورینیکه به دفتر می رفتند. و یا قوای عسکری که یونی فورم عسکری ... عسکری و پولیس داشت، باقی کله پیراهن تنبان می پوشید.
در بعضی مناطق بخاطر گرم نگاه کردن خود اه... چپَن می پوشیدند، کرتی می پوشیدند،
اه... در بعضی مناطق یک چیزی را گوپیچه میگویند، در طرف مزار از آن می ساختند. پیراهنهای کلان کلان در بینش پنبه می ماندند می پوشیدند.

احمد: آن پتلونش هم داشتند از آن نی؟

جاوید: از آن پتلونش هم در..در..بود به نام یکچیز دیگری یاد می کردند.
اما بصورت عموم همان پیراهنش رواج بود در سمت شمال.

احمد: بلی.

جاوید: اه ... دیگر در قسمتهای دیگری افغانستان اه... این چیز میپوشیدند، بالاپوش یا کرتی میپوشیدند. و در بالای از آن یک چیزی را به نام چادر میگفتند یا قدیفه میگفتند.

احمد: یا پتُو.

جاوید: یا پتُو میگفتند از آن میپوشیدند.

---

[54] The speakers on this selection are Ahmad and Javid they attended high school in Afghanistan and Javid is a graduate of Kabul University and has a slight Kabuli accent and Ahmad speaks Kohdamani dialect of Dari.

National Dress

Ahmad: In Afghanistan people in each region had a separate custom.

In one area, people would wear karakul hats, and in another area people would wear turbans, and in another area people would wear some kind of hat called a taqen hat, they would wear that, and in another area they would wear chapan and overcoats and things like that.

In each different place there was a custom for that area, for example. All Afghans (lit. all of Afghanistan) didn't wear the same kind of clothes.

Javid: Yes indeed, in different parts of Afghanistan, people's clothes were different. But one thing was universal across all of Afghanistan, which is the perahan and tonban.

Ahmad: OK.

Javid: Everybody in Afghanistan wore a perahan and tonban except office workers and military personnel because they had military and police uniforms. The rest all wore a perahan and tonban.

In some regions people would wear a chapan and or a coat to keep warm.

In some areas people [wore] something which is called gopecha. They used to make gopecha in the Mazar area. They are long shirts; they filled the lining with cotton and wore those.

Ahmad: They had pants for it too, didn't they?

Javid: There were pants for it, too. They called it something else.

But generally speaking, this shirt was common in northern Afghanistan.

Ahmad: Yes.

Javid: Um... in other parts of Afghanistan, they wore an overcoat or jacket. Over that, they wore something called a chadar or qadifa.

Ahmad: Or patu.

Javid: Or it is called a patu. They would wear that.

احمد: پَتُو بسیار گرم نگاه میکرد یا نی؟
جاوید: بسیار گرم نگاه میکرد. و زیادتر پَتُو بافت داخل افغانستان هم بود. از پاکستان هم پَتُو میآمد.
احمد: پِتُوی کشمیری.
جاوید: پِتُوی کشمیری، پَتُوی پشاوری، پَتُوی پنجابی، پَتُوئیکه در داخل افغانستان بنام ده مسکین و رباط جور میکردند آن پَتُو هم خوبش بود.
دیگر در افغانستان در بعضی قسمتها دستار میپوشیدند که زیادتر نفوس افغانستان دستار میپوشید.
احمد: بلی.
جاوید: یکتعداد مردمیکه نسبتاً وضع اقتصادیش خوبتر بود، کلاه قره قول میپوشید که آن هم از حاصلات افغانسان بود.
احمد: کلاه قره قول خصوصاً طرف شمال مردم زیاد میپوشید.
جاوید: کلاه قره قول مردم شمال بسیار زیاد میپوشید وکسهای از مردم جنوب کسهائیکه در شهرها رفت وآمد داشتند قره قول زیاد میپوشیدند. یکتعداد نفوس افغانستان مثل مردم اه... مشرقی کلاه سفید میپوشیدند. یکتعداد مثل مردم نورستان پَکُول میپوشیدند رواج مردم بود.
احمد: مردم قندهار یک چیز دیگر بود.
جاوید: یکقسم کلاه گک داشتند. اینطور پیش رویش ...
احمد: تاقین واری.
جاوید: هان، تاقین واری بریده گی بود. از آن میپوشیدند و در سرش دستار بسته میکردند.
این قسمتهای مختلف افغانستان لباس مختلف داشتند.

Ahmad: A patu kept you warm, didn't it?

Javid: It would keep you very warm. Most patu were woven in Afghanistan, and patu were imported from Pakistan also.

Ahmad: Kashmiri patu.

Javid: Kashmiri patu, Peshawari patu, Punjabi patu, and patu which is made in the Dehmoskeen and Rabat districts of Afghanistan. Those were good patoos also.

In some regions in Afghanistan people would wear turbans. Most Afghan people wear turbans.

Ahmad: Yes.

Javid: People who were financially set would wear a karakul hat. That is an Afghanistan production.

Ahmad: People, especially in the northern region, would wear a karakul hat.

Javid: People, mostly from northern Afghanistan, would wear karakul hats and also people from southern Afghanistan who visit cities often would wear karakul hats. Some people in the eastern region would wear white hats. Some people, like Noristanis would wear pakool. It was the peoples' custom.

Ahmad: The people of Kandahar would wear something else. They had some kind of hat. It looked like taqen in the front.

Javid: They had a little had... like this in the front.

Ahmad: Like taqen

Javid: Yes, like taqen had a cut. They would wear that and then they would wear a turban over it.

Different regions in Afghanistan had different customs of dressing up.

Vocabulary

تاقن *colloquial* طاقین *n* an embroidered cap with curved top (often worn under a turban)
گـوپیـچـه *colloquial* *n* warm pants with a lining filled with cotton (people wear then in northern Afghanistan)
پَتُو *colloquial* *n* coarse woolen cloth use by men as an outer garment
ده مسکین و رباط *n* name of two villages in northern Kabul

تفریح[55]

احمد: در افغانستان دیگر ساعت تیری زیاد تر همین چیز بود، در وقتهای میله ها بود. میلهٔ عید و نوروز و اه... خصوصاً در کابل که ما می رفتیم باز در همان کوتل خیرخانه.
در آنجا این چیز میشد اه... قُچ جنگی می شد و مثلاً سگ جنگی می شد و گودی پران بازی میشد و این همین میله های ... چی... دَوش میشد و تیرانداختن و نیزه انداختن، سنگ انداختن خصوصاً که کی سَنگ را پیش می اندازد این گپها بود. اه... شما هم بسیار در این میله ها و چیزها رفتید دیگر حتماً.

جاوید: بلی، هان، در افغانستان قسمت تفریح و ساعت تیری که میگویند، این زیادتر در وقت زمستان می بود. چون در زمستان مردم در کار و بار زراعت خود مصروف نمي بود یا در باقی کارها زمستان معتل می بود مردم به تفریحهای مختلف فرضاً سگ جنگ میداختند، بودنه جنگ میداختدن، مرغ جنگ میداختند، بزکشی بسیار زیاد اجراعات میکردند در طرف شمال افغانستان.

احمد: هان ... راستی بزکشی خو بسیار یک... این چیز بود باصطلاح یک سپورت و ورزش بسیار قوی.

جاوید: سپورت بسیار .... سپورت و ورزش عنعنوی افغانستان است. این چیزها را دیگر گودیپران بازی میکردند، دیگر در زمستان اکثراً مردم عروسی در زمستان میکرد. بخاطریکه فرصت میبود و حاصلات تابستان را میبرداشتند یک چند روپی میداشتند باز در آن ساز و موسیقی میآوردند.
سازهای محلی بنام دهل و سرنای داشتند. و سازهای دیگر خاننده های محلی بود، این قسمتها ساعت تیری مردم است.
و همچنان در قسمتهای دیگر ساعت تیریشان فرضاً توپبازی، ما توپ دنده میگفتیم توپ همراه دنده مثلیکه اینجا بیس بال میگویند همینطور یک قسم.

[55] The speakers on this selection are Ahmad and Javid they attended high school in Afghanistan and Javid is a graduate of Kabul University and has a slight Kabuli accent and Ahmad speaks Kohdamani dialect of Dari.

Recreation

Ahmad: Recreation in Afghanistan is mostly during festivals, Eid festivals, and New Year's festivals. Um... especially, when we used to go to Kabul, to Khair Khana pass.

There were bighorn sheep fights, and, for example, dogfights, kite-flying and also there was a running festival, and archery, javelin, and stone-throwing. Especially, [to see] who throws the stone farther? Oh... you must have gone to these festivals a lot.

Javid: Yes, all right, entertainment in Afghanistan mostly takes place in the winter. Since people were not busy working in their farms and most other work is stopped, they would have entertainment. For example, they would make dogs fight, they would make quails fight, they would make chickens fight and they would have the buzkashee, mostly in the northern region of Afghanistan.

Ahmad: Yes, ...indeed buzkashee was very good and a powerful sport.

Javid: Sport... it is Afghanistan's traditional sport. People used to fly kites and things like these. Another thing was that people would get married in the winter because people have more time in the winter and also they would have money from selling produce over the summer. So they could afford to have music at their wedding.

They had local traditional music; it is called drum and oboe. And also they had the folkloric music. This is the entertainment that people have.

People also had other kinds of entertainment, like playing ball, we called it "toop danda." It is a ball with a bat. It is like what they call baseball over here. It is something like that.

احمد: مثل بیس بال امریکائی واری.

جاوید: امریکائی واریست. آن در افغانستان زیاد رواج داشت.
اه... دیگر مردم سگها را خوب صحیح نگاه میکرد، آن را غذا میداد، چاق میکرد قوی می ساخت. باز هرکس میآورد و میدان جور میشُد و باهم و این سگها را جنگ میندا ختند.
و باز در وقت میلهٔ نوروز که میشد در چند نقطه یکی در مزارشریف بسیار مردم جمع میشد بنام میلهٔ نوروزی یا گل سرخ. در خود کابل در زیارت سخی جمع میشدند. یکی دیگر از طرف حکومت بنام روز دهقان در زیر کوتل خیرخانه تجلیل میشد، که در آنجا دهقانهای هرمنطقهٔ اطراف کابل میآمدند. حیواناتیکه خوب تربیه کرده بودند به نمایش میآوردند.
اه... باز بخاطر تفریح و ساعت تیری مردم آن همان اسپ دوانی بود و نیزه بازی بود و سگ جنگی بود و گودیپران بازی بود. این ساعت تیریها را مردم در آنجا داشتند.

Ahmad: It is like American baseball.

Javid: It is like American. It was very popular in Afghanistan.

Oh... another thing was that they kept dogs, they fed them, made them big and strong. Then everyone would bring their dog to the dog field then they would have the dogs fight.

Also people would gether at the New Year festival or red flower festival in Mazar-e-Sharif. They would also gather in Zearat-e-Sakhi in Kabul.

Also Labor Day was a government holiday and was celebrated at the Khair Khana pass.

And the farmers around Kabul would come to the festival and would bring livestock, which they raised, for the festival show.

Oh... then, to entertain people they would have horse racing, throwing a lance, dog fights, and kite fights. Those were the entertainments that people would have.

Vocabulary

ساتیری *colloquial* تفریح *n* entertainment, having a good time
میِ ورداشتن *colloquial* میبرداشتند، جمع میکردند *v* they would harvest
سازای *colloquial* سازهای، موسیقیهای *n* music
بیس بال *colloquial* *n* baseball
چاغ *colloquial* چاق *adj* fat, a heavy person or animal
آستا آستا *colloquial* آهسته آهسته *adv* slowly

موسیقی[56]

جاوید: در افغانستان خو موسیقی بود از بسیار سابق بود من نمی فهمم در زمان شما وقتیکه من در افغانستان نبودم.
موسیقی به کدام درجه بود؟ چه قسم بود؟ مردم علاقه داشت نداشت چطور بود؟

احمد: هان ... در موسیقی خو بسیار مردم علاقه داشت خصوصاً در وقتی که ... در وقت داودخان و در وقت خلقیها و در وقت پرچمی ها خصوصاً در جشنها که میشد باز هر وزارت از خود یک کمپ داشت. باز در هر کمپ باز خواننده های اه... در آنجا بود و همان گروپ خواننده های شان به اصطلاح مثلاً در کمپ وزارت زراعت یکسال احمد ظاهر می خواند.
احمد ظاهر یک اه... خوانندهٔ بسیار مشهور افغانستان، که مردم بسیار خوش داشتش خصوصاً در شهرها.
باز هر وزارت از خود یک خواننده داشت.
باز در اطرافها که بود اه... به اصطلاح همان خواندنهای محلی بود که یک نفر یک تنبور داشت و باز یک نفر دیگر یک تبله داشت. و باز می نشستند میخواندند خصوصاً در عروسیها که میشُد باز اه... مردم جمع میشُد شب که ناوقت میشُد بعد از ده بجهٔ شب باز ساز شروع میشُد تا دم صبح دیگر.
باز اه... رقص بود اه... چی موسیقی بود و خواندن بود اه... خاندنهای محلی باز در همان طرف اطراف و قریه جات و این جایها بسیار رونق داشت.
اه... باز در وقت خلقیها باز موسیقی، باز موسیقیهای بسیار پیش رفته که از آلات موسیقی که الکترونی بود یا برقی استفاده میکردند که آن را ازخارج میآوردند.
اه... باز همانطور آهسته آهسته دیگر اه... موسیقیشان پیشرفت کرده بود بسیار زیاد.

---

[56] The speakers on this selection are Ahmad and Javid they attended high school in Afghanistan and Javid is a graduate of Kabul University and has a slight Kabuli accent and Ahmad speaks Kohdamani dialect of Dari.

Music

Javid: Music has been influential in Afghanistan since the ancient time, but I don't know how it was in your time because I wasn't there

At what level was the music? What was the music like? Were people interested in music or not?

Ahmad: Yes, ... people were interested in music especially in Daud Khan time and Khalqis and Parchamis time, and especially during independence day celebrations. During that time every ministry had its own tent and there was a music group to perform in each tent. For example, Ahmad Zahir performed in the department of agricultural tent once.

Ahmad Zahir was a very famous Afghan singer. People liked him very much, especially people in the cities.

Then, every ministry had its own singer.

Then, in the countryside, there was folkloric music. One person would play sitar and one person would play bongos. They would sit and sing especially when there was a wedding party. People would get together and the music would start from 10 at night until morning.

Oh... they would have dancing music and singing. Folkloric music was very popular in the countryside and in the villages. Oh... music was developed during Khalqis, there were electrical music instruments, which run on electricity. They would import those from abroad. Oh... the music was well-developed slowly.

جاوید: از این در آن وقت شما همین خواننده های مشهور رادیو که در بین مردم هم بسیار شهرت داشت کی ها بودند؟

احمد: اه... در آن وقت دیگر اَحمدظاهر بود و ناشناس بود و اه... حبیب شریف بود و رحیم بخش اُو خو سابقه بود اما در آن وقت هم بسیار مشهور بود.
و اه... در طرف ... اطراف عالم میگفتند و فیظ کاریزی و هماهنگ و حاجی سیفو که بسیار مشهور است اُو آدم بیسواد بود. أما خواننده بود مردم بسیار همانطور خوش داشتش بخاطر از این که ساعت تیری بود.

Javid: Who was very popular among those singers who sung over the radio station?

Ahmad: Oh... at that time they were Ahmad Zahir, Nashinas and oh... Habib Sharif, Rahim Bakhash, he was the oldtimer but he was famous at that time.

And oh...in the countryside ...countryside there was somebody called Alem and Faiz Karazi and Hamahang and Hagi Saifo; he is very famous and illiterate. He was a singer that people liked because he was an entertainment for people.

ورزش[57]

احمد: اه... در افغانستان اه... سپورت و ورزش هم بسیار زیاد بود. خصوصاً در شهرهای بزرگ. اه... مثلاً فتبال بسیار مشهور بود. و والیبال که شق خودم بود من هم والیبال را بسیار خوش دارم والیبال هم بسیار زیاد بود. و مردم علاقه داشت چرا یک بازی اجتماعی.

بود و باز در مناطق اطراف پهلوانی بود و اه... دویدن و این سپورتهای اه...این چیز اولمپیک هم زیاد بود و چیزها.

شما هم در این سپورتها اشتراک کردید اه... فکر میکنم شما فتبال میکردید یا نی؟

جاوید: هان بلی، سپورت در افغانستان رواج داشت. در بین مردم عوام اه... سپورت بزکشی بود، پهلوانی بود، دویدن بود اه... اما...

احمد: خیز انداختن کاکایم یگان دفعه میگفت.

جاوید: خیز انداختن بود بلی. اما در بین طبقهٔ تحصیل یافته و مکتبی و پوهنتون اینجا یا به سطح حکومتی در این سپورتهای پهلوانی، بوکس، دویدن، فتبال، والیبال، بزکشی همهٔ از این... جمناستک رواج داشت. من دیگر در دوران مکتب... زیاد فتبال میکردم.

احمد: بلی.

جاوید: اما در دوران پوهنتون باز یک چند مدت کراته کردم. بعد از آن یک مدتی تقریباً یکسال جمناستک کار کردم. اه... دیگر تقریباً در سپورتها در کلش علاقه داشتم و حالا هم علاقه دارم.

سپورت چیزِ بسیار خوب است. در تنها چیزیکه در افغانستان سپورت را یعنی تق... مانع رُشد بیشترش میشُد آن خرابی وضع اقتصادی افغانستان بود فرضاً، وسائل ابتدائی بود. وسائل پیشرفته، وسائل خوب برای تعلیم افراد نداشتند.

غذا بسیار محدود بود برای یک سپورتمَین غذای کافی ویتامین کافی ضرورت است، در حالیکه در افغانستان برای مردم کم میرسید. لباس سپورت نبود فرضاً، کرمچ کسی نداشت. همیشه پای لوچ میدوید فوتبال همراه...

---

[57] The speakers on this selection are Ahmad and Javid they attended high school in Afghanistan and Javid is a graduate of Kabul University and has a slight Kabuli accent and Ahmad speaks Kohdamani dialect of Dari.

Sport

Ahmad: Oh... in Afghanistan oh... there were various sports especially in the big cities. Um... soccer was very popular and volleyball that is my hobby and I like it very much. People played a lot. People liked volleyball because it is a good social game.

Then in the countryside they had wrestling oh... running, these kinds of games. They had Olympic games too.

Did you participate in these games also? I think you did. You played football. Didn't you?

Javid: Yes. People would do sports. People in the countryside would play buzkashee, and do wrestling and they would race. But in this...

Ahmad: My uncle said they used to do the long jump.

Javid: Yes, there was long jump. But educated people, school students, and college students would participate in games like wrestling, boxing, racing, football, volleyball, buzkashee and gymnastics. These games were traditional games. Then I used to play football a lot when I was in school.

Ahmad: OK.

Javid: But when I was in college I practiced martial arts for awhile. Then I practiced gymnastics for a year. Oh... then I was interested in all kinds of sports and I am now too.

Sport is a very good thing. The only thing that prevents the people of Afghanistan from doing sports is the bad economic situation of Afghanistan. For example, they had ordinary facilities. They did not have advanced facilities and equipment to train people.

There was limited food. An athlete would need enough nutrition and vitamins, while in Afghanistan people had little.

There were not athletic clothes. For example, nobody had athletic shoes; people would run and play football barefoot, with no shoes.

احمد: ما...

جاوید: پای لوچ فتبال میکردند.

احمد: حالی ما خود ما والیبال را که شروع کردیم نی کرمچ داشتیم نی دیگر. توپ والیبال را هم نمی فهمیدیم. یک توپ سخت را گرفته بودیم که زود خراب نشود. از خاطریکه اه... نداشتیم زور خریدنشه.
باز پای لوچ والیبال میکردیم. و راستی هم که در افغانستان دیگر مردم توان از این را نداشت.

جاوید: مردم استعداد بسیار خوب دارد ولیکن توان اقتصادی و توان وقتش را ندارند.

احمد: بلی هان، باز در این جیز افغانستان تیمهای این چیز هم داشت نی؟... که در اولمپیک اشتراک میکرد. فکر میکنم که پهلوانی افغانستان قویترین تیمش در این چیز بود، در اولمپیک یا... یا نی؟

جاوید: بلی هان، در افغانستان اه... تیم پهلوانی افغانستان در اولمپیک می رفت.

احمد: باز بعضی این چیز اه... کوچهای روسی میآمد مردم را تربیه میکرد در افغانستان والیبال و چیزها در وقتهای خلقیها و این جا.

جاوید: نی کوچ از کشورهای خاریجی نمیآمد در افغانستان.

احمد: خو... نمی آمد. تنها تیمهای میآمد که مسابقه کُند؟

جاوید: بلی.

احمد: خو بسیار خوب.

Ahmad: We...

Javid: They played football barefoot.

Ahmad: Myself, when I started playing volleyball, we didn't have athletic shoes or anything like that. We didn't know what volleyball was. We bought a hard ball, so it would last longer, because we could not afford to buy the right one.

Then we played barefoot. Actually people could not afford that.

Javid: People have talent but economically they are not able and they don't have time for it.

Ahmad: Yes indeed. Did Afghanistan have teams or things, like the one to participate in the Olympics? I think the wrestling team was the strongest team from Afghanistan to participate in the Olympics, or not?

Javid: Yes indeed, Afghanistan's wrestling team used to go to the Olympics.

Ahmad: Some of those oh... Russian coaches used to come to Afghanistan and train volleyball and other things during Khalqies, and here.

Javid: No, the coaches would not come from abroad to Afghanistan.

Ahmad: OK... so they didn't come. Only the teams came that competed.

Javid: Yes.

Ahmad: Ok, very good.

Vocabulary

شوق *colloquial* رشته، مسلک *n* hobby *n* major
کوچ *colloquial* *n* coach

مقاومت افغانها در مقابل اشغال شوروی[58]

احمد: وقتیکه روسها در افغانستان آمدند افغانستان را اشغال کردند، روسها خو یک قدرت جهانی بودند به اصطلاح اَبَر قدرت بودند.
اه... آفرین مردم افغانستان که این ضد روسها مقاومت کرد و روسها را شکست داد.
اه... فکر میکنم که اه... همین اه... که افغانستان یک مملکتی بود مردمش به دین پابند و اه... بخاطر از این که، بخاطر وطن و آزادی خود جنگ کردند به این خاطر شاید روسها را شکست داده باشد.
و اه... شما در همین باره یک روشنی میاندازید.

جاوید: بلی هان، روسها که در افغانستان آمدند قبل از خود یک دسته ای را روان کرده بودند بنام کمونستها که حزب خلق[59] و پرچم بود. مردم افغانستان از حزب خلق و پرچم بسیار نفرت داشتند.

احمد: بلی.

جاوید: و آنها بسیار گروه اقلیت بودند. یکبار خو مردم در ضد از آنها شروع کرد مبارزه را. وقتیکه آنها به شکست مواجه شدند، روسها خودشان آمدند مردم از روسها هم بیشتر به دو سه علت نفرت داشتند
یکی این که روس قبلاً آمده بود، آسیایِ میانه را گرفته بود، هویت ملِی و هویت مذهبی مردم آن منطقه را از بین بُرده بود. مردم بسیار بد می بُرد.
دیگر این که مردمیکه در... از آنجا فرار کرده بودند قصه های از ظلمهای قوای عسکری روس در آن منطقه میکردند.

احمد: مردم بخارا و ازبکستان و...

[58] The speakers on this selection are Ahmad and Javid they attended high school in Afghanistan and Javid is a graduate of Kabul University and has a slight Kabuli accent and Ahmad speaks Kohdamani dialect of Dari.

[59] There were two communist parties in Afghanistan, the Khalqi and the Parchami.

Afghans Resist Russian Invasion

Ahmad: When the Russians came to Afghanistan and invaded Afghanistan, they were the world's most powerful people. In other words they were the superpower.

Oh... bravo to the Afghan people that they resisted the Russians and defeated them.

Oh... I think that...oh... this thing...oh... it was a country where the people were dedicated to religion and oh...they fought for their country and freedom and that is why they defeated the Russians.

And oh... would you explain this subject.

Javid: Yes indeed. Prior to their arrival in Afghanistan the Russians sent the Communists who consisted of the Khalqies and Parchamies parties. The people of Afghanistan felt hatred toward the Khalqies and Parchamies.

Ahmad: Yes.

Javid: And they were a minority group. Suddenly the people started a campaign against them. When they were about to be defeated, the Russian themselves came. People felt an even stronger hatred toward the Russians, for two, three reasons.

One, the Russians came and invaded Central Asia one time before. And they destroyed the people of that region, their traditional and religious identity. People hated that.

And also the people, who were exiled from there, would tell the story about oppression that the Russian military did in that region.

Ahmad: The people of Bukhara and Uzbekistan and...

جاوید: بخارا، بلی هان... اینها این قصه ها را که میکردند مردم بسیار زیاد نفرت پیدا کرده بود در برابر روس.
و دیگر این که مردم می فهمید که روس کمونست است به خدا ایمان ندارد. و از این خاطر بسیار آنها از آنها نفرت می کردند.
به اساس همین نفرتیکه مردم از روس داشت، مقاومت را به ضد روس شروع کرد. وقتیکه مقاومت را شروع کرد. در وقت... در مقاومتش جهان اسلام و جهان دیمکراسی آزادی غرب همه از مجاهدین بشدت پشتیبانی کردند. فرضاً، فیصله های ملل متحد از افغانستان بسیار صورت گرفت.

احمد: اه... مردم افغانستان خو نی سلاح داشت و نی اه... پول داشت نی دیگر داشت اینها چطور توانستند که ضد روسها و ضد کمونستها جهاد را شروع کنند و مقاومت کنند. این آفرین شان.
اینها از دست خالی شروع کردند یا اینها کَتِ همان سلاح های سابقی که داشتند، اینها چطور به این قسم اه... مقاومتَ اه... مقاومت کردند ضد روسها؟

جاوید: هان... مردم افغانستان مردم عوام بصورت عموم سلاح هیچ نداشتند. تنها یکتعداد مردم افغانستان که در قوای عسکری بود و نوانستند یکتعداد اسلحه را بدست بیاورند از قطعات عسکری با همان شروع کردند.
باز سلاح های کهنه ای که از زمان انگریزها در افغانستان بود به آن اسلحه شروع کردند. مجردیکه اینها مقاومت را شروع کردند از داخل اُردو و پولیس با اینها کمک صورت گرفت. هم اسلحه برشان کمک... داخل ... از داخل رسید هم مهمات برایشان رسید و اینها تقویه شدند.
وقتیکه جنگ کمی جان گرفت، دنیای آزاد هم کمکهای خود را شروع کرد.
فرضاً امریکا و عربستان سعودی و پاکستان و ایران و ساحر... مصر و چین و اینها هم به مجاهدین کمک های اسلحه را شروع کردند.
بتدریج مجاهدین به سطحی رسید که می توانستند هم از خود دفاع کنند و بعداً قوای روسی را در شکست مواجه ساختند.
این مقاومتها یعنی یک جنبۀ جهانی را بخود گرفت و از طرف ملل متحد فیصله های چند بار شد که با گروپهای مجاهدین باید از طرف دنیا هم اسلحه کمک شود هم لباس کمک شود هم غذا کمک شود. مگر تا آخر اسلحه... کمک اسلحه به مجاهدین رسید اما بر مجاهدین کمک اقتصادی، غذائی، البسه نرسید و با همان داشته ای که از خود داشتند حاصلات محیط خود و وطن خودشان بود به همان زنده گی خود را پیش می بُردند.

Javid: Bukhara, yes indeed. They would tell these stories and the people had built a hatred toward the Russians.

Another thing, people knew that the Russians were Communists and they didn't believe in God. Also because of this people would hate them.

Based on this hatred that the people had toward the Russians, they started a resistance against the Russians. As they started resisting the Russians, at the same time the Islamic world and the western democracy world strongly supported the Mujahedeen resistance. For example, the summits at the United Nation were mostly about Afghanistan.

Ahmad: Oh... people of Afghanistan neither had weapons, oh... nor money and nothing, how were they able to start a Jihad and resistance against the Russian and the Communists? Bravo to them.

Did they start empty-handed or with old weapons that they had? How could they oh... resist like that?

Javid: Oh... people of Afghanistan, especially civilians, in general civilians did not have weapons. Only some people who served in the military could obtain some weapons from the military bases.

Then they started with the old weapons that were left from the British time in Afghanistan. When they started, they got help from personnel inside the police and the military. They received weapons and ammunitions from inside the police and the military and they were strengthened.

When the war revived, the liberal world also started helping. For example, America, Saudi Arabia, Pakistan, Iran, and all... Egypt, and China they also started helping the Mujahedeen with weapons.

Gradually, the Mujahedeen were at the level that they were able to defend themselves and confronted the Russians with defeat.

These resistances gained worldwide attention and a decision was made in the United Nations to help Mujahedeen's groups with weapons, clothes, and food. But until the end, weapons... the Mujahedeen were helped with weapons but not with economic aid, food, or clothes. They lived on produce and products that they had in their regions.

احمد: فکر میکنم مجاهدین از روسها هم بسیار غنیمت گرفتن سلاح مثلاً کلاشنکوف و تفنگچه و این سلاح ثقیله مثل دهشکه و توپ و چیزها.
وقتیکه روسها را میزدند که میگریختند باز این چیزها را می ماندند اینها.

جاوید: بلی مجاهدین از قوای عسکری روس هم اسلحه های مختلف الشکل غنیمت گرفتند. کلاشنکوف کلاکوف شینکوف اه... اقسام مختلف اسلحه را از قوای عسکری روس اینها به غنیمت گرفتند.
و حتی اسلحهٔ بسیار سری روس که داشتند و آوردند در جنگ افغانستان استعمال کردند مجاهدین آن را گرفتند و آن نمونه ای از آن بدست خبر رسانیهای جهان رسید، بدست کشورهای پیشرفتهٔ دیگری دنیا رسید و آنها را یعنی تخنیک روس را افشا ساخت.
بهترین طیاره های خود را روس در افغانستان به جنگ آورد که طیاره هایش سقوط داده شد.

احمد: فکر می کنم همین ستنگر در افغانستان بسیار موثر واقع شد که امریکا کَت مجاهدین کمک کرد. همان بسیار هلیکوپترهای روسها را زد که باز روسها را بیخی اه... گلَمشان را جمع کرد به اصطلاح.

جاوید: هان بلی ... اَه... روسها یکنوع هلیکوپتر بنام اه... هلیکوپتر ضد مرمی یا...

احمد: هان، گنشیپ.

جاوید: گنشیپ آورده بود استعمال میکرد که با سلاح دست داشتهٔ مجاهدین آن سخت مقابله میکرد سلاح مجاهدین سرش کار نمیکرد.
بعداً که امریکا کمک را شروع کرد... کمک ستنگر داد به مجاهدین. آن هلیکوپتر زیادش سقوط کرد. بعد از آن از صحنهٔ جنگ خارج شد، تلفاتش بیشتر شد.
به این لحاظ روسها محدود شدند در ساحات شهرها و در قطعات عسکری و باز مواجه شدند به شکست. و بالآخره حاظر شدند از افغانستان خارج شوند.

Vocabulary

بد می بُرد *colloquial* نفرت داشت *v* hated, was against
تانستن *colloquial* توانستند *v* were able, had the ability
انگریزا *colloquial* انگلیسها *n* the British

Ahmad: I think that the Mujahedeen got a lot of weapons from the Russians as booty. For example, they seized Kalashinkovs, handguns, and heavy weaponry like anti-aircraft guns and artilleries.

When they attacked the Russians, the Russians would run away and they would leave these things.

Javid: Yes, the Mujahedeen seized a variety of weapons from the Russians as booty. They seized a variety of weapons like Kalashinkovs, Kolikovs, and Shinkovs from the Russians as booty.

The Russians even brought their secret weapons and used them in the fight in Afghanistan. The Mujahedeen seized them, then the media worldwide got a sample of them. Developed countries also obtained them, and the Russian technology was thereby divulged.

The Russians brought their best fighter aircrafts in the war in Afghanistan and they were shot down.

Ahmad: I think the stingers, which America gave to the Mujahedeen, were very effective in Afghanistan. They shot a lot of Russian helicopters, then the Russians were completely incapacitated (lit. packed up to leave).

Javid: Yes indeed, oh… the Russians used some kind of helicopter that was bulletproof.

Ahmad: Yes, gunships.

Javid: They brought and used gunships, which would resist the guns that the Mujahedeen had, and the Mujahedeen weapons were not affecting the gunship.

Later on when started helping… gave stingers to the Mujahedeen, then that helicopter was shot down. They were destroyed and they disappeared from the war zone.

Because of that the Russians were eliminated in the cities and in the military bases, then they were defeated. Finally, they were ready to withdraw from Afghanistan.

ستنگر *n* stinger missile

گلَمشانه جمع کرد *colloquial* شکست داد *v, phrase* defeated them, *n, phrase* fold their carpet or rug

گنشیپ *colloquial* *n* gunship helicopter

دعوت به نان شب[60]

ناهید: مصطفی جان سلام.
احمد: سلام و علیکم. خوب هستید؟
ناهید: چه حال دارید خوب هستید؟ جور بخیر؟
احمد: صحت شما خوب است؟ خیر خیرت؟
ناهید: تشکر، شما چه حال دارید؟
احمد: تشکر.
ناهید: فامیل همه گی خوب استند؟
احمد: الحمدلله، شما فامیل ها همه گی خوب هستند؟
ناهید: زنده باشید، والده صاحب چطور هستند؟
احمد: والده صاحب خوب هستند. کَمَکی مریض بودند فضل خدا خوب شدند حالا.
ناهید: خو بسیار خوب. بلی شنیدم که یَک کمی. چه تکلیف داشتند؟
احمد: تکلیف فشار خون داشتند.
ناهید: هان... خو حالا انشاءالله که زیر تداوی داکتر هستند چطور؟
احمد: بلی هان ، بلی دوا میگیَرند و زیر تداویستند، فضل خدا صحتشان خوب است.
ناهید: خو بسیار خوب. همشیره ها همگی خوب هستند؟ قبله گاه صاحب، کُلگی خوب استند؟
احمد: بلی صاحب، فضل خدا.
ناهید: خو، خوب است که والده صاحب یکذره صحتش بهتراست، صباح شب اگر بتوانید خانۀ ما بیاید و یک چند نفر دیگر را هم خواستیم، خواهرم هم از طرفهای شمال آمده. شما را هم گفتم والده صاحب را تکلیف می دهم اگر برای نان شب بیآید صباح خانۀ ما.
احمد: خو، انشاء الله چرا نی، من پرسان می کنم.
ناهید: خو.
احمد: اه... چه پخته می کنید؟

---

[60] In this selection the speakers are Ahmad and Nahid. Ahmad attended high school in Afghanistan and speaks the Kohdamani dialect of Dari. Nahid finidhed college in Afghanistan, obtained her master's degree in the U.S., and speaks the Kabuli dialect of Dari.

Dinner Invitation

Nahid: Hello, dear Mostapha.

Ahmad: Hello, how are you?

Nahid: How are you and how is your health, are you in a good health?

Ahmad: Is your health good, are you in a good health?

Nahid: Thanks, how is everything with you?

Ahmad: Thank you.

Nahid: How is everybody in your family?

Ahmad: Thank God. How is everyone in your family?

Nahid: I wish you longer life. How is your mother?

Ahmad: She is fine; she was a little sick. By the grace of God, she is better now.

Nahid: OK, very well. Yes, I heard that she was a little (sick). What was her difficulty?

Ahmad: She had difficulty with blood pressure.

Nahid: Oh…God willing. Is she under a doctor's treatment now or what?

Ahmad: Yes, indeed. Yes, she takes her medicine and she is under a doctor's treatment. By the grace of God, her health is good.

Nahid: OK, very good. How are your sisters, and how is your father?

Ahmad: Yes, ma'am by the grace of God everyone is good.

Nahid: OK, it is good that your mother's health is good. If you could come to my house tomorrow... you and your mother are invited for dinner. We invited a few more people; my sister is coming from the north. Please forgive us for the difficulty your mother might have.

Ahmad: Yes, God willing, why not? I will ask.

Nahid: OK.

Ahmad: Oh… what are you going to cook?

ناهید: چه پخته می کنیم.

احمد: مهم هم خو نیست، خو باز هم.

ناهید: شما بگوید که چی، والده صاحب چی خوش دارد؟

احمد: والله والده صاحب دیگر اه... آنها خو برنج بی نمک می خورند و...

ناهید: خو خو...

احمد: گوشت بی نمک از خاطر فشار خون.

ناهید: فشارخون. بسیار خوب شد که گفتید. خو، من دل من است که یک ذره آشک پخته کنم و آشک را می توانمِ بی نمک پخته کنم. دیگر قابلی پلاو پخته می کنم برایتان. اه... چلو مِیشود و کتِ سبزی یا قورمه یا یک... هر چیزیکه شما فرمایش میدهید.

شما اگر بگوید من آنقدر زیاد به پخت و پز بلد... آشنائی ندارم اما می توانم (یک جول خود را از آب کشیده می توانم)

احمد: منتو چطور؟

ناهید: منتو والله منتو را زیاد تجربهٔ پخته کردنش را ندارم.

احمد: نداری. قابلی پلاو چه قسم پخته میشود؟

ناهید: قابلی پلاو، خو اُنه برنج را مثل... برنج را جوش میدهیم اول، باز صافش می کنیم، باز برنج را که دم می کنیم در همان وقت دم کردن، یا پیاز آدم بریان می کند که رنگش را... بخاطر رنگ دادنش یا اینَکه بوره را هم آدم می تواند که بسوزاند که رنگ نسواری پیدا کند.

اما بعد از آن باز اُنه زردک را خلال می کنیم، در روغن سرخ می کنیم، باز کشمش را هم در روغن سرخ می کنیم وقتیکه پلاو را دم کردیم باز زردک و کشمش را کَتیِش می اندازیم. این حالی بعضی وقتها من همین گوشت مرغ را هم در همین بغلهای،... بعد ازینکه برنج پخته می شود در همین سر دیگ می مانم که یکذره گگ تف بکشد بعضی وقت. بعضی اوقات این را من جدا پخته می کنم.

مرغ را جدا پخته می کنم باز وقتیکه نان را می کشیم مرغ را البته اُنه شما آشنائی دارید که مرغ را اول در سر غوری می مانیم در سرش برنج را می اندازیم. دیگر من خو اینهمین رقَمی پخته کردیم.

Nahid: What am I going to cook?

Ahmad: It is not that important, just because...

Nahid: You tell me what. What does your mother like?

Ahmad: Oh, God… my mother, oh… she eats rice without salt and…

Nahid: OK…OK.

Ahmad: Meat without salt because of blood pressure.

Nahid: Blood pressure. That is good you told me. OK, I am planing to cook some aushak. And I can cook aushak without any salt. Then I will cook qabilee palove for you. Oh… chalov would go with spinach or qorma or one…

whatever you like to order. If you ask me... I am not very familiar with cooking. But I know enough to get by.

Ahmad: How about mantoo?

Nahid: Mantoo, God, I don't have experience in cooking mantoo.

Ahmad: You don't have? How do you cook qabilee palove?

Nahid: Qabilee palove, it is like you take rice… first you boil water, then pour the water out, then we will steam the rice at that time; you either fry onion for color… for giving the rice some color, or one can burn sugar until it becomes brown.

But after that, we will slice carrots thinly then, we will sauté it in oil, then we also sauté raisins in oil. Then we steam the palove; we will add the carrots and the raisins. Now, sometimes we can put chicken meat around the rice and let it cook. After the rice is done, we will put it on the top of the dish so it gets steamed. Some times I cook this separately.

I cook chicken separately. Then when we take the food out of the dish... you are familiar with how we would put the chicken on the plate first then we will top it with rice. Then, this is the way I have cooked.

احمد: والله همین حالا آدم گشنه می شود صدای این چیزی که می شنود.
ناهید: البته والده صاحب و همشیرهٔ شما من میفهمم که بسیار زیاد قابل استند. خو یک چیز خجالتی می شود که من...
احمد: نی خواهش می کنم.
ناهید: دیگر آشک، آشک خوب است، اگر والده صاحب بتوانند که همراه همشیره صاحب اینها کُلَگی وقتتر یکذره بیایند که کَتِ من کُمَک کنند.
باز ... بخیلم که مهمانهای من خواهرم و اینهَا آمده نمی توانند از راه، از راه دور می آیند یک کَمَکِی شاید تال بخورد.
اگر شما والده صاحبِ را روزِ وقت بیاورید که در همین آشک پُر کردن یکذره گگ... شما بلَد هستید آشک پُر کردن.
احمد: والله آشک من بلَد نیستم خودم اما دیدیم.
ناهید: دیدین
احمد: که چه قسم درست می کنند اما صحیح...
ناهید: نمی فهمی
احمد: همین موادش را نمی فهمم که چه، می فهمم که گندنه است. اما نمی فهمم که چه قسم.
ناهید: مردهای، مردهای افغان دیگر نان پخته نمی کنند، معلومدار. و خو من گندنه را خریدم من یگان دفعه کَتِ کندنه همین گشنیز را هم این چیز می کنم، ریزه می کنیم بر از اینکه خوش مَزه می شود.
بعضی کسها آشک، در مابین آشک کوفته هم پُر میکنند. من کَتِ گوشت زیادتر این چیز نمی کنم، فقط همان گندنه و گشنیز را میده می کَنم...
احمد: بلی.
ناهید: یک کَمَک واری مرچ و مصاله اش را، اُنه روغن و مرچ سرخ و مرچ سیاه و نمک از خاطر والده صاحب نمک نمی اندازمِ دیگر این همین همان این چیز اش می شود، موادش می شود. باز فقط برای پُر کردنش یکذره گگ کُمَک کار است.
احمد: خو به چشم.
ناهید: که اگر زحمت نشود اگر والده صاحب همشیره واینها خانم برادرتان را هم بگویید.
احمد: بلی به چشم.

Ahmad: Oh God, one hears this conversation and will get hungry.

Nahid: I know of course that your mother and sister are very good at it. I might embarrass myself.

Ahmad: No, please pardon me.

Nahid: Next, aushak, aushak is good. If your mother, sister, and everyone else could come earlier, so they can help me.

Then… I think my guests, my sister and others (lit.them) can't come; they come from a long distance; they might be a little late.

If you bring your mother earlier in the day, so she can help a little… you know how to fill aushak.

Ahmad: By God, I don't know how to make aushak but I have seen...

Nahid: You have seen.

Ahmad: How it is been done. But I exactly...

Nahid: You do not know.

Ahmad: (I) don't know the ingredients, I only know that there are leeks, but I don't know how.

Nahid: Afghan men don't cook. I have bought leeks, and sometimes I chop cilantro and add (it) to taste better.

Some people would add ground beef also in the aushak. I don't do it much with meat. Only, I chop leeks, cilantro...

Ahmad: OK.

Nahid: A little pepper and spices, some oil, red and black pepper, and because of your mother I will not add salt. And this is the thing, the ingredient. The ingredient can be done; only for filling it, help is needed.

Ahmd: OK, with pleasure (lit. with my eye).

Nahid: If it is no trouble, would you tell your mother, sister, and your sister-in-law, all of them?

Ahmad: Yes, with pleasure.

ناهید: شما همه گی را میآورید باز زود زود میشود انشاءالله.
احمد: اما من خودم دستها را بر میزنم برایتان انشاءالله پُر می کنم.
ناهید: شما، والله تعجب می کنم من.
احمد: مرا مقصد نشان بدهید که چه قسم می شود باز همراه تان کُمَک می کنم.
ناهید: تعجب می کنم، شما را خانم تان اجازه میدهد که دست بزنید به آشپزی افغانی؟
احمد: هان بلی، هان بلی.
ناهید: خو. در خانه کُمَک می کنید؟
احمد: کُمَک می کنم بلی هان، اما زیادتر غذا را آنها پخته می کنند.
ناهید: هان معلومدار... وظیفه... وظیفهٔ زنهاست، بلی؟
احمد: چرا همین قسم در کلچر ما وشماست. وظیفهٔ شان خو نیست، همان قسم کلچراست آمده دیگر.
ناهید: مردها میروند سر کار، و میآیند میگوند که نان تیاراست یا نیست.
احمد: بلی هان.
ناهید: اگر نان تیار باشد خوب، اگر نباشد پیشانیشان تُرش می شود.
احمد: بلی هان پیشانیشان ترش میشود. از خاطریکه همین قسم کار خانه تقسیم شده نی.
ناهید: بلی
احمد: مثلاً، مردها میرود در بیرون...
ناهید: درست،درست.
احمد: کار می کند، و زنها همان اه... مسلهٔ نان پختن است.
ناهید: وظائف خانه است...
احمد: و وظائف خانه است، و...

Nahid: When you bring everybody, God willing, it can be done faster.

Ahmad: But I myself will rool up my sleeves and, God willing, I will fill.

Nahid: You! I am surprised.

Ahmad: You just show me how it is done, then I will help you.

Nahid: I am surprised. Does your wife allow you to touch Afghan cooking?

Ahmad: Indeed, yes, yes.

Nahid: OK, Do you help at home?

Ahmad: Yes, I help indeed. But she cooks the food.

Nahid: Of course indeed, job of… it is a woman's job.

Ahmad: Wy, this is how it is in our culture. It is not their job, but it is part of the culture.

Nahid: Men go to work and come back and ask, "Is the food ready or not?"

Ahmad: Yes indeed.

Nahid: If the food would be ready everything would be good; otherwise, they would be frowning.

Ahmad: Yes, indeed, they would be frowning. Because in this way housework in a family is divided, or not?

Nahid: Yes, right, right.

Ahmad: For example, men go...

Nahid: Right, right.

Ahmad: And work outside of the house. Then, there is oh… cooking matter.

Nahid: There is house work.

Ahmad: Housework…

ناهید: اولاد داری و این گپها

احمد: اولاد داری و ..بلی.

ناهید: شما اولادها خو، اولادها را هم میاورید همراه تان بلی.

احمد: والله از من دیگر یک طفلک است همان را هم شاید بیاورم دیگر.

ناهید: نی، معلومدار دیگر. اینطور است که در رسم و رواج ما خو همان است، که هر جایکه میرویم اولادهای خود را کتِ خود می بریم.
اولادها برای اولادها اگر میگوید منَ چیز مخصوص، میگوید برایشان تیار می کنم. مکرونی و این چیزها را اگر خوش دارند آن را می توانم برایشان تیار کنم.

احمد: نی، ببخشید به زحمت می شین. همان آشک و برنج می تانن بخورند.

Vocabulary

تکلیف می تُم *colloquial phrase* please pardon the trouble *phrase*

صبا *colloquial* فردا *n* tomorrow *n* morning

سرخ *colloquial v* sauté *n* red

کَتیش *colloquial* همرایش *adj* with it

می مانیم *colloquial* می گذاریم *v* we will let, we will wait *v* we will lay, we will put, we will allow

نان *colloquial* غذا *n* food, meal, dinner or lunch

نانه *colloquial* غذا را *n* food, dish, dinner or lunch

همیالی *colloquial* الآن، حالا *adv* now, right now

وختر *colloquial* زوتر, وقتر *adj* earlier

بخیلم *colloquial* به فکر م، فکر میکنم، به خیالم *v, phrase* I think, I assume

تال *colloquial Arabic* معطل *adj* delayed *adv* postponed

Nahid: Raising kids and things like these.

Ahmad: Yes, raising children and these kinds of matters.

Nahid: Do you have children? Yes,are you going to bring the children with you? Yes.

Ahmad: By God, I have one child; I will bring him with me.

Nahid: No, of course you will. It is part of our culture that, wherever we go we take our children with us.

Also the children... if you would like I can make something special for the children. If they like macaroni or things like that, I will make it.

Ahmad: No, please do not go to any trouble (LIt. please pardon the trouble). They can eat the aushak and the rice.

بَلَد *colloquial* آشنا، وارد *adv* knowledgeable *n* city, town
باضی *colloquial* بعضی *n* some, few, portion
کَمَکی واری *colloquial* کمی *n* like a little
دستهاره ور میزنیم *colloquial phrase* I will fold up my sleeves
کلچر *colloquial English* کلتور، فرهنگ *n* culture
پیشانیشان تُرش میشه *colloquial* قهر میشوند، نا راحت میشوند *phrase* (lit. their foreheads would become sour) they will be unhappy
مکرونی *colloquial English n* macaroni
آشَک *n* Afghan dish prepared with dough, leeks, "quroot," and served with yogurt sauce, similar to a dumpling

مکتب نسوان[61]

احمد: خو نوریه جان، شما مکتب در کابل رفتید نی؟

ناهید: بلی هان در کابل مکتب.

احمد: مکتب ابتدائیه و مکتب لیسه و...

ناهید: بلی من در سه صنف اول در مکتب ملالی بودیم. بر از اینکه آن وقت در همان طرفها زنده گی میکردیم. باز صنف سوم را که خلاس کردیم بابۀ مرا خدا ببخشد اه...

احمد: خدا ببخشد ایشان را.

ناهید: بلی تشکر مرا آورد خانۀ ما در ده بوری بود. در چوک ده بوری خانۀ نَو گرفته بودیم باز مارا آورد ... در... من را در مکتب رابعۀ بلخی درکارتۀ چهار بود، در آنجا داخل کرد.

احمد: رابعۀ بلخی خوب مکتب مشهور بود دیگر.

ناهید: شما می شناسید رابعۀ بلخی را. بلی اینطور بود که مکتب ملالی به خیالم اه... بسیار مشهور بود بعد از آن مکتب زرغونه بعد از آن مکتب رابعۀ بلخی. باز در مکتب رابعۀ بلخی، اگر چه من صنف سه را در مکتب ملالی خلاص کرده بودم آن وقت بابه ام من یادم است بسیار که به مدیرۀ مکتب گفت که دخترم چون خوردترک است همین صنف سه را باز بخواند و دیگر آن وقت سر من آنقدر تأثیر نکرد، اما پسان که دیدم که یکسال ما تکرار کردیم صنف سه باز تا آخره دیگر در مکتب رابعۀ بلخی بودم.

احمد: مکتب تان از اه... مکتب بچه ها جدا بود دیگر؟

ناهید: بلی هان دیگر خو در افغانستان خو اینهمین رسم و رواج است بچه ها...

احمد: تا صنف دوازده.

ناهید: تا صنف دوازده بلی آن وقتها خو دختر و بچه شاید بعد از ما اگر مکاتب یک بچه ها و دختر ها را یکجای کرده باشند در وقت ما هیچ نبود، در هیچ جای نبود. ما دیگر دورۀ اول این چیز هم بودیم، دورۀ اول رابعۀ بلخی هم بودیم.

---

[61] In this selection the speakers are Ahmad and Nahid. Ahmad attended high school in Afghanistan and speaks the Kohdamani dialect of Dari. Nahid finidhed college in Afghanistan, obtained her master's degree in the U.S., and speaks the Kabuli dialect of Dari.

Girls' School

Ahmad: OK, dear Noria, you went to school in Kabul, didn't you?

Nahid: Yes indeed, to school in Kabul.

Ahmad: Elementary or high school?

Nahid: Yes, the first 3 classes I went to Malalia School because we used to live in that area. Then, when I finished third grade, God bless my father…

Ahmad: God blesses him.

Nahid: Yes, thank you. Then we moved to Dehbori. We bought a new house in Dehbori square, then he moved us there. Then he got me admission at Rabia Balkhi School, which was located in Karti Char.

Ahmad: Rabia Balkhi was a popular school, for sure.

Nahid: Do you know Rabia Balkhi? Yes, but I think it was like this, the most popular school is Zarghona School, then it is Rabia Balkhi school. Then Rabia Balkhi School. Even though I finished the third grade in Malalia School, my father told the school principal that "My daughter is very little; it is better for her to study in third grade again." It didn't affect me at that time but later on I realized that I repeated the third grade one more year. Then I attended Rabia Balkhi School until the end.

Ahmad: Was your school separate from the boys' school, of course?

Nahid: Yes, of course. This was the tradition and the culture in Afghanistan.

Ahmad: Until twelfth grade.

Nahid: Until twelfth grade boys and girls were separate. Maybe after I was gone, they mix boys and girls, but it wasn't so anywhere at my time. We were the first ones, the founding class of students to open Rabia Balkhi.

احمد: بلی.

ناهید: دوازده بود یا چهارده نفر بود که از مکتب دورهٔ اولش بودیم.

احمد: نام خدا.

ناهید: که فارغ تحصیل شدیم.

احمد: بسیار خوب. معلمهای تان زن بود یا مرد هم بود؟

ناهید: معلمها، معلم زبان پشتو یک مرد بود و رسام ما هم یک مرد بود. رسام مرد بود، معلم پشتو مرد بود دیگر یادم نیست این آدمها. فکر می کنم که کل معلمهای دیگر زنها بودند، بلی.

احمد: خو خو...

ناهید: مدیرهٔ مکتب ما هم یک خانم بود، اه... آنقدر مردها نبود اما یکنفر دیگر به خیالم که، ... بلی هان در وقتیکه من در صنف یازده و دوازده بودم یک کمَک واری در همین اه... کیمیا و فزیک همینجا کُمَک کار داشتم. باز یک معلم خانگی گرفته بودم. آن معلم این چیز مرد بود. دیگر معلمها کله زن بود.

احمد: خو بسیار خوب. بعد از رابعهٔ بلخی که فارغ شدید باز به فاکولته نرفتید؟

ناهید: نخیر دیگر من در وقتیکه در صنف یازده و دوازده بودم در وزارت زراعت کار می کردم به حیث سکرتر باز آنهمانجا وقتیکه من در وزارت زراعت بودم یک سکالرشیپ آمد به وزارت. یکنفر خانم را می خواستند، یک دختریکه فارغ تحصیل مکتب شده باشد، می خواستند که امریکا روان کنند.
باز آنهمانجا من کاندید بودم و متأسفانه که سه سال من منتظر شدم تا که برای من اجازه دادند که از افغانستان برآیم.

احمد: خوشبخت بودید دیگر.

ناهید: بلی بلی ، معلومدار براز اینکه اولین دختری هم بودم که از افغانستان من رسمی به این رقمی برایم... معلومدار بسیار یک گپ بسیار کلان بود.

احمد: نام خدا.

Ahmad: Yes.

Nahid: It was either twelve or thirteen of us to start the school for the first time.

Ahmad: Bravo (lit. in the name of God.)

Nahid: That we were graduated.

Ahmad: Very good. Were your teachers males or were they all women?

Nahid: Teachers, the Pashto language teacher was a man and also the art teacher was a man too. The art teacher was a man and the Pashto teacher was a man; I don't remember the other people. I think the rest of the teachers were women. Yes.

Ahmad: Good, good.

Nahid: Our school principal was a woman also. Oh…there were not too many men. I think there was one more person, that… Yes indeed, when we were in either eleventh or twelfth grade, I needed a little help in chemistry and physics. Then I had a private tutor and he was a male teacher; the rest of the teachers were women.

Ahmad: Good, very good. After you were graduated from Rabia Balkhi School, did you go to college?

Nahid: No, I didn't. When I was in eleventh or twelfth grade, I worked as a secretary in the ministry of agriculture. When I worked at the ministry of the agriculture, the ministry received a scholarship. They were looking for a highschool graduate woman to give her the scholarship and send her to America.

Then I was the candidate; unfortunately I had to wait three years to get permission to go out of Afghanistan.

Ahmad: You were lucky, obviously.

Nahid: Yes, yes. Obviously, because I was the first girl who traveled out of Afghanistan officially like this. Obviously, it was a big deal.

Ahmad: Bravo (lit. In the name of God).

ناهید: برای ما برای فامیل ما دیگر، خوش بختی در اینجا بود که فامیل اجازه دادند که من تنها بیآیم به امریکا باز آن هم، سه سال بعد ازینکه از مکتب خلاص شدم آمدم امریکا، درسهای فاکولته و ماستری خود را در امریکا خوانده ام.

احمد: بسیار خوب، بسیار خوب. دیگر دخترهای که از لیسه فارغ می شدند آنها خو به فاکولته می گرفت ایشان را.

ناهید: بلی هم صنفی های ما کل شان در فاکولتهٔ حقوق و در دندان سازی و طب و جاهای مختلف در افغانستان در فاکولته.

احمد: بلی.

ناهید: یعنی وقتیکه من... تا وقتیکه من در افغانستان بودم کل شان دیگر تقریباً در صنف سه فاکولته رسیده بودند... آن وقتیکه...

احمد: نام خدا.

ناهید: بلی... بلی همه گی همانجا بود.

Nahid: For me and my family… I was so lucky that my family gave me permission to come to America by myself. Then, then three years after I graduated from school, I came to America. I finished my college studies and my master's in America.

Ahmad: Very good, very good. The other girls who graduated from high school, would they be accepted in college?

Nahid: Yes, my classmates were all attending colleges like law, dental, medicine and other colleges in Afghanistan.

Ahmad: Yes.

Nahid: That means, my classmates were in their third year of college and I was still in Afghanistan… when…

Ahmad: Bravo (lit. In the name of God).

Nahid: Yes… yes everybody was there.

Vocabulary

ده بوری *n* name of a district in Kabul
اچی *colloquial* چیز *prep* thing
همیجه *colloquial* همینجا، اینجا *prep* here
گُله *colloquial* همه *pro* everyone, all
خانمه *colloquial* خانم، زن *n* woman

تفریح دخترها

احمد: شما در افغانستان که بودید اه... برای تفریح چه می کردید همراه دخترهای خالهٔ تان یا همراه همشیرهایتان همراه دخترهای کاکا؟

ناهید: هان بلی از ما یک همشیرهٔ خورد من است دیگر دخترهای عمهٔ ام بود و بعضی... بعضیِ اوقات مثل... مثل ... همراه شاگردهای... هم صنفی های مکتب خود مثلاً. یا میگریختیم یا همانطو اجازه گرفته از خانه می رفتیم بیرون بعد ازمکتب یا سینما می رفتیم، سینما درِ شهر نَو که بود.
اه... یا می رفتیم درِ کدام جای دیگر مثلاً برای چای خوردن و چیزها و فامیل را نمی گفتیم، پت پُت. بعضی... بعضی اوقات هم در خانهٔ مثلاً، رفیقهای خود اجازه می داشتیم از فامیل خود می رفتیم بر ... یا خود ما ساز می کردیم اگر آن کسهائیکه استعداد وعلاقه داشتیم یا موسیقی گوش می کردیم.

احمد: بلی.

ناهید: این رقم باز وقتهای خود را... تیر... وقت را تیر می کردیم.

احمد: بسیار خوب، اه... اه... در آنجا برای دخترها اه... والیبال و فتبال و چیزها بود یا دخترها زیادتر نمی کردند.

ناهید: والله نی، نی در وقت ما خو هیچ چیز نبود، در مکتب هم نبود در بیرون هم نبود و در وقتیکه من مثلاً در افغانستان بودم و در آنجا در مکتب بودیم هیچ.
ما در خانه یک میز پنگ پانگ داشتیم حتی همان هم برای دخترها آنقدر ما تشویق نمی شدیم.
برادرهای من، من چهار برادر دارم از این چهارتا دوتایش پنگ پانگ باز بسیار مشهور برآمدند. ما را یگان دفعه اجازه می دادند مثلاً در خانه پنگ پانگ بازی می کردیم همراه از آنها. یا دیگر تختهٔ کرمبول، خو شما بلد هستید؟

احمد: بلی هان، کرمبول بسیار کردیم.

ناهید: کرمبول در خانه میکردیم ما مثلاً، آنطور اه... بازی هایکه مثلاً دیگر نفرها هم همرایش باشد، در بیرون باشد، یا مثلاً فتبال یا والیبال این چیزی را که شما گفتید آن چیزها برای ما مهیا نبود متأسفانه.

Girls' Recreation

Ahmad: When you were in Afghanistan, what did you do with your cousins and your sisters for fun?

Nahid: Yes, we have a younger sister and there were my cousins... then sometimes for example... for example.... With the students, with our classmates, used to skipping school or getting permission from home, and we went out of the school to the movies and Shahre-Now.

Oh... or we used to go somewhere else for tea and things. We would not tell the family and went secretly... secretly. Sometimes in the house, for example. We used to get permission from parents to bring in friends. Or we played music with the people who had the talent and liked and listened to the music.

Ahmad: Yes.

Nahid: This is the way we spent our time sometimes.

Ahmad: Very good, oh...oh... for the girls there...oh girls wouldn't play volleyball or football very much.

Nahid: By God no, no, there wasn't any in our time. There wasn't any in school or outside. When I was in school in Afghanistan there was nothing. We had a ping-pong table in our house; we the girls, were still not encouraged.

My brothers, I have four brothers. Two of the four became very popular ping-pong players. They would let us play with them once in awhile. Another thing is carom. Do you know how to play?

Ahmad: Yes indeed, I played carom a lot.

Nahid: We played carom at home, for example. Oh... but we didn't play games that involve other players, or were played outside, for example football, volleyball. And things you mentioned, unfortunately, were not available for us.

احمد: یگانه چیزیکه یاد من میآمد که دخترها می کردند، جزبازی یا لشپی بازی که می گفتند.

ناهید: من... من آن را نمی فهمم. جز بازی چه بود؟

احمد: اینطور خط که می کشیدند...

ناهید: هان بلی، بلی.

احمد: باز این چیز را می انداختند خیز می زدند.

ناهید: آن همان که خیز می زدند نامش یادم رفته بود، بلی.

احمد: جزبازی میگوند آن را.

ناهید: یکی دیگر ریسمان بازی ما میکردیم بسیار زیاد.

احمد: بلی هان ریسمان بازی هم دخترها زیاد میکردند.

ناهید: در همین، کَت رفیقهای دَور و پیش خانه.

احمد: بلی.

ناهید: که همسایه ها، همسایه های ما بود یک دختر یک دوتا بچه همسایهٔ ما بود کَت از آنها بازی می کردیم در بیرون.

احمد: باز ما که خورد بودیم همراه دخترهای خورد دیگر اه... ما یکچیزی را چشم پتکان می گفتیم.

ناهید: بلی هان.

احمد: از آن یکی که چشمای خود را پت می گرفت باز...

ناهید: که دیگر را پیدا کنید، بلی.

احمد: پت می کرد خود را باز می رفتی پیدا می کردی.

ناهید: پیدایش می کردی. ما در زمستان بسیار ساعت ما تیر بود برازیکه خانهٔ ما بسیار کلان بود حویلی بسیار کلان داشتیم. برف که میبارید باز یک یخمالک بسیار کلان می ساختیم مثل یک کوه واری بلند.
برف را این چیز می کردیم تیار می کردیم باز می رفتیم پت پت از خانه، همین لگنیکه در حمام می بُردند لگن را می گرفتیم باز کَت از این یخمالک می خوردیم.

Ahmad: The only thing I remember that girls would play was hopscotch or they would call it leshpai.

Nahid: I… I don't know that. What was hopscotch?

Ahmad: They would draw lines...

Nahid: OK, yes...yes.

Ahmad: On the ground then they would throw the thing then they would hop.

Nahid: OK, yes, yes, I forgot the name of hopping, yes.

Ahmad: They call it juzbazee.

Nahid: Another thing we did a lot was skipping rope.

Ahmad: Yes indeed, the girls would also skip rope a lot.

Nahid: With friends around the neighborhood.

Ahmad: Yes.

Nahid: The neighbors, a girl and two boys were our neighbors, and we used to play outside.

Ahmad: When we were little, we played a game with girls and we called that game hide-and-seek.

Nahid: Yes, OK.

Ahmad: It was like you had to close your eyes and…

Nahid: To find the other person, yes.

Ahmad: They would hide and you would have to find them.

Nahid: You had to find them. We had a great time in the winter because our house was big and it had a large backyard. When there was snow we used to make a sledding hill from snow as high as mountains

We used to do things, we used to make the snow ready, and we had to go out of the house secretly, and we took the bathing tub and slid with it.

احمد: خو.

ناهید: کل اولادها از دَور و پیش و از همسایه گی اینها جمع شده بودند. ما دیگر تقریباً سه چهار نفر خود ما و یک پنج شش نفر هم از همسایه ها وقت در زمستان این کار را می کردیم. یکروز دیدیم که همین لگن کونش سوراخ شده. اینقدر ترسیدیم که توبه برای از اینکه لگن حمام بود نی، خو در اش آب میگیرند که خود را بشورند.

باز بسیار وارخطا شدیم. بردیم این لگن را پس در همان جای ظرفهای حمام ماندیم و در خیالم که کس سر ما خبر نشد. در زمستان ساعت ما بسیار زیاد تیر بود برای از اینکه مکتبها رخصت است و برف جنگی می کردیم مثلاً، در حویلی خود دیگر همسایه ها می آمدند...

احمد: بلی.

ناهید: بازی میکردیم ساعت ما در زمستان زیادتر تیر بود. در تابستان دیگر گرمی تکلیف میداد بسیار زیاد و یکذره در خانه هم دخترها دیگر مسئولیت داشت، باید خانه میآمدند و کَت مادر خود کُمَک می کردیم برای نان پختن و برای این گپها.

احمد: بلی، بسیار خوب.

ناهید: از آن خاطر زیاد ما تشویق نمی شدیم که بریم بیرون برای بازیهای سپورت و این گپها.

احمد: بلی بسیار خوب.

Vocabulary

خالیتان *colloquial* خالهٔ تان *n* your aunt

همشیرایتان *colloquial* همشیره هایتان *n* your sisters

پُت پُت *colloquial* پنهان، مخفیانه *adv* secretly, concealed *n* close, coverd

دوتایش *colloquial* دو نفر، ایشان، دونفر آنها *phrase* two of them

کرمبول *n* carom

جزبازی *n* a children's game similar to hopscotch played with a (potshard)

لشپی بازی *colloquial* لشپاک بازی، جزبازی *n* a children's game similar to hopscotch played with a (potter shard)

Ahmad: Good.

Nahid: All the children in the neighborhood would gather. We were approximately three or four ourselves, and five or six people were neighbors; together we did these things. One day I looked and I saw a hole at the bottom of the tub. I was scared because it was a bathing tub. They fill it with water so they can take a bath, then I was worried.

Then we took the bathing tub and put it where the bathing equipment was and I think nobody noticed us. We had a lot of fun in the winter because schools were closed. We used to snow fight, for example, in our house and our neighbor used to come over.

Ahmad: Yes.

Nahid: We used to play around in the winter, we had a lot of fun. In the summer, the heat gave us a hard time very much. And also girls had responsibility. We would come home and help our mother with cooking and things like this.

Ahmad: Yes, very good.

Nahid: That is why we were not encouraged to go out to play and do sports and things like that.

Ahmad: Yes, very good (OK).

چشم پُتَکان *colloquial* *n* hide and seek
لگن *colloquial* تشت *n* tub, tray
کونش *colloquial* زیر *n* bottom
دَ اش *colloquial* در آن *phrase* in it, with it
وارخَطا *colloquial* *pash* *adj* nervous, confused, hesitant
برف جنگی *colloquial* *n* snowball fight
حولی *colloquial* حویلی *n* house, courtyard
تیر *colloquial* *pash* خوب گذشت *adj* good, fun *adv* the act of passing, the act of crossing *n* an arrow, a dart *n* the fourth month of the Persian solar year

رویهٔ طالبها با زنها[62]

احمد: نظر شما در بارهٔ رویهٔ طالبها در مقابل زنهای افغانستان چه است و شما چه فکر می کنید که رویهٔ که طالبها در مقابل زنهای افغانستان کردند، در وقتی که قدرت داشتند در افغانستان.

ناهید: والله مصطفی[63] جان من بیخی... برای من بسیار قابل تعجب است، برای از اینکه من در یک فامیلی کلان شده ام که، اگر چه مادر من مثلاً مکتب نرفته بود در پیش یک خانم درس خوانده بود. یا قرآن را یاد گرفت، خواندن قرآن شریف را یاد گرفته بود اما ما همیشه تشویق می شدیم که باید درس بخوانیم که آیندهٔ خوب داشته باشیم. برای... باید کار کنیم که برای فامیل بتوانیم کُمَک شود.

دیگر اینکه طالبها که زنها را بیچاره ها را به این رقم همراه شان وضیعت میکرد که هم از کار کردن ماندند هم از درس خاندند ماندند هم از بیرون رفتن ماندند، این بیخی دیگر بهتراست که در بندی خانه اینها را بندازد. من تعجب می کنم که چطور یک بشر، یک انسان میتواند که به یک انسان دیگر اینقدر ظلم کُند.

احمد: بلی.

ناهید: به نظر من این فقط ظلم است که یک انسان نا دان، و نافهم به مقابل یک خواهر خود که ما، میگویند که ما این کارها را می کنیم به خاطر از اینکه اینها را جای شان در خانه باید باشند یا در بیرون برای شان محفوظ نیست یا امنیت نیست یا چه رقمی.

اما ما در قرن بیست بیست و یک زنده گی میکنیم. این وقت از این نیست که خانمها را در خانه نگاه کنیم که باش که اینها محفوظ باشند این دیگر یک جرم بسیار بزرگ در مقابل بشریت است. من فکر می کنم.

احمد: بلی من خبر شدم که حتی یک زنیکه شوهرش در جنگ کشته شده بود و یک طفلک داشت آن طفلکش مریض بود و این زن می خواست که برود دوا بگیرد برایش...

---

[62] In this selection the speakers are Ahmad and Nahid. Ahmad attended high school in Afghanistan and speaks the Kohdamani dialect of Dari. Nahid finidhed college in Afghanistan, obtained her master's degree in the U.S., and speaks the Kabuli dialect of Dari.

[63] Mostafa is Ahmad's nickname.

The Taliban Treatment of Women

Ahmad: What is your opinion about the Taliban's behavior toward women? And what do you think of the Taliban's behavior toward women when the Taliban had power in Afghanistan?

Nahid: By God, dear Mostapha. I am totally surprised. Because I was raised in a family that, although my mother did not attend school and she learned from a woman, learned Quran, learned how to read the holy Quran, still we were always encouraged to study to have a good future, to do that to be able to help our family.

Another thing, the way the Taliban treated those helpless women so they couldn't work, they couldn't study and they couldn't go outside. Even being in jail was better than that. I am surprised, how could a human oppress another human this much.

Ahmad: Yes.

Nahid: In my opinion it is oppression that an ignorant and uneducated person would treat their sister like that so that they stay home because it is not safe for them to go outside or something like that.

But we live in the twentieth and twenty-first centuries. This is not the time to make women stay home so they can be safe; this is a big oppression toward humanity I think.

Ahmad: Yes, I heard that even a woman at home, her husband was killed in the war, she had a baby and the baby was sick, and she wanted to go and buy medicine for the baby…

ناهید: بلی، بلی.

احمد: برای طفلک خود اُو از خانه بر آمده نتوانست چون دوا هم نامد. همان طفلکش بیچاره مُرد.

ناهید: طفلکش مُرد.

احمد: باز همان زن بیچاره قصهٔ خود را به یک ژورنالست، اچیز خبرنگار انگلیس گفته بود باز اُو نوشته کرده بود. این بسیار یک قصهٔ بسیار تراژید و بسیار غم... غمناک است.

ناهید: ...دلخراش است، بلی. بلی من از این قضیه خو شخصاً خبر نشدیم اما بعضی چیزهائیرا که مثلاً در فلم و در اینجا می بینم اه... من یک چند وقت در پاکستان بودم در آنجا بعضی مؤسسهای خیریه یا بعضی کلنیکها برای خا... برای صحت نی، صحت عامه این چیزها داشتند حتی آنجا هم زنها را بسیار به ندرت می دیدند.
مثلاً مردها طفلکهای خود را می بُردند، خو می فهمید که هم زن مریض می شود هم طفل مریض می شود هم مرد مریض، اما زنها بخاطریکه داکترها مرد بودند اجازه نداشتند که مثلاً بروند به داکتر مرد اینها را معاینه کند در آن صورت اینها بیچاره ها همانطور می ماندند دیگر. اینقدر ظلم دیگر خو.

احمد: حالا سیل کن که اینها چقدر بی منطق استند زنهای خود را پیش داکتر مَرد نمی مانند و زنهای خود را هم نمی خواهند که داکتر شوند، که باز زنهایشان را تداوی کند نی. اگر زن نرود مکتب نخواند...

ناهید: بلی بلی درست. درست میگوید.

احمد: مثلاً یاد نگیرد، داکتر نشود، باز آن زنها را کِی تداوی کند.

ناهید: پس در این صورت در اه... از هر نقطهٔ نظریکه این را ببینید این برای زنهان ظلم است نی، برای از اینکه نمی توانند درس بخوانند که کُمک به دیگرها کنند نمی توانند که خودشان مثلاً وقتیکه مریض میشوند پیش یک کسی بروند که... من فکر میکنم حماقت است.
این کارها کُلَش از حماقت است. یک آدمیکه عقل سالم داشته باشد، این کارها را اصلاً نمی کند.

Nahid: Yes, OK.

Ahmad: She couldn't go out for her baby and they couldn't have the medicine. That poor baby died.

Nahid: Her baby died.

Ahmad: Then that helpless woman told a journalist her story. She told a British journalist and the journalist has written it. This is a very sad and tragic story.

Nahid: Yes, personally I wasn't aware of this story but when I see some other things in video oh… I was in Pakistan for some time; there were some aid organizations and some clinics for health and the department of public health care, even there the women were discriminated against.

For example, men would take their children to the doctor. We know that women also get sick, children also get sick and men also get sick. But since the doctors were male, women were not allowed to go to the doctor for a check-up. In this case those helpless would remain like that. This much oppression!

Ahmad: Now look! How ignorant they are that they neither allow their women to go to a male doctor nor do they let their daughter become a doctor so then they would be able to do a medical examination on their wives. If women don't go to school and don't learn….

Nahid: Yes, you are saying the right thing.

Ahmad: For example, if they don't learn, and don't become a doctor, then who will medically examine those women?

Nahid: Then in this case oh… if one looks at it from any angle, it is oppressing to women. Isn't it? Because they can't go to school so they could help others, and they can't go to a doctor by themselves when they are sick; I think this is all ignorance.

These actions are all ignorance. Someone who has a healthy brain would not take these kinds of actions at all.

احمد: نمی کند. باز، باز اینها دین را ملامت می کنند. اصلاً دین اسلام هیچ وقت نگفته که زن نخواند. دایم دین اسلام در چند جای تکرار کرده که زنها باید درس بخوانند علم یاد بگیرند ولو که در هر جائی باشد.

ناهید: تشویق کرده. بلی، بلی، بلی درست، درست میگوید بلی. من متأسفانه به این بدبختی در سر مردم ما آمده دیگر مخصوصاً در سر زنهای افغان این بدبختی از چند، بیست سال به این طرف است.

احمد: بلی بیست سال.

ناهید: خدا امید وار هستیم که حالا در... بعد از این یک آیندهٔ روشن در پیش روی داشته باشیم.

احمد: انشاء الله.

Ahmad: They would not do it. Then, then they blame the religion. Actually Islamic religion never says, "Women should not study." Always Islamic religion in several places repeated that "Women should study and learn knowledge wherever they can."

Nahid: They were encouraged. Yes, yes, yes, right. You are telling the truth, yes. I… unfortunately, our people are undergoing hardship, especially the women. How long this misfortune has been, since twenty years.

Ahmad: Yes, twenty years.

Nahid: We have hopes now that God will give us a bright future.

Ahmad: God willing.

Vocabulary

نتانست *colloquial* نتوانست *v, phrase* was not able to, could not

ژورنالست *colloquial English* خبرنگار *n* journalist

تراژید *colloquial* غمناک *n* tragedy

اقه *colloquial* اینقدر *adv* this much, that much

سَیل کُو *colloquial* ببین *imperative v* look, see

یاد نگره *colloquial* اگر یاد نگیرد *v, phrase* if he/she would not learn

نمی تانن *colloquial* نمی توانند *v, phrase* they are not allowed *v, phrase* they are not able, they can't

خریداری زنها[64]

احمد: شما در اچیز کابل که بودید نی.

ناهید: هان.

احمد: اه... وقتیکه لباس خریدن یا مثلاً بوت خریدن و این چیزها می رفتید. اه... باز به اچیز می رفتید نی، در همان ده افغانان یک جایکی بود، در پائینش یک سرای نَو جور کرده بودند که طلاه فروشی هم بود در پهلویش دکانهای هندو که بود.

ناهید: به دکانهای هندو، من خو اینهمین هیچ یادم نمی آید. اما در دکانهای هندو ما که می رفتیم همیشه برای تکه می خریدیم نی که باز...

احمد: بلی هان.

ناهید: تکه را می بُردیم بر خیاط که برای ما کالا بسازد.

احمد: بلی.

ناهید: همان را میگوید اما من ده افغانان یاد من نمی آید که گفتید زیر زمینی بود؟

احمد: هان زیر زمینی جور کرده بودند شاید آن وقت شما در آنخا نبودید دیگر.

ناهید: هان چهل سال پیش شاید.

احمد: بلی هان. تقریباً یک بیست و پنج سل پیش جور کردند.

ناهید: نی خی آن بعد از من درست شده. برای از اینکه هیچ یاد من نمی آید. اما یاد من همینقدر میآید که ما خاله ام و مادرم و من می رفتیم ، ما می خواستیم یک برادرم را نامزد کنیم.

احمد: خو خو.

ناهید: باز اگرچه آن نامزدی هم نشد اما پیش از اینکه این گپها را شروع کنیم، باز می رفتیم در همین، چه میگویند. بزازی میگویند؟

احمد: بلی هان...

ناهید: بزازی میگویند.

احمد: بزازی تکه که می فروشند. بلی هان.

ناهید: تکه می فروشند. هان. و همیشه اینها تکه فروشها هندوها بودند نی.

---

64 In this selection the speakers are Ahmad and Nahid. Ahmad attended high school in Afghanistan and speaks the Kohdamani dialect of Dari. Nahid finidhed college in Afghanistan, obtained her master's degree in the U.S., and speaks the Kabuli dialect of Dari.

Women Shopping

Ahmad: You were in Kabul, weren't you?

Nahid: Yes.

Ahmad: Oh… when you shopped for clothes or shoes or other things, oh… then you had to go somewhere, somewhere called Deh-Afghanan. Underneath, they had built a new shopping center where they had jewelry stores and there were (Afghan) Hindu stores.

Nahid: To Hindu stores (Afghan Hindus), I don't remember this at all. But when we went to Hindu stores, we bought fabric. Wasn't it then…?

Ahmad: Yes indeed.

Nahid: Then we would take the fabric to a tailor to make dresses for us.

Ahmad: Yes.

Nahid: They talked about it, but I don't remember Deh-Afghanan. Did you say that it was underground?

Ahmad: Yes, they built underground, maybe you were not there at that time then.

Nahid: Yes, it was forty years ago.

Ahmad: Yes indeed, it was built approximately twenty-five years ago.

Nahid: No, OK, it was built after I left there because I don't remember it at all. I only remember that my aunt, my mother, and I would go. We wanted my brother to get engaged.

Ahmad: Good, good.

Nahid: Then even though the engagement didn't occur, and prior to these issues, we used to go somewhere. What was it called? It was called bazazi.

Ahmad: Yes indeed...

Nahid: They call it bazzar.

Ahmad: They sell fabric in bazazi. Yes indeed.

Nahid: They sell fabric. Yes, and usually the Hindus would sell fabric. Wouldn't they?

احمد: بلی هان.

ناهید: در همان بازار نزدیکهای شوربازار.

احمد: لاله می گفتیم.

ناهید: لاله بلی هان. یکی در همان نزدیکهای شوربازار بودند آن همانجا می رفتیم تکه می خریدیم. برای از اینکه برای خود لباس می ساختیم که برویم خواستگاری برای برادرم.

باز آه... بوت را پرسان کردید بخیالم. بوت را خو معلومدار ما پیش بوت دوز می رفتیم اندازهٔ پای ما را می گرفت و اُنه فرمایش میدادیم. باز مثلاً پیش از پیش بوتِ برای راه رفتن یا بوت فیشنی برای پارتی و این گپها بر... از طرف شبَ آن را خو فرمایش می دادیم، برای ما می دوخت بوت.

دیگر تکه را می گرفتیم پیش خیاط می بُردیم و آنکه اندازه ات را می گرفت باز برای ما می ساخت.

احمد: فابریکهٔ بوت آهو یادتان است؟

ناهید: فابریکهٔ بوت آهو هم بعد از من شده.

احمد: خو، در اینطرف وزارت دفاع که بود.

ناهید: بلی.

احمد: پائین طرف دریا که می رفتی. دریای کابل. در آنجا یک...

ناهید: هان نخیر، در وقت من نبود آن.

احمد: بلی، یک فابریکهٔ بوت آهو بود بسیار بوتهای خوب جور می کرد. زنانه، مردانه، طفلانه.

ناهید: خو آن خو نبوده پیشم... فقط یگانه فابریکه ای که در افغانستان در وقتیکه من بودم بود، اه... نساجی بود.

احمد: فابریکهٔ نساجی... بلی هان.

ناهید: اه... نام نفر هم یادم رفته اینحالی. اما فابریکهٔ نساجی بود که تکه های بسیار خوب...

احمد: در طرف پلچرخی بود، طرف خورد کابل.

Ahmad: Yes indeed.

Nahid: Somewhere near Shore Bazaar.

Ahmad: We would call them Lala.

Nahid: Lala, yes indeed. There was one near Shore Bazaar; we used to go there and buy because we would make ourselves dresses to go to my brother's marriage proposal.

Then oh…I think we asked about shoes. Of course we would go to a shoemaker for shoes. He would measure our feet and we would order. Then, if it was shoes, like walking shoes, dress shoes, party shoes, and shoes to be worn at nighttime, we would order those. Then he would make it for us.

Then we would take the fabric to the tailor; he would measure it and make dresses for us.

Ahmad: Do you remember the Aho shoe factory?

Nahid: The Aho shoe factory was also there after I left.

Ahmad: OK, it was near the defense ministry.

Nahid: Yes.

Ahmad: One would go down toward the river, the Kabul River.

Nahid: OK. No, it wasn't in my time.

Ahmad: There was an Aho shoe factory that would make good shoes, men's, women's, and children's.

Nahid: OK, it wasn't there before… just, the only factory in Afghanistan, when I was there oh… was Nasaji.

Ahmad: Nasaji factory…

Nahid: Oh… I forget the name of that person now. But it was the Nasaji factory that made good fabric.

Ahmad: It was toward Pule-Charkhi, toward Khord Kabul.

ناهید: بلی، بلی، سید مرتضی خان، سید مرتضی خان فابریکهٔ نساجی ساخته بود، اُو بسیار مشهور بود. دیگر در غیر از آن این همین دکانک های خورد و ریزه میرفتیم و برای بوت در دکان بوت دوزی و برای لباس در دکان خیاط و اینها.

احمد: بوتهای لیلامی در اُو وقت شما هم بود، میآوردند؟

ناهید: بوتای لیلامی نی، از دکانهای.... بوتهای مثلاً اگر ساخته گی می خواستیم بخریم، درشهر نَو باز بوت فروشها و این گپها بود میخریدیم بوت ... لیلامی نه خیر.

احمد: بوت های لیلامی از جرمنی و از اوروپا زیاد می آمد.

ناهید: مستعمل یعنی؟

احمد: بلی هان.

ناهید: مقصدتان مستعمل است از لیلامی؟

احمد: نی یعنی اه... از آن جایها...

ناهید: که ارزان شده.

احمد: که از مود می رفت. ارزان میشد. باز در افغانستان میآوردند.

ناهید: خو خو خو بلی بلی هان. ما دیگر نمی فهمیدیم که لیلامی بود یا چی بود. ما در دکان....

احمد: بلی هان، باز به قیمت ارزان می فروختنش.

Nahid: Yes, yes. Sayed Mortaza Khan, Sayed Mortaza Khan has built the Nasaji factory. He was very famous. Then beside that we used to go to those small and tiny stores; for shoes we used to go to a shoemaker store, and for clothes to a tailor store, and this.

Ahmad: Were there wholesale shoes in your time, would they bring them?

Nahid: Not wholesale shoes, when we wanted to buy shoes from stores, for example, if they were already made, we would buy them from a shoe store in Share-Now. Not wholesale, no. How was that?

Ahmad: Wholesale shoes were imported from Germany and Europe a lot.

Nahid: Does it mean used?

Ahmad: Yes indeed.

Nahid: Do you mean wholesale is used?

Ahmad: No, mean oh… from those places.

Nahid: The ones that became cheaper.

Ahmad: The ones that are out of fashion. Then they would bring them to Afghanistan.

Nahid: OK, OK, OK. Yes, yes indeed. We wouldn't know if they were wholesale or what. We in the store…

Ahmad: Yes indeed, then they would sell them cheaper.

ناهید: ما در دکان که می رفتیم فکر می کردیم که این بوتهای نَواست دیگر آن همان...

احمد: بلی هان.

ناهید: بوتهای مود روز است می خریدیم.

احمد: بلی هان، آنجا که از مود می افتاد باز ارزان می شد..

ناهید: باز می آمد در افغانستان. یکی در همان وقتهای عید که می شد یاد من است که اه... پدر ما را خدا ببخشد ، فوت کرد ما خورد و ریزه بودیم دیگر ما شش تا، شش اولاد در خانه. مادرم نمی توانست که برای کلگی در هر عید لباس نَو و این چیزها بسازد باز کوشش می کرد که مثلاً غم بچه ها را اول بخورد و باز دخترها را.

احمد: بسیار خوب.

ناهید: دیگر در آن وقت ما لباس اِچِی نَو می ساختیم در عید برای خود.

احمد: بسیار خوب.

ناهید: تشکر.

Nahid: When we went to the store, we would think that they are new.

Ahmad: Yes indeed.

Nahid: These shoes are the style and we would buy them.

Ahmad: Yes indeed, when they were out of style there, they would be sold cheaper.

Nahid: They would come to Afghanistan. One thing, whenever it was Eid, I remember that, "God blesses my father he passed away," we were very small and tiny and six of us, six children in a house. And my mother wouldn't be able to make new clothes for everybody, then she would try, for example, to take care of the boys first then the girls.

Ahmad: Very good.

Nahid: Then, at that time, we would make ourselves new clothes for Eid.

Ahmad: Very good.

Nahid: Thank you.

Vocabulary

بسازه *colloquial* بسازد *colloquial* to make, to create
لاله *colloquial n* a polite word used for a Hindu male in Afghanistan
فیشنی *colloquial English adj* fashionable
پارتی *colloquial English* مهمانی، مجلس *n* party
ششتا *colloquial* شش شخص ،شش نفر *phrase* six siblings, six persons (تا used between number and countable nouns)

عید مبارکی[65]

لیدا: سلام سیما جان.
سیما: سلام لیدا جان. چطور استید؟
لیدا: تشکر. شما خوب استید؟
سیما: تشکر زنده باشید.
لیدا: فامیل همه گی خوب استند؟
سیما: همه گی خوب. شما چطور استید؟
لیدا: البر جان همه گی خوب استند؟
سیما: تشکر خوب استند سلام می گفتند. خودت چه حال داری؟
لیدا: بد نیستم.
سیما: از مادرجانت شان احوال داری، خوب هستند؟
لیدا: همه گی خوب هستند سلام می رسانند.
سیما: خوب تشکر. ایام... عید گذشتهٔ تان مبارک.
لیدا: عید شما مبارک سیماجان.
سیما: داخل حاجی ها و غازیها باشید.
لیدا: باشد...

[65] In this selection the speakers are Sima and Lida. Sima finished university in Afghanistan and speacks the Kabuli dialect of Dari, Lida was born in Herat Afghanistan and emigrated to Iran at a very young age and then she came to the U.S. and she is a high school graduate. Lida speaks the Herati dialect of Dari, which is influenced by the Iranian Farsi.

Greeting during Eid

Lida: Hi dear Sima.

Sima: Hi dear Lida, how are you?

Lida: Thanks, are you well?

Sima: Thanks, I wish you longer life.

Lida: Is everyone in the family well?

Sima: Everybody is well. How are you?

Lida: Is dear Alber and everyone else well?

Sima: Thanks, they are well; they said hello. How are things with you?

Lida: I am not bad.

Sima: Do you have any news from your mother? Is she well?

Lida: Everybody is fine; they send regards.

Sima: Good, thanks. Happy past Eid days.

Lida: Happy Eid to you, dear Sima.

Sima: May you be among the pilgrims and heroes.

Lida: I shall.

سیما:	باشد. جایی نرفته بودید به عید؟
لیدا:	نخیر نی کار بودِم شما چه کردید؟
سیما:	من هم کار بودم، متأسفانه مسجد و این جایها هم رفته نتوانستم.
لیدا:	خو.
سیما:	دیگر منتها اولادها را عیدی دادم. خواهر زاده ها و برادرزاده ها ره عیدی دادم که بفهمند که در عید ما چی می کنیم.
لیدا:	خو چند ساله هستند؟
سیما:	اولادهای غزال جان یازده ساله، هشت ساله، هفت ساله.
لیدا:	نام خدا.
سیما:	هان. دیگر دخترکهای ناهیدجان چندساله است؟
لیدا:	ناهید... سمعیه یازده ساله است، سحر هشت شده.
سیما:	خو خو بسیار خوب.
لیدا:	امروز یکیشان عیدی شان کم شد، بخاطر ازیکه روی خود را نشسته بود صبح که خیست.
سیما:	خو خو.
لیدا:	روی چتل نان می خورد، باز پدرش پنج دالر از عیدیش کم کرد.

Sima: I shall, didn't you go somewhere in Eid?

Lida: Not really, no, I was at work. What did you do?

Sima: I was also at work. Unfortunately, I could not go to a mosque or a place like that.

Lida: OK.

Sima: Then, but I gave my children their Eid presents. I gave my sister's children their Eid presents so they know what we do on Eids.

Lida: OK, how old are they?

Sima: Dear Ghazal's children are eleven years old, eight years old, seven years old.

Lida: God blesses.

Sima: Yes. Then, how old are dear Nahid's daughters?

Lida: Nahid… Samia is eleven years old; Sahar has turned eight.

Sima: OK, OK. Very good.

Lida: The present for one of them wasn't enough because when she woke up, she didn't wash her face.

Sima: OK, OK.

Lida: Her face was dirty while she was eating breakfast. Then her father reduced her Eid present by five dollars.

سیما: کم کرد خو. خو از مادرکلانت شان چه احوال دارید؟
لیدا: مادر کلانم خوب است، بخانه است همیشه.
سیما: امریکا خوشش آمده؟
لیدا: به آن صورت نی، زیاد نی بخاطر از اینکه...
سیما: چون به خانه استند همیشه.
لیدا: دِق میشود به خانه است، کُلَگِی میروند اُو را تنها میمانند.
سیما: خَو صحیح.
لیدا: دیگر به پاکستان که بود خاله ام شان اولادهایش همیشه خانه بودند.
سیما: کُل در خانه بودند هان صحیح.
لیدا: از لحاظ لسان هم دیگر به تلویزیون هم چیزی نمی فهمد.
سیما: خو معلومدار لسان بسیار تاثیر دارد.
لیدا: لسان بسیار سخت است برایش.
سیما: هان راست میگوید.
لیدا: یک نفر کار دارد که بیست و چهار ساعت اُو را...
سیما: ترجمه کرده برود.
لیدا: نی بیست و چهار ساعت اُو را نگهداری کُند و از اُو...
سیما: که تشناب ببرد و نان پخته کند.
لیدا: هان دیگر مثل بچهٔ خورد میشود.

Sima: He reduced, OK, OK. What news do you have from your grandmother?

Lida: My grandmother is well; she is always at home.

Sima: Does she like America?

Lida: Not that much, not very much because...

Sima: Because she always stays home.

Lida: She gets bored staying at home; everybody goes and they leave her alone.

Sima: OK, right.

Lida: Then, when she was in Pakistan, my aunt's children were always home.

Sima: They were all home. Yes, right.

Lida: It is because of language also. She doesn't understand anything on TV either.

Sima: OK, of course, language has a big effect.

Lida: Language (English) is difficult for her.

Sima: Yes, you are telling the truth.

Lida: She needs a person who can be 24 hours…

Sima: To keep translating.

Lida: No, to take care of her 24 hours and for her…

Sima: To take her to the bathroom and cook for her.

Lida: Yes, then she would be like a little baby.

سیما: خو خو صحیح. خو دیگر همراه کار و بار خودت چطور هستی؟
لیدا: کار وبار، کار هفته ای پنج روز، شش روز کار هستم سیماجان.
سیما: خو بسیار خوب، خوب است مصروفیت باشد خوبتر است.
لیدا: لیکن مسافرت باشد بهتر است.
سیما: هان، خو معلومدار فیکیشن هم در بین می باشد. منتها کار هم خوب است که باشد.
لیدا: شما چی، از جرمنی دیگر بعد از آن قصد مسافرت ندارید؟
سیما: نی دیگر به این زودیها نی، برای از اینکه اه... باید یک کَمَکِی همین فیننس و وضع اقتصاد خانه را پس صحیح کنم. من تازه ریفایننس کردم خانهٔ من قسط خانه را دوباره تجدید کردم.
لیدا: بلی هان.
سیما: دیگر آن مصرفش سرم بسیار زیاد بود. و از همان خاطر کار دوم خود را هم دوام می دهم.
لیدا: خو.
سیما: دیگر تا که یک کَمَکِی شرایط اقتصادی صحیح شود باز آهسته آهسته دیگر کار دومم هم صحیح می شود.

Sima: OK, OK, correct. Then, how are you doing with work?

Lida: Work and things, I work five or six days a week, dear Sima.

Sima: OK, very good. It is good; it is better to be busy.

Lida: However, if it was travel, it would be better.

Sima: Yes, obviously, there should be vacation in between. But work is also good to have.

Lida: What about you? After going to Germany, don't you have any travel plan?

Sima: Obviously not. Not any soon, because, oh… I have to help to get the finances and financial situation back in shape. I recently refinanced my house. I renewed the payment of my house.

Lida: Yes indeed.

Sima: Its payment was too much for me. That is why I still do the second job.

Lida: OK.

Sima: Then, when the financial condition gets better, my second job will slowly get better.

Vocabulary

خواهرزاداره *colloquial* خواهرزاده هارا *n* my sister's children (sons and daughters)
دق *adj* sad, depressed
برش *colloquial* برایش *prep* for him/her
فیننس *colloquial* تجدید قسط *n* finance
سرم *colloquial* برایم *phrase* for me, to me, on me
خودام *colloquial* خود را هم *phrase* also my

زنها در زمان حکومت طالبها[66]

لیدا: به طالبها و آیندۀ افغانستان چیست، چی فکر میکنید، نقش زن، آیا می تواند زن آن آزادیهائیکه قبلاً به وقت شما داشتند پیدا کنند چند وقت طول میکشد یا چی فکر میکنید شما؟

سیما: والله با از بین بُردن طالبها حالی امید واری بسیار زیاد است. برای از اینکه سابق هم به افغانستان قسمیکه شاید و باید یک زن استقلال می داشت و اینها به اندازۀ کافی نداشت.

لیدا: بلی.

سیما: بسیار محدودیت ها داشت... نظر به مرد، مگر حالا شرایط اینقدر تغیر کرده که بسیار امید واری زیاد شده. حتی من فکر میکنم که از آن دوره های سابق هم که حداقل زن میتوانست مکتب برود البته به شهر کابل.

لیدا: بلی.

سیما: که مرکز بود.

لیدا: ویا شهرهای کلان.

سیما: یا شهرهای کلان مثل هرات و مزار شریف و بدخشان هم شاید یا اینها، در همان شهرهای کلان زن می توانست مکتب برود. اقلاً یعنی (پارت) همین اچی حصه داشته باشد به جامعه.

لیدا: بلی هان.

سیما: منتها قسمیکه به دنیا زن حقوق مساوی داده شده.

لیدا: به غرب.

سیما: به ممالک غربی مخصوصاً...

لیدا: بلی.

سیما: زنهای شرقی که آسیائی و اینها هستند آنقدر زیاد نی، خو مگر حالا امیدواری به بسیار زیاد است.

---

66 In this selection the speakers are Sima and Lida. Sima finished university in Afghanistan and speacks the Kabuli dialect of Dari, Lida was born in Herat Afghanistan and emigrated to Iran at a very young age and then she came to the U.S. and she is a high school graduate. Lida speaks the Herati dialect of Dari, which is influenced by the Iranian Farsi.

Women during the Taliban Government

Lida: What would the future of Afghanistan be under the Taliban? What do you think about women's roles in the future? Could women have their freedom like you had in the past? How long would it take? What do you think?

Sima: By God, there is a big hope that the Taliban would be removed. Because women also in the past did not have freedom the way they are supposed to. They did not have enough freedom.

Lida: Yes.

Sima: Women were more restricted than men were. But now, with the rapid change of circumstances, there is more hope. I think even in the past, at least women could go to school in the city of Kabul.

Lida: Yes.

Sima: That was in the central city.

Lida: Or the big cities.

Sima: Or, large cities like Herat, Mazar-e-Sharif, Badakhshan were the cities where women would go to school. That is to say, places where women could be part of the society.

Lida: Yes indeed.

Sima: However, the way women have equal rights in the world…

Lida: In the western world.

Sima: Especially in the western countries…

Lida: Yes.

Sima: Not Eastern or Asian women, but there are hopes now.

لیدا: و دلیلش فکر می کنید رشته و اساس (بیس) همین مسئله که زنها آزادی و چیزشان را ندارند به آن قسمت دنیا بخاطر چیست؟ اساسش؟

سیما: والله چندین چیز، چندین چیز باعث است. خود همین (پارت) کلچر ماست.

لیدا: کلچر از چی اساس میگیرد؟

سیما: کلچر اساسش از این است که از علمیت خود جامعه، خود جامعه حتی کسهایش که عالم هم بودند ، ادیب بودند، خواندن و نوشتن را می فهمیدند میتوانستند که استدلال خوب کنند، نظر به شرایط... من نمی خواهم تنها بگویم که مذهبی باعث این گپ است.

لیدا: بلی.

سیما: تن... نظر به اینکه قدامت تاریخی اینهمین که زن همیشه باید به همان شکل نگاه شود. و نه ... مانده نشود که زن همسری و برابری به مرد کُند.

لیدا: بلی.

سیما: آن باعث شده که زن همیشه به همان یک...

لیدا: آن خو در اینجا هم به پنجاه سال اخیر بود دیگر.

سیما: هان معلومدار به ممالک غربی هم از ابتداء نبوده، بمرور زمان حالا که ما می بینیم. فرضاً من از وقتیکه به امریکا آمده ام می بینم که فرق بین زن ومرد آنقدر زیاد نیست حتی اه... (سلری) یا (انکم) که همین آید، مزد کاریکه زن و مرد دارد یک کمی تغیر دارد به آن هم تلاش به این است که آن هم از بین بُرده شود که بسیار چیز خوب است.

منتها به افغانستان حالا من از سابق هم کرده بسیار امیدواری زیادتر حالا دارم برای اینکه حتی اه (پرایمنستر) یا صدر اعظم انگلستان خانمش، اسمش هم به یادم نیست اُو رسماً تقاضا کرد که از جملهٔ اعضای کابینهٔ نَو افغانستان یک یا دو زن حتماً حصه داشته باشد.

لیدا: بلی هان، پس امیدواری زیاد است.

Lida: What do you think the base and foundation of women not having freedom and things like that in that part of the world is? And the foundation?

Sima: By God, many, there are many things causing this. Of course this is part of our culture.

Lida: What is the foundation of a culture?

Sima: The foundation of a culture is from the knowledge of a society and the society itself. Even the people who were knowledgeable, literate, who were able to read and write, and the ones who could justify well, depending on the situation…
I don't want to say that only religion is the cause of these issues.

Lida: Yes.

Sima: Close-minded… according to the past history women were always left behind like that. Women have never been given a chance to compete with men and be equal to them.

Lida: Yes.

Sima: That is the reason why women have always been like that.

Lida: Here was also like that in the past fifty years.

Sima: Yes, of course it was not like this in ancient western countries either, if we look at it, over a period of time, it changed. For example, since we first came to America, I have noticed that there is not much difference between men and women. Even oh… salary or income, the income of men and women differs a little. They are trying to even change that, which will be a good thing.

However I am more hopeful for Afghanistan now than ever before. Because even the Prime Minister of England's wife, whose name I forgot, officially requested that at least two women should be members of the Afghan new cabinet.

Lida: Yes indeed, so there are a lot of hopes.

سیما: باورت... بسیار زیاد است. باور کن که این همین که در امریکا و اروپا راجع به زن افغان همیشه گپ زده شده و حق شان به صدای بلند خواسته شده. اینقدر سر روحیات زنها تأثیر کرده که حتی زنهائیکه سالها در همینجا بود آنها جرأت نمیکردند که در مجلسهای کلان گپ بزنند. حالا می بینم که بسیار به فصاحت و بسیار به جرأت گپ می زنند حتی حصه میگیرند به موسیقی و آواز خوانی و اینها از بس که یک خوشی و ...

لیدا: امید واری برایشان.

سیما: امیدواری برایشان... خوده عضو جامعه فکرمی کنند. (آلریدی). نی؟

لیدا: بلی هان.

سیما: دیگر امیدواری بسیار خوب است برای زنها به صورت عموم برای افغانستان، مخصوصاً برای طبقهٔ اناث برای زنها بسیار امیدواری فوق العاده است.

Sima: You must believe that there are conferences and discussions in America and Europe about Afghan women's rights in a loud voice.

This has a psychological effect on women. Even women who didn't have the courage to speak in big conferences now I see that they speak enthusiastically and bravely. They even participate in music and singing and things like that. And for the joy of it.

Lida: They are hopeful.

Sima: They are hopeful...they think of themselves as members of the society, already.

Lida: Yes indeed.

Sima: Then there is a good hope for women, generally in Afghanistan, especially for women. Women are extraordinarily hopeful.

Vocabulary

چیستک *colloquial* چی اس *phrase* what is
پارت *colloquial English* جزء *n* part
بیس *colloquial English* اساس *n* base
بودک *colloquial* بود *v* was
سلَری *colloquial English* معاش *n* salary
انکَم *colloquial* عایداد *n* income
پرایمنستر *colloquial English* صدر اعظم *n* prime minister
باورت *n* your beliefs

کار زنها در خانه[67]

لیدا: خانه داری چه قسم بود سیما جان به افغانستان؟ آیا امکاناتیکه به امریکا است مثل ماشین کالاشوئی، ضرف شوئی امکانات بود، یا نی، یا چه قسم؟ یک زن کلگی کارها را پیش می بُرد؟

سیما: معلومدار مسئولیت زن و خانه خو عین مسئولیت است که نان پخته می کردند اه... کالاشوئی بود، اولادداری، جمع و جاروی خانه و این گپها. ماشین کالاشوئی در همین آخرها رواج شده بود یک اندازه.

لیدا: آخرها به چه سالهائی؟

سیما: در سالهائیکه فرضاً من در سال هشتاد برآمدم سالهائی... که من نَو عروسی کردم، سالای هفتاد و هشت، و هفتاد و نه.

لیدا: اواخر سال.

سیما: اواخر سالها. آن همان وقتها ماشین کالاشوئی و اینها پیدا شده بود. معلومدار یخچال بود این گپها، منتها ماشین ظرف شوئی آنقدر من ندیده بودم در افغانستان.

لیدا: بلی.

سیما: که ظرف خوراک شوئی منظور من است.

لیدا: بلی.

سیما: منتها اه... یگانه شرایطی که از اینجا فرق دارد اگر کسیکه وضع اقتصادش ایجاب می کرد می توانستند که یک کُمَکی بگیرند فرضاً.

لیدا: یک نفر که کارهای خانه را انجام بدهد.

سیما: یک نفریکه کارهای خانه را کُند یا سودای بازار را بیآورد یا کالاشوئی همراه زن خانه همکاری کُند جمع و جاروی خانه را کُند اولاد خورد را بگیرد تا و بالا کند آن چیزها میسر بود.

لیدا: بلی.

---

[67] In this selection the speakers are Sima and Lida. Sima finished university in Afghanistan and speacks the Kabuli dialect of Dari, Lida was born in Herat Afghanistan and emigrated to Iran at a very young age and then she came to the U.S. and she is a high school graduate. Lida speaks the Herati dialect of Dari, which is influenced by the Iranian Farsi.

Women's Work at Home

Lida: How was housekeeping in Afghanistan, dear Sima?

Were such luxuries that are in America for example, washing machine, dishwasher, or there were not, or how was it? Does a woman do all the housework?

Sima: Of course, the responsibility of a woman and a house is the same. They would do the cooking oh... do the laundry, raise children, straighten up the house and do the vacuuming and thing like that. Lately there were some washing machines.

Lida: What year lately?

Sima: In the years that I left, and I got married, in the years of 78 and 79.

Lida: Late that year.

Sima: Late those years. At that time there were washing machines and things like these. Of course there were refrigerators and things like that. However, I have not seen dishwashers that much in Afghanistan.

Lida: Yes.

Sima: I mean dishwasher.

Lida: Yes.

Sima: However, oh... the only difference between here and there is the financial situation. If people could afford it they would have servants.

Lida: Somebody to do housework.

Sima: Somebody to do housework, to buy groceries from the bazaar, help the housewife to do laundry, sweep and straighten the house, help to carry children around, things like that. Things like that were available.

Lida: Yes.

سیما: مگر مسئولیت زن خانه به مراتب از اینجا کرده زیادتر به این خاطر بود که اینجا یک کَمِی علمیت مردها زیادتر شده ومنظور من از آن این است که همکاری.

لیدا: مردهای افغان منظور تان؟ که همکاری می کنند.

سیما: مردهای افغان یاد گرفتند که باید همکاری به کارهای خانه همراه زن خانه کنند.

سابق من نمی فهمم بدبختانه جزء همین کلتور ما این بود که برای یک مرد بسیار شرم است که کار خانه را کُند و من خوشبختانه در این آخرها دیده ام که همین محیط اوروپا و امریکا و اینها یگانه تأثیر خوبی که کرده سر مردها این است که...

لیدا: تأثیر مثبت.

سیما: دیگر این را عیب نمی دانند.

لیدا: بلی هان.

سیما: که ولَو زن خانه بیرون کار می کُند یا نی مرد خانه.

لیدا: خو اینجا هر دو نفر کار میکنند.

سیما: اکثراً همه کار می کنند، و لَو زنیکه اولاد خورد دارد و نمی تواند یا نمی خواهد بیرون کار کُند، مرد خانه احساس مسئولیت می کُند که باید همکاری همراه زن خود، همراه خانم خود کند. منتها به افغانستان من این گپ را نمی دیدم.

لیدا: بلی.

سیما: و امید است که با این تغیرات خوبی که به افغانستان میآید امیدوارهستیم شاید همین، همین رواج را همراه خود ببریم آنجا پس.

لیدا: اولادها چه قسم بودند؟ اولادها مثل امریکا از خانه بیرون می شدند؟ یا چه قسم...

سیما: در هیچ صورت

لیدا: خو.

سیما: در هیچ صورت. این را من نمی فهمم خودت چند ساله بودی که بر آمدی.

لیدا: بیرون منظورم این که به اینجا...

Sima: However, the responsibility of a housewife is way more than it is over here. Because men here are more knowledgeable; I mean they are helpful.

Lida: Do you mean Afghan men are helpful?

Sima: Afghan men learned how to help women with housework.

I didn't know before. Unfortunately, it is shame for a man in our culture to do housework. Fortunately, I see lately that the only good influence the European and American environment has on men is…

Lida: Positive influence.

Sima: It is not a shame for them anymore.

Lida: Yes indeed.

Sima: No matter if a woman works a job other than housework, the man in the house…

Lida: obviously both persons work here.

Sima: Most of them work. Women who have young children, even though they don't want or they can't work outside of the house, men in the house take the responsibility to help their women or their wives. However, I have not seen such a thing in Afghanistan.Lida: Yes.

Lida: Yes,

Sima: There is a hope and we have hope that with a good change in Afghanistan we will take this custom back there with us.

Lida: How were children. Would they move out like they do in America? Or… OK.

Sima: Not in any case.

Lida: OK.

Sima: Never, I don't know. How old were you when you left?

Lida: Out, I mean like here.

سیما: جدا زنده گی کنند.

لیدا: که هفده هژده ساله می شوند جدا می شوند. جدا زنده گی میکردند؟

سیما: می خواهند بروند. هان من همین را گفتم، هان هیچ وقت.

لیدا: چه قسم جدا می شدند پس؟

سیما: این به عروسی به ازدواج.

لیدا: تنها راه شان این بود که عروسی کنند که از خانهٔ پدر و مادر بِروند.

سیما: ازدواج، هان. اگر یعنی که فاکولته می خواندند مجبور نبود که یِک جوان خودش کار کُند خودش مصرف خود را پیدا کُند.

لیدا: بلی.

سیما: این هیچ قابل سوال نبود، پدر و مادر کل مسئولیت مادی و معنوی و همه چیز یک اولاد به دوشش بود و هیچ این توقع نمی شد از یک دختر یا بچهٔ جوان که برود کار کُند و جیب خرچی خود زا پیدا کُند و اینها و کار هم، راست بگویم به افغانستان اینطور کاری نبود. بدون کسهائیکه از فاکولته یا مکتب خلاص می شد و به قسم دائیمی مامور یک...

لیدا: حد کار زیاد نبود دیگر... که کار بگیرد.

سیما: هیچ اصلاً هیچ، همین (بزنس) های یا همین کارهای خورد و ریزه ای که فرضاً در این محیط آدم می بیند آنجا هیچ وجود نداشت.

لیدا: بلی هان.

سیما: اگر داشت بدبختانه یک کار بد بود. فرصاً یک نفریکه تکسی ران می بود به افغانستان بسیار از مردم سطح پائین حساب می شد.

لیدا: خو هر کس دیگر. هر کاری را به افغانستان بد می دید.

Sima: To live separately.

Lida: When they become 17 or 18 then they live separately.

Sima: They want to leave. Yes, I meant this, yes, never.

Lida: Then how would they be separated?

Sima: By getting married, by marriage.

Lida: Was it the only way to leave a parent's house, to get married?

Sima: Marriage, yes. If, for example, they studied in a college, a young person didn't have to work to earn their expenses.

Lida: Yes.

Sima: There was no doubt about it that parents had financial and moral responsibility for their children. They never expected their young son or young daughter to work and earn their expenses. They are not used to work either, to be honest with you; there were not these kinds of work in Afghanistan, except the people who graduated from a college or high school and would work permanently as a clerk.

Lida: There were not many jobs… to get a job.

Sima: None, never at all, the businesses or small jobs one could find in this society, cannot be found there at all.

Lida: Yes indeed.

Sima: If there were one, it would be considered a bad job. For example, a taxi driver in Afghanistan would be considered a very low-class person.

Lida: Everybody considers any kind of job a bad job in Afghanistan anyway.

سیما: یا فرضاً، اگر کسی رستوران می داشت نامِش را آشپز می ماندند، دیگر آن یک کار آبرو مند نبود. بدبختانه همین ذهنیتِ مردم اینطور پائین بود که می گفتند نی باید حتماً آن نفر قابل عزت است در محیط که یک رئیس ومدیر و وزیر و این چیزها باشد کار دفتری داشته باشد و فامیلش یک فامیل بهتر حساب می شد.

مگر حالا من اکثر افغانهائیکه در این ده بیست سال برآمدند از افغانستان می بینند که آن گپ واقعیت نداشته هر کسیکه در محیط، در جامعه بهر شکلی فعال شود، یک پول بیآورد بدست و فامیل خود را کُمَک کُنَد.

لیدا: کار خو ننگ نیست.

سیما: نی کار ننگ نیست. یعنی این هم از جملهٔ خوبیهائیکه بضمن بدبختیهایکه ما افغانها مواجع شدیم در این بیست سال آخر یگان چیزهای خوبی از آن برگشت کرد که یکی هم از همین چیزهاست که مردم یک کمی فکرشان روشن شد که کار کردن عیب نیست.

اینکه چه نوع کار است به همین اندازه ایکه زحمت می کشد یک نفر و پول را بدست می آورد که زنده گی آبرومند برای فامیل خود بسازد مهم نیست که رستوران است، مهم نیست که تکسیران است یا اینکه پیش یک نفر کار می کند.

لیدا: بلی هان.

سیما: این را حالا عیب نمی دانند مگر آن زمانهائیکه من به افغانستان بودم بسیار عیب کلان بود که فلان نفر به رستوران آشپز است. در حالیکه حالی اینجا افتخار می کنند که (شف) است و بهترین معاش دارد و بهترین (انشورنس) و (کفرج) و یعنی چیزهای خوب دارد.

لیدا: بلی هان. مادر و پدرها چه قسم بودند؟ مادرکلان یا اه... اگر یک پدر کلان تان یا مادر کلان تان پیر می شد تا آخر عمر اُو را کی نگاه می کرد آنجا؟

سیما: اُو بلی.

لیدا: مثل اینجا اه... خانه ای که کلان سالها است آنجا هم بود یا نی؟

سیما: هیچ وقت.

لیدا: همین چیز، رشت و بافت فامیلی چه قسم بود؟

سیما: بسیار زیاد محکم بسیار، قابل سوال نبود که نفریکه سنش زیاد شده بود جای از اُو در بالاسرخانه بود. هرکسیکه خانه می آمد اولین کاریکه میکرد، احترام خود را بجای میکرد. اول پیش کلان خانه میرفت، دست پرسی و سلام علیکی میکرد.

Sima: Or, for example, if somebody owned a restaurant, people would call him a cook. Then it wasn't a respected job. Unfortunately, people's mentality was so poor that they would say, "He has to be a well-respected person; in that society, he has to be a manager or director or a minister and things like that, or to have an office job and has to be from a high-class family."

However, now when I look at Afghans who left Afghanistan in the last 10 or 20 years, I realize that mentality wasn't a fact. Anybody who becomes active in different ways in this society or environment, and earns some money and helps their family…

Lida: Working is not a shame.

Sima: No, working is not a shame. That is to say, this is one of the good fortunes in the course of the misfortunes that we Afghans were all engaged in in the past 20 years. There was some good influence, like people became open-minded and working is not a shame for them anymore.

No matter what kind of work it is. As much as they work hard so they can earn some money and to have a respected life with their family. It is not important that they have a restaurant job or they are taxi drivers or they work for someone else.

Lida: Yes indeed.

Sima: Now they don't consider it a shame, but when I was in Afghanistan, working in a restaurant as a cook was a big shame. Although people here are proud being a chief, having a high salary, having the best insurance coverage, in other words it has good benefits.

Lida: Yes indeed. What were parents like? When your grandmother or... grandfather were old, who would take care of them for the rest of their lives?

Sima: Them, yes.

Lida: Did they have a nursing home there like it is here?

Sima: Never.

Lida: This thing… how was the relationship among family members?

Sima: Very strong, very much. When someone became old, no doubt that they are well-respected and well-treated in a family. When someone comes to the house, the first thing they do is greet and show respect to and shake the hands of the elderly.

لیدا: احترام.

سیما: احترام تقدیم میکرد. و آن کلان خانه اصلاً به... چون خودش خسته و ضعیف می بود، معلومدار اگر زیاد پیر نمی بود یگان همکاری همراه زن خانه می کرد اگر نمی توانست به بسیار احترام، به بسیار خوبی غذایش پیشش تیار برده می شد، لباس از اُو از همه بهتر ششته و اُتو می شد عزت و احترامش به جای می شد.

لیدا: پس مادرکلان و پدرکلان و فامیلی کُلَگی همراه هم دیگر زنده گی می کردند.

سیما: همه یکجا بودند یک فامیل پانزده نفره می توانستند در یک اتاق کلانیکه به این همین اندازهٔ این همین سالون است. می توانستند زنده گی کنند که آن عبارت از زن و شوهر پدر یا مادر زن. یا... زن خو نی حتماً مرد یک هفت هشت دانه اولاد هم همراه شان کل از یک سر توشک هموار می شد. نی همین عامیانیش همین چیز بود. باوجودیکه باز پسانها فرضاً اینک من خودم که یادم می آید، یک اتاق خواب من و... ما و خواهرم علیحده بود. از پدر و مادرم علیحده بود دیگر خوارهایم ...سه خواهر دیگریم.

لیدا: چندتا خواهر و برادر استید سیما جان؟

سیما: من... دو برادر و شش خواهر هستیم.

لیدا: ماشاءالله.

سیما: منتها یعنی به قسم عامیانهٔ عادی حالت عادی یکنفریکه ده، پانزده نفر هم در عضو فامیل می بود می توانستند در یک سالون کلان همه زنده گی کنند.

لیدا: بلی هان.

سیما: بدون چون وچرا یک چیز قبول شده بود هیچ کس شکایت نمی کرد آن جزء زنده گی روز مرهٔ مردم بود.

لیدا: بلی.

Vocabulary

خانه داری *colloquial* کار خانه *n* housework *n* having a house *n* getting in bed with a spouse

آخرا *colloquial* اواخر *adv* lately

تا و بالا *colloquial* *v* to take care of the children putting down and lifting up

جیب خرچی *n* pocket money

بزنس *colloquial English* تجارت *n* business

سطح پایین *colloquial* طبقهٔ پایین *n* low class

Lida: Respect.

Sima: S/he would greet with respect. In reality the head of the house… oh since s/he is old and weak of course if s/he is not very old sh/he would help the house-women some if s/he was not able to do so, s/he would receive their meal and their clothes would be washed and be ironed. S/he would be well-respected.

Lida: Thus grandmother and grandfather and everyone in the family lives together.

Sima: Everybody was together; a family of 15 people could live together in a room the size of this living room. And the family consists of the wife, the husband, father or mother of the wife, maybe not the wife's, certainly the man's. There would be seven or eight children, and there would be beds for them on the floor.

No, the ordinary people would be like this. Even though, later on I remember that my sister and I had one separate room. Then my parents' room was separate. Then my sisters… my other three sisters.

Lida: How many brothers and sisters do you have, dear Sima?

Sima: We are two brothers and three sisters.

Lida: Whatever God wished.

Sima: However, for example, in an ordinary way a person with 10 or 15 people in the family could live in a living room.

Lida: Yes indeed.

Sima: Without any problem, this situation was expected and no one would complain. It was part of people's daily lives.

Lida: Yes.

رستورانت *colloquial English* رستوران *n* restaurant
تکسیران *n* taxi driver
شف *English* آشپز *n* chief
انشورنس *colloquial English* بیمه *n* insurance
کفرج *colloquial English* مورد بیمه *n* coverage
پسانا *colloquial* اواخر *adv* lately, later on
چون و چرا *colloquial* شک *n* doubt

معاشرت قبل از ازدواج[68]

لیدا: سیما جان به افغانستان چه قسم همدیگر را، دختر و بچه چه قسم همراه همدیگر برای ازدواج آشنا می شدند؟ آیا مثل اینجا... همدیگر بیرون می رفتند یا از طریق فامیلی ازدواج اچی می شد یا چه قسم؟

سیما: هان خو معلومدار افغانستان هیچ این مضوع نبود که دختر و بچه باید به هم ... اجازهٔ رسمی نداشتند که به هم ببینند و تصمیم بگیرند.
از طریق فامیل این گپها اچی می شد، تصمیم گرفته می شد. اکثراً فامیل بچه مدنظر می گرفت یک چند دختر را، البته مقبولی دختر هم رول داشت و فامیلش بسیار رول داشت.

لیدا: بلی.

سیما: که باید یک فامیل خوب باشد که آیندهٔ بچهٔ شان یعنی خوب باشد. وقتیکه فامیلها تصمیم گرفته بودند باز فامیل بچه معلومدار می رفت پیش فامیل دختر خواهش و تقاضای این گپ را می کردند.
اگر فامیل دختر رضایت می داشت، البته باز اجازهٔ این گپ داده می شد و بسیار رسمیات و موضوعات مادی و این گپهایش باز در جریان می افتاد.

لیدا: بلی هان.

سیما: در این آخرهایکه فرضاً من به حافظهٔ من است، یا من ازدواج کردم.
موضوعات مهر... مهر نی بلکه طویانه می گفتند یک اصطلاحی بود که برای دختر یک قیمت می ماندند.

لیدا: بلی هان ، که به فامیل دختر پیسه می دادند.

سیما: که باید اینقدر پول... پیسه باید می دادن. این گپها از بین رفته بود. اه ... اقلاً در کابل از بین رفته بود. معلومدار مهر یک چیز مذهبیست که به قرآن شریف هم آمده که چون مخصوصاً شرایط زن چون در این ... در آن شهرها و در آن ممالک بسیار محدود و چیست. که نمی تواند زن متکی به خود باشد. به آن اساس...

---

[68] In this selection the speakers are Sima and Lida. Sima finished university in Afghanistan and speacks the Kabuli dialect of Dari, Lida was born in Herat Afghanistan and emigrated to Iran at a very young age and then she came to the U.S. and she is a high school graduate. Lida speaks the Herati dialect of Dari, which is influenced by the Iranian Farsi.

Courtship

Lida: Dear Sima how did a boy and a girl meet to get married? Did they go out with each other like they do it here (America) or did they have arranged marriage and how?

Sima: Yes, of course, there wasn't such a thing in Afghanistan for the girl and boy to see each other. They did not have official permission to see each other and decide.

The family would decide and deal with these kinds of issues. Usually the boy's family would check out a few girls, of course the beauty of a girl would be considered and the family reputation would be considered very much.

Lida: Yes.

Sima: She has to be from a good family so their son would have a good future. When families from both sides made a decision, and then of course the family would go to the girl's family and propose.

If the girl's family was satisfied, then obviously they would have the permission to talk. The other issues like financial issues would be talked about.

Lida: Yes indeed.

Sima: Lately what I remember, or when I got married, the meher issues… not meher but they would call it toyana … it is a tradition that they issue a price for the girl.

Lida: Yes indeed, that they would give money to the girl's family.

Sima: They would have paid a certain amount of money. Those things don't exist anymore. At least it did not exist in Kabul. Obviously meher is a religious thing that is written in the holy Quran too. That is because opportunities for women are limited in those countries. Women cannot be undefended, in that case.

لیدا: بلی از لحاظ مادی.

سیما: از نگاه مادی حق المهر برایش تعین می شود که اگر یک واقعه می شود که این زن و شوی ازدواج شان دوام نمی کُند. اقلاً زن یک چیز مالی برایش باشد که اُو بتواند زنده گی خود را پیش ببرد.

منتها طویانه در این آخرها بالکل از بین رفته بود. در همین شهرهای کلان یا فرضاً من در کابل بودم طویانه و این گپها کس نمی گرفت.

لیدا: باز عروسی را کی می گرفت، خرج عروسی و اینها کی میداد؟

سیما: البته فامیل بچه.

لیدا: بلی کُلَگی خرج عروسی؟

سیما: همه خرج عروسی، لباس خریدن، فرضاً به شرینی خوری. البته وقتیکه یک شرینی می دادند دختر را، اولین کاریکه فامیل بچه می کرد یک مقدار پولیکه نظر به سویهٔ اقتصادی خود. البته، کسی بود که ده هزار افغانی می ماند، کسی بود که پنجاه هزار می ماند، کسی بود که پنجصد افغانی می ماند.

مربوط از این بود که چقدر توانائی دارد باز بعد از آن معلومدار موضوعات شرینی خوری اکثراً ما... فامیل دختر می کرد.

لیدا: بلی.

سیما: باز در دورهٔ نامزادی هم اینطور رسمی اجازه نداشت که دختر و بچه تنها باشند به هم. هیچ وقت اینطور تنها هم اجازه نبود.

لیدا: همراه فامیل می رفتن.

سیما: حتی اگر یک سینما یا دِر یگان کانسرت ایهنا می رفتند یکتعداد اعضای فامیل را همراه خود باید می بُردند.

لیدا: بلی.

سیما: چون دورهٔ نامزدی بود. دورهٔ نامزدی آنقدر آزادی قایل نبودند.

لیدا: عروسی چه قسم بود، تا جایکه من یادم استه یگان تا عروسی دوسه شب چهارشب بود. عروسیها چه قسم بود؟

Lida: In financial terms.

Sima: Due to the financial situation they issue meher. In case something happens and the marriage of wife and husband would not continue. The wife should have at least some property to continue with her life. But lately toyana did not exist. In the big cities or when I was in Kabul they would not accept toyana or things like that.

Lida: Then who would pay for the wedding? Who would pay for expenses of the wedding and these things?

Sima: Obviously, the boy's family.

Lida: All the wedding expenses?

Sima: All the wedding expenses, buying clothes, for example, the engagement party. When a girl gets engaged, the first thing the boy's family does is to pay some money to the girl's family. And the amount depends on their financial ability. However there were people who would pay 10,000 Afghani, there were people who would pay 50,000 Afghani, and there were people who would pay 500 Afghani.

It depends on their ability. Then obviously there was the engagement party financial issue. The girl's family usually does that.

Lida: Yes.

Sima: Then, during the engagement period the boy and the girl were not permitted officially to be alone together. They were never permitted to be by themselves.

Lida: They would go together with the family.

Sima: Even when they went to the movies or to some concerts, they would have to take some family members with them.

Lida: Yes.

Sima: Because it was the engagement period. They didn't have that much freedom during the engagement period.

Lida: How was the wedding? As long as I remember, some of the weddings were two, three, or four nights long. How were weddings?

سیما: واللّه، عروسی هایکه عموماً در شهرهای ام... به کابل این همین چیز نبود که خودت میگوی دوسه شب. من همین را شنیدیم که فرضاً در مزار و همین بعضی شهرهای دیگر هرات و اینها این شب خویش خوری و پیش خوری و شب خینه.

لیدا: بلی سه چهار شب بلی.

سیما: باز شت نمی دانم...... کل چیزها آخرین شب شب خینه بود که باز عروس را همان شب همراه خود می بُردند.

لیدا: بلی.

سیما: فامیل داماد باز عروس را همان شب همراه خود می بُردند و معلومدار دیگر باز برای یک مدتی عروس نمی توانست دوباره پس پیش فامیل خود بیآید که تا یک ماه چهل روز تیر نشود و یک مجلس بسیار فوق العادهٔ کلان فامیل (بچه).... دختر می گرفت و دخترِ خود را پس پای وازی میکردند می خاستند.

لیدا: ماه عسل و این چیزها هم نبود به اصطلاح.

سیما: واللّه ماه عسل را من هیچ وقت نشنیده بودم.

لیدا: خو، در ایران فقط استه. به افغانستان نبود؟

سیما: به افغانستان نبود ماه عسل با وجودیکه در این آخرهایکه من بودم گپ میزدند. منتها شرایط اقتصادی مردم قسمی نبود، در خود مجلس عروسی اینقدر از نگاه اقتصادی مخصوصاً فامیل بچه را اینقدر ورشکست می کرد که تا چندین سال دیگر از نگاه اقتصادی اُو نمی توانست...

لیدا: بلی هان.

سیما: که جزئیترین کار دیگر کند.

لیدا: منتها تمام این عروسی و چیزها برای چی بود که؟

سیما: برای فامیل برای فامیلها و اینکه مخصوص....

لیدا: چهارصد، پنجصد نفره.

سیما: باید خبر باشد هر قدریکه مصرفش زیادتر میشد، نام بهتر می کشیدند.

لیدا: بلی هان.

Sima: By God, the weddings that took place mostly in cities.... in Kabul, as you mentioned were not two or three nights long. I have heard, for example in Mazar, some other big cities like Herat, and those, there were relatives feasting night, in advance of the feasting night and the henna night.

Lida: Four nights, yes.

Sima: Then I don't know the night... of everything. The very last night was the henna night, that is the night when they take the bride with them.

Lida: Yes.

Sima: Then the groom's family would take the bride with them that night. Obviously the bride would not return to her family for awhile. She would not return to family for a month or forty days until her family throws an extraordinary party and they give their daughter paiwazi.

Lida: There was no honeymoon or things like that, for example.

Sima: By God, I would have never heard of a honeymoon.

Lida: OK, it is only in Iran. Wasn't it in Afghanistan?

Sima: There was no honeymoon in Afghanistan. Lately, when I was there, they would talk about it. However, people didn't have that kind of economic situation. The groom's family would go broke spending money at the wedding party.

Lida: Yes indeed.

Sima: So he would not be able to do anything else.

Lida: However, what were the wedding and all these things for?

Sima: For the family, families, and especially...

Lida: Four hundred, five hundred.

Sima: They had to invite people. The more money he spends the more famous he becomes.

Lida: Yes indeed.

سیما: منتها بدبختانه بعضی نفرها اینطور مجلسهائی می گرفتند که ...گفتی که ... خودت گفتی که سه چهار شب و، چهارصد پنجصد نفر را خبر می کردند بدبختانه کلش به قرض و اینها باز به ماه ها و سالهای آیندۀ عروس و داماد به جگرخونی تیر می شد.

لیدا: بلی هان.

سیما: صرف بخاطریکه نام بکشَند، مجلس کلان می گرفتند منتها پسانها تا که اقتصاد از اینها پس به حالت عادی می آمد بسیار رنج را تیر می کردند.

لیدا: بلی.

سیما: دیگر منتها همه مصرفش سر فامیل بچه بود. فامیل دختر هیچ حتی شرایط می ماندند که باید این کار را کنید، این کار را کنید منتها فامیل دختر هیچ نوع خرج نداشت.

Sima: However, unfortunately some people threw parties like you mentioned three, four nights long. They would invite four or five hundred people, and unfortunately they would do all that with loans and then the bride and the groom would spend months and years in frustration.

Lida: Yes indeed.

Sima: Only so they can show off. They would throw big parties and then, until they would get to their normal situation, they would be very frustrated.

Lida: Yes.

Sima: However, the boy's family would pay for all the expenses. The girl's family would demand things like he has to do this and that. However, the girl's family would not have any expenses.

Vocabulary

اجازی رسمی *colloquial* اجازهٔ رسمی *n* official permission
چیسته *colloquial* چی هست *phrase* what is it
بتانه *colloquial* بتواند *v* to be able
سینما *English* *n* cinema
کنسرت *English* *n* concert
کمر شکست *colloquial* کم پول *n* broke

چند زنه[69]

لیدا: نظر شما راجع به این مردهایکه سه چهارتا زن داشتند و کلگی را به یک خانه نگاه می کردند این چیست؟

سیما: هان، بسیار یک چیز بدبختانه و لَو من درست است مسلمان هستم.

لیدا: خو این یک قسمت از دین است.

سیما: هان، این یک قسمتی از دین است که من شدیداً مخالفش هستم. باوجودیکه فلسفه ای که مردمهای مذهبی میگویند بخاطر حضرت محمد این موضوع را خواست که شَود که جنگها زیاد بود مردها زیاد کُشته می داد زنها زیاد می ماندند، از آن کرده که زنها بدون شوهر و که اولادداری و اینها.

لیدا: سرپرست.

سیما: بدون سرپرست پیر میشدند و می مُردند. بالآخره گفت، حضرت محمد گفته خی عوض یک زن می تواند یکمرد سه یا چهار زن کند.

لیدا: تعداد زنها بیشتر بود.

سیما: هان، چون تعداد زنها زیادتر بود. منتها باز در پهلویش بسیار شرایط شدید مانده بود که هر زن از ... خانۀ مستقل داشته باشد و اعاشه و اباتیش شدید هر زنه به همان سویه ای که لازم است باید می بود. مگر باز پسانها بدبختانه از این موضوع یک تعداد مردها استفاده می کردند...

لیدا: بلی.

سیما: بلی. دو سه زن میکردن و آنها را نمی توانستند که اعاشه و اباتۀ صحیح کنند و آن زنها بسیار به رنج، به فقر و اولادهایشان هم به بسیار فقر و بدبختی تیر میکرد.
منتها من این از جملۀ یگانه بعضی چیزها است که در اسلام من راستی همیشه پرابلوم داشتیم همراه اش و چند... برای از اینکه..

[69] In this selection the speakers are Sima and Lida. Sima finished university in Afghanistan and speacks the Kabuli dialect of Dari, Lida was born in Herat Afghanistan and emigrated to Iran at a very young age and then she came to the U.S. and she is a high school graduate. Lida speaks the Herati dialect of Dari, which is influenced by the Iranian Farsi.

Polygamy

Lida: What is your opinion about men who have three or four wives and they would keep them in one house?

Sima: Yes, it is unfortunate, even though it is true that I am a Muslim.

Lida: OK, it is part of the religion.

Sima: Yes this is part of the religion and I oppose it. Even though the religious people falsify and say "Prophet Mohammed implemented this because there were too many wars and the death toll of the men was high, there were too many women without husbands, and to have children," and these.

Lida: Guardian.

Sima: Without a guardian they would get old and die. Finally, Prophet Mohammed said, "Instead of one wife, a man can marry four wives."

Lida: The number of women was more.

Sima: Yes, because the number of women was more. However, he implemented conditions along with that, every woman should be given a separate house, every woman should be given enough livelihood and place to live according to their need. But, unfortunately, later on, some men would take advantage of this issue...

Lida: Yes.

Sima: Yes, and marry two, three women, then they would not provide them with food and houses then those women and their children would live in poverty and a burdened life.

However this is one of the things in Islam that I have always had problem with. And because of...

لیدا: بلی، زن هیچ اچیز نداشت، سر از اینکه مرد تصمیم مرد تصمیم از اُو بود که که اگر زن ... زن دیگر بگیرد.

سیما: هیچ هان، زن دیکر بگیرد هان. هیچ کدام دلیل هم نداشت مرد که نظر به چه شرایط بتواند زن دیکر بگیرد آزاد بود. همینقدر که می توانست که زورش می رسید از نگاه اقتصادی اُو می توانست زن کُند بدون چون و چرا و البته زن باز به هیچ صورت حق نداشت که ... معلومدار خو به کل دنیا همین طور است که وقتیکه یک زن ازدواج می کُند اُو معلومدار کل خواص و همه فکر و همه چیزش به همان یک مرد منحصر میشد و معلومدار اولادش وهمه چیز.
منتها زن بدون از آن دیکر حق نداشت مگر مرد بر عکس قانون دنیا آزادی بی نهایت داده شده بود نظر به اینکه تعداد زنهائیکه می گرفت و یا بهر شکلیکه زنده گی را پیش می بُرد.

لیدا: بلی هان.

سیما: باوجودیکه در آخرها چون مردم بسیار تحصیل کردند، فهمیدند که اُو کدام... شاید از نگاه... من نمی فهمم چه... نه تنها... ببخشید که من این را هم باید بگویم، نه تنها از نگاه شهوانی و این گپها شهوت و اینها برای خودنمائی و برای خود را یک نفر بسیار مهم نشان دادن و هم بعضی مردم می خواستند این کار را کنند.

لیدا: و تعداد اولاد هم به همآن قسم.

سیما: به همان اندازه زیاد. منتها در آخرها هرقدریکه مردها زیادتر درس خواندند و فامیده شدند این گپها کم شده بود.

لیدا: بلی هان.

سیما: این گپها بسیار کم شده بود و.

لیدا: تعداد مردهایکه بیشتر از یک زن داشته باشند.

سیما: هان آنقدر من زیاد نمی دیدم. اقلاً در همان محیطیکه من بودم به کابل من آنقدر زیاد نمی دیدم که آنطور میشد.

Lida: A woman has never had the thing to make a decision. A man would decide if he wanted to marry more women.

Sima: Yes, never, to marry another woman, yes. And a man did not have an excuse, why and under what condition he should marry another woman. As long as he could afford and had economic ability without any hesitation he would marry another woman. Of course, the woman had no right to... obviously it is like this in the entire world, when a woman is married, she and her children would be surrendered to a man.

However, women had no right besides that. In contrast, men were given unlimited rights in the world according to the number of wives they could marry, and live in any way they wanted.

Lida: Yes indeed.

Sima: Even though people are educated lately, they learn that which... maybe in perspective of... I don't know what... not only... excuse me I have to say that, not only from a sexual perspective and these things, sex and these things are for showoff. Some people would do that so they can show people how important they are.

Lida: And having many children is also like that.

Sima: Like those many. However, lately, the more people study and learn knowledge, the less they would have this kind of issue.

Lida: Yes indeed.

Sima: These issues are becoming less.

Lida: The number of men who have more than one wife.

Sima: I have not seen too many. At least in that society where I was, in Kabul, I have not seen that many to be that way.

Vocabulary

اباتیش *colloquial* اباته اش *n* her/his shelter and clothing
پرابلم *colloquial* مشکل *n* problem

کودکستان[70]

لیدا: اُشتوکها چه قسم بود به افغانستان سیما جان، از چی سن به کودکستان می رفتند، آیا کودکستان بود یا نی، واز چی سنی شروع به مکتب رفتن می کردند؟

سیما: اولادها ام... به یک تعداد کودکستانها به شهر کابل بود.

لیدا: بلی.

سیما: معلومدار برای کُل اولادها میسر نبود به یک تعداد محدود یگانه کودکستانیکه فرضاً در منطقهٔ که کارتهٔ چهار بود که من آنجا فرضاً غزال خواهرم جزء همان کودکستان بود و به شهر نَو هم کودکستان بود و قلعهٔ فتح اللّه هم یکی دوتا کودکستان.

لیدا: از چه سن می رفتند.

سیما: از پنج سالگی می رفتند از چهار یا پنج سالگی می رفتند تا به هفت سالگی. باز صنف اول از صنف... از هفت سالگی شروع می کردند.

لیدا: بلی هان.

سیما: منتها تعداد کودکستانها بی حد محدود بود.

لیدا: بلی هان.

سیما: شاید یک یا دو فیصد اولادها به آن سن می توانستند شامل کودکستان شوند.

لیدا: بلی، یکجای می رفتند دختر و پسر مکتب یا...؟

سیما: هان، در کودکستان دختر و بچه یکجای بود.

لیدا: نی، به مکتب چی؟

سیما: مگر به مکتب، باز مکتب دخترها و بچه ها جدا می شد.

لیدا: بلی.

سیما: از صنف اول تا صنف دوازده جدا می شدند معلومدار به چهار سال فاکولته پس یکجای می شدند.

---

[70] In this selection the speakers are Sima and Lida. Sima finished university in Afghanistan and speacks the Kabuli dialect of Dari, Lida was born in Herat Afghanistan and emigrated to Iran at a very young age and then she came to the U.S. and she is a high school graduate. Lida speaks the Herati dialect of Dari, which is influenced by the Iranian Farsi.

Kindergarten

Lida: How were kids in Afghanistan, dear Sima? At what age would they go to kindergarten? Was there kindergarten or not? And what age would they start going to school?

Sima: Children also… there were some kindergarten schools in Kabul City.

Lida: Yes.

Sima: Obviously, not all children could afford that. For a limited number… there were some kindergartens, for example in Karti-Char, where my sister Ghazal and I went, there was only that one. And there were kindergartens in Shar-e-Now. And there were one or two kindergartens in Qalah-e-Fatullah.

Lida: At what ages would they go?

Sima: From the age of five they would go. They would go from the ages of four or five until they are seven years old. They would start the first grade when they are seven years of age.

Lida: Yes, indeed.

Sima: However, the number of kindergartens was very limited.

Lida: Yes, indeed.

Sima: Maybe one or two percent of children in that age would attend kindergarten.

Lida: Yes, did girls and boys go to school together or…?

Sima: Girls and boys were together in kindergarten.

Lida: No, how about school?

Sima: But in school, girls and boys were separate.

Lida: Yes.

Sima: From grade 1 until grade 12 they would be separate, obviously in four years of college they would be together again.

لیدا: خو. و درسهایشان چه قسم بود؟

سیما: درسها عین پروگرام بود. فرضاً، کتابهای مکتبهای بچه ها ومکتبهای دخترها عین چیز بود ام... مکتب بچه ها اکثراً معلمهایشان مرد می بود. مکتب زنها، یگان مردانه هم معلم می بود. اکثراً معلمها زنانه می بود. مگر درسشان اینها پروگرامهای درسی اکثراً عین چیز.

لیدا: بلی.

سیما: و البته زنهایکه مکتب خوانده بودند و فاکولته ای بسیار استعداد فوق العاده و خوب نشان داده بودند.

لیدا: بلی.

سیما: به هیچ صورت معنی از این را نمی داد که زن افغان نتوانسته بود که درس را صحیح بخواند، یا رشتهٔ ره که شروع کرده بود حتماً بهترین شاکرد می بود در آن رشته.

لیدا: باز وضع کار چه قسم بود، اگر زن تحصیلات خود را میداشت یا چیز، حقوق کار مساوی بود برای زن و مرد... شرایط؟

سیما: واللّه، کار زنانه مخصوصاً برای زنها، ولَو هر قدرکه عین فاکولته را زن هم می خواند، برای مرد شرایط کارش زیادتر بود. به بسیار زودی قبول می شد.
اکثراً زنها به همان خاطر هم بود که آن زنهایکه بعد از ازدواج خود می توانستند کار کنند یا اجازهٔ فامیلی داشتند که کار کنند برای از اینکه اکثر زنها شوهرهایشان اجازه نمی داد.

لیدا: بلی هان.

سیما: منتها در این آخرها چون وضع اقتصاد و این گپها هم حصه داشت و باز زنهایکه کار می کردن اکثراً کوشش می کردند که معلم مکتب شوند. برای از اینکه مکتب ها تا یک... چاشت رخصت می شد و می توانستند به زنده گی خانگی خود هم بِرَسَند و یک تعداد بسیار محدود بود که به وزارت خانه ها کار می کردند.

لیدا: پس کار بسیار ربط داشت به اینکه زن هستی یا مرد هستی. یکزن نمی توانست هر کار را داشته باشد.

سیما: زن یا مرد بسیار. به آسانی البته نی.

Lida: OK, how were their classes?

Sima: Classes were the same. For example, books for girls' and boy's school were the same, but... teachers in boys' school were male. In girls' school, there were a few male teachers also. Most of the teachers were women. But their classes and study programs were mostly the same.

Lida: Yes.

Sima: And, however, women who have gone to school and college have shown incredible talent.

Lida: Yes.

Sima: It doesn't ever mean that Afghan women are not able to study right or would start in a major and would not be the best student in that major.

Lida: Then how was the situation for jobs? If a woman had her education or something, would the job opportunity be equal for a man and a woman? Conditions.

Sima: By God, women's jobs especially for women, even though a woman has a degree from the same college, the job opportunity was more for a man. He would be hired very soon.

Some women could work even when they were married, because they have permission from their family. Then, because most women, their husbands would not permit them.

Lida: Yes indeed.

Sima: However, since the effect of the economic situation lately, then women who wanted to work, they would try to be a schoolteacher. Because school was until one... she would get off in the afternoon, so she was able to do the housework. Limited women had jobs in the ministries.

Lida: So getting a job very much depended on whether you were a man or a woman?

Sima: Man or woman, obviously not very easy.

لیدا: بلی.

سیما: دیگر، منتها زنهایکه حق داده شده بود به یک رشته، ای بسیار لیاقت و فامیده گی از خود نشان داده بود همیشه. فرضاً من داکترهای زن را می شناسم که بی نهایت لایق بودند بسیار خوب.

معلومدار مرد... داکترهای مردی هم بود که بسیار لایق، مگریعنی زنها هم از خود بسیار لیاقت و فهمیده گی نشان داده بودند. تا جایکه برایشان حصه داده شده بود.

لیدا: بلی برای تحصیلات چطور آیا زن یا مرد می توانست خارج از افغانستان مسافرت کُند، به اُروپا تحصیل کُند یا خارج از افغانستان از زمان شما یا بیست سال پیش؟

سیما: واللّه، هان، خارج از افغانستان از من نمی فهمم که تنها تا حالی هم پیش من سوال است که تنها وضع اقتصادی ما مردم بود که باعث از این شده بود که نتواند مردم بخارج برود تحصیل کُند.

بسیار یک تعداد محدود برایشان این چانس میسر می شد که یا کدام بورسی برایشان داده شود ویا خودشان شخصاً بتوانند بروند در یک ممالک خارجی مخصوصاً غربی اینها بروند درس بخوانند، بسیار تعداد از آن نفرها کم بود و همان نفرهایکه به اصطلاح در همان دورهٔ دولتی همان زمان قدرت زیاد داشتند. اکثر اگر کدام فیصدی محدودی هم که اگر آن کار را می کردند همان نفرهای بودند که دست رسی داشتند در این گپها. اکثراً مردم جدا نگاه شده بود از این چیزها.

لیدا: چیز افغانستان، همین درصد زن و مرد مساوی بود یا... جمعیت افغانستان چه قدر بود و به همان وقت شما؟

سیما: واللّه، اینطور مقایسوی من هیچ وقت،... فکر میکنم شانزده ملیون، هم پیش از این تلفاتیکه در دورهٔ جنگ ما دادیم.

Lida: Yes.

Sima: Another thing, however, the women were hired in a field for which they have shown great talent and knowledge. For example, I know women doctors that were extremely talented and very good.

Obviously, a man. There were some talented male doctors, also. But it means that women also have shown great talent and intelligence as long as they were given chances.

Lida: How did a man or a woman travel and get their education outside of Afghanistan, or get education in Europe or outside of Afghanistan in your time, or twenty years ago?

Sima: By God, outside of Afghanistan, I don't know that only, I still have a question that, is it only the economical situation that causes people not to get their education abroad? Very limited people would have a chance or have a scholarship or were personally able to study in a foreign country, especially in the western countries.

The number of those people is limited and they were the people who, for example, had power in the government at that time. Usually a small percentage of people would do that; those people were knowledgeable in these issues. Most people were kept away from these things.

Lida: The thing, Afghanistan, were the number of men and women equal or... what was the population of Afghanistan at your time?

Sima: By God, I have never compared ... I think it is 16 million before the losses we had during the war.

لیدا: شانزده ملیون جمعیت افغانستان بود.

سیما: که شانزده ملیون نفوس داشت، که من موثق نمی فهمم که از نگاه اناث یا مرد و زن کدامش اکثریت بود. اینش را تا حالی نمی فهمم، منتها بقراریکه من از روی خبرها میشنوم تقریباً ده الی دوازده ملیون ما تلفات دادیم.

لیدا: بلی چهار و پنج ملیون.

سیما: و چهار پنج ملیون مهاجر شدند. مهاجرت و بسیار زیاد از دست دادیم.

لیدا: بلی پس چیز افغانستان در حال حاضر چه فکر می کنید باشه، چه جمعیت به افغانستان باقی مانده؟

سیما: اگر... اگر همین (ریفوجیهای) که به آسترلیا، امریکا و هر نقطهٔ اُروپا هستند اگر دوباره بروند، واللّه فکر نکنم که از شش الی هفت ملیون زیاد شود.

لیدا: خو.

سیما: هان، بالکل نفوس حداقل از نیم پائین تر مانده.

Lida: The population of Afghanistan was 16 million.

Sima: I don't know if the population was 16 million. Regarding the population of men and women, and which one is the majority, I don't know this part. But according to the news I have heard, our losses were approximately 10 to 12 million people.

Lida: Yes four, five million.

Sima: And four, five took refuge. Refuge and we had a lot of losses.

Lida: Yes, then what do you think the thing of Afghanistan would be now; what is the remaining population of Afghanistan?

Sima: If... if these refugees who live in Australia, America, and all over Europe go back to Afghanistan, I think they would exceed 6 to 7 million.

Lida: OK.

Sima: Yes, entirely, and at least the population has dropped by less than half.

Vocabulary

کارتی چار *colloquial* کارتهٔ چار *n* a small district in Kabul
بِرسَن *colloquial* برسند *v* to get to do something, to get somewhere
چانس *colloquial English* فرصت *adj* chance
بورسی *colloquial French* یک بورس *n* scholarship
بِرَن *colloquial* بروند *v* they go
در صد *colloquial* فیصدی *adv* percentage
جمعیت *Persian* نفوس *n* population
ایشه *colloquial* اینش را *adv* this one
تالی *adv* تا الآن، تا الحال yet, until now
ریفوجیهای *colloquial English* مهاجرین *n* the refugees

مراسم عروسی[71]

لیدا: رسم و رسومات عروسی چه قسم بود به افغانستان، سیما جان؟ همین...

سیما: محفل عروسی اصلاً بسیار فرق داشت، باوجودیکه در آخرها بسیار ساده تر شده بود و تنها به یک شب آن را ختم می کردند، منتها در سابق اینطور بود که محفل عروسی از سه چار پنج روز وقتتر شروع می شد. قسمی بود که حمام را قروق می کردند، مثلیکه اینجا میگویند (چارتر)، نی؟

لیدا: بلی.

سیما: حمام را قروغ می کردند و عروس را به حمام می بُردند و کل فامیلهای زن و مرد و اینها حمام های عمومی بود. از آن شروع می شد تا اینکه شب خویش خوری. به شب خویش خوری فامیل بچه هم قومهای خود را خبر میکرد به خانۀ خود، و فامیل دختر قوم و خویش خود را خبر میکرد به خانۀ خود.

لیدا: بلی.

سیما: و بسیار نانهای زیاد پخته می شد. و عقارب... و همسایه کله می آمدند و ساز می بود و رقص می بود و سازهای خانگی بود. فرضاً رقاصهای خانگی بود که تا دَم صبح اینها میرقصیدند و بسیار ساعت تیری می بود. باز بعد از خویش خوری، شب پیش خوری...
به این معنی که پیش از شب حنا یا شب خینه پیش خوری بود که یعنی پیش از پیش آماده گی می گرفتند باز هم. آن بازهم یک حمام قروق میشد و زن به آرایشگاه میرفت و عروسی... پیش از عروسی و البته بسیار دیگر ترتیبات زیورات و چندین دست.

لیدا: کالا و...

[71] In this selection the speakers are Sima and Lida. Sima finished university in Afghanistan and speacks the Kabuli dialect of Dari, Lida was born in Herat Afghanistan and emigrated to Iran at a very young age and then she came to the U.S. and she is a high school graduate. Lida speaks the Herati dialect of Dari, which is influenced by the Iranian Farsi.

Wedding Party

Lida: What was the custom and tradition of the wedding party in Afghanistan, dear Sima?

Sima: Actually, wedding parties vary. Even though it has become very simple lately, it would it would last only one night; however the way it was in the past, the wedding party would start three, four, and five days earlier.

They used to reserve the bathhouse. Like they say (charter) here too.

Lida: Yes.

Sima: They would reserve the bathhouse and the boy's and the girl's family would take the bride there. These were public bathhouses. They would start with that until the relatives' dinner party began. At the relatives' dinner party, the boy's family would invite his relatives to their house and the girl's family would invite her relatives to their house.

Lida: Yes.

Sima: And many dishes would be cooked. And the share...and all neighbors would come and there would be music and dancing and there would be a family band and family dancing. They would dance until dawn and there would be so much fun. Then after the relatives' dinner party it was the prior dinner party...

that means before the henna or night of the henna, there was a prior dinner party. That is to say, they would get ready in advance, also then. Again the bathhouse would be reserved and they would take the bride to a beauty salon ... Prior to the wedding, obviously jewelry would be arranged, and a few sets.

Lida: Clothes and...

سیما: بسیار حالی به همین شبهای خویش خوری و پیش خوری در همانِ دوره های قدیمیکه مادرم قصه می کرد، هر کس بکس کالای خود را می بُرد در یک شب چهار پنج دست لباس زری و لباسهای بسیار قیمتی و زیورات بسیار مقبول را می پوشیدند.

و معلومدار آن را می کشیدند و باز دیگرش را می پوشیدند باز شب همانجا خواب می کردند. صبحش هم صبح چای صبح بسیار فوق العاده می خوردند وچاشت نان هم.

لیدا: بلی.

سیما: باز شب دیگرش شب خینه می بود عین موضوع ساز این گپها منتها به شب خینه باز کل فامیل عروس و داماد یکجای می شدند عموماً جای کلانترِ هم می گرفتند باز بسیار ساز خوب و معلومدار مجلس زنانه و مردانه اکثراً جدا می بود در آن دوره ها.

باز در این دوره های که من بودم و دوستهای ما عروسی کردند و خودم عروسی کرده ام، این موضوعات خویش خوری و پیش خوری و اینها کم شد.

لیدا: بلی.

سیما: منتها شب عروسی بود در هوتل کُلَ می رفتند و مرد و زن هم یکجای بود.

لیدا: مثل عروسیهای اینجا واری.

سیما: مثل عروسیهای اینجا واری. و لباس عروسی هم لباس سفید بود برای زن. و مرد همیشه دریشی سیاه می پوشید و زن لباس درازِ سفید با چادرِجالی و گُلِ دَست و همه چیزهایکه من به عروسی اینها می بینم اینجا.

لیدا: بلیِ هان.

سیما: بسیار شباحت داشت و البته خویش خوری و پیش خوری و این گپها خلاص شده بود منتها صبح بعد از شب نکاح همه به خانهٔ عروس می رفتند، ناشتائی بردند.

لیدا: بلی هان.

سیما: و ناشتائی عبارت از بسیار چیزها بود دیگر خوراکهای بسیارخوب ...

لیدا: آن چه قسم خوراکها...

Sima: Nowadays very much about the… relatives' dinner party and the prior dinner party and those old days that my mother would tell the story about how "Everyone would take their suitcase and they would change into four different outfits in one night and they would wear golden wefts clothes, very expensive clothes and beautiful jewelry.

Obviously they would take off one and wear another one and then they would sleep there. The next morning, in the morning, they would have an extraordinary breakfast and they would have lunch too.

Lida: Yes.

Sima: Then the next night would be the henna night. Music and these things would be the same, however the family of bride and groom would get together. Generally they would have a bigger place then they would have good music. Obviously the women's party and the men's party would be separate back then.

Then in my time, when my friend got married, and I got married myself, these relatives' dinner parties and prior dinner parties and things like these were not very popular.

Lida: Yes.

Sima: However, it was wedding night, everybody would go to the hotel and men and women would be together.

Lida: Like the weddings over here.

Sima: Like the weddings over here. And the wedding dress was also white for the woman. And the man would always wear a black suit and the woman would wear a long white dress and bridal veil and a bouquet and everything I see in the weddings over here.

Lida: Yes indeed.

Sima: It was very similar. However, the relatives' dinner party and prior dinner party no longer existed. However, the next morning of the ceremony night, everybody would go to the bride's house and take breakfast there.

Lida: Yes indeed.

Sima: And the breakfast consists of many good foods...

Lida: What kind of food was that?

سیما: ماغوت[72] و کباب های رقم به رقم می بود و بولانی و...
لیدا: منتو.
سیما: منتو و این گپها می شد و بعضی ها گوسفند هم می توانستند ببرند جزء همین ناشتائی و این گپها باز آن همان کل روز آنجا می بودند. باز آخر همان روز داماد می رفت پدرسلامی. پدر سلامی معنیش این است که داماد می رفت پیش خُسُر خود.
لیدا: بلی.
سیما: به اسم به احترام به اصطلاح بود نامش را داماد سلامی می گفتند که داماد میرود سلامی برای خُسُر خود میدهد. البته دخترشان نمیرفت تنها داماد خودش تنها میرفت و عروس تا وقتیکه باز یک پای وازی کلان مادر و پدرش می کرد باز آن وقت می رفت.
منتها از نانها حالی یاد کردی بسیار نانهای خوب معلومدار جزء از آن ناشتائی هم بود و البته که نانهایکه در عروسی و این چیزها می شد عبارت از قابلی پلَو و چلَو و سبزی و قورمی آلوبخارا وقورمی برانی بادنجان و بولانی و معلومدار مربوط فصل بود اگر فصل زمستان می بود کچری قروت، و بته شلغم و این گپها جزء همین...
لیدا: بسیار نانهای خوشمزه.
سیما: هان بسیار نانهای خوشمزه و چیزهای خوب بود.
لیدا: خودتان هم بسیار آشپز خوب استید سیما جان.
سیما: واللّه کوشش می کنم، منتها اینکه چقدر خوب است دیگر آن به قضاوت دیگرهاست. منتها کسیکه علاقه به خوراک داشته باشد مجبور است یاد بگیرد برای از اینکه دیگر کس برای آدم پخته نمی کند، غیر از اینکه خود آدم برای خود پخته کند آدم.
لیدا: دیگر نان می دادند و بعد از آن.

[72] Dessert make with rice flower, sugar, milk and other ingredients (like rice pudding.)

Sima: There were Maghoot, variety of kebabs and bolony and...

Lida: mantoo.

Sima: There would be mantoo and these things. And some people would take a whole (cooked) sheep for breakfast and things, and then they would stay all day. Then at the end of that day the groom would go to the father-in-law greeting. Father-in-law greeting means that the groom would go to his father-in-law out of respect.

Lida: Yes.

Sima: And they would also call it groom greeting, the groom would go to his father-in-law to greet him. However their daughter would not go; the groom would go by himself. And the bride would go when her parents invite her to a paiwazi party.

However, now that you mentioned about food, obviously it was also part of the breakfast. Actually, the food that would be served in weddings consists of qhabili-palov, chalov, sabzi, Bukhara plum qhorma, eggplant qhorma, and *bolony*. And obviously it depended on the season; if it was winter, there would be kichriqhoroot, batashlgham and things like that would be part of...

Lida: Very delicious food.

Sima: Indeed there was delicious food and good things.

Lida: You are a very good cook also, dear Sima.

Sima: By God, I try. However, to judge how good it is, depend on others' judgement. However, people who are interested in eating have to learn because nobody else would cook for you, except one would cook for her/himself.

Lida: They would serve food. Then what?

سیما: نانهای بسیار فوق العاده، باز راستی به روزیکه همین صبح عروسی که روز ناشتائی بود باز فامیل دختر همراه ناشتائی در جهیز و این گپهائیکه خودِ دختر برای خانهٔ شوهر خود در طول سالهای جوانی خود پس انداز کرده بود،.
فرضاً یک دختریکه جوان می شد از چهارده پانزده سالگی فرضاً بعضی وقتها می دید یگان سامان خانه یا یک چیزی خُوشِش می آمد آن را می خرید و نگاه می کرد یا اقلاً اگر خودش نمی کرد...

لیدا: اُو را جهیز می دادند.

سیما: هان، خودش اگر نمی کرد از حیا مادر و پدر عموماً آمادگی جهیز و جهیزهٔ دختر خود را پیش بین بودند و باز همراه ناشتائی جهیز دختر خود را هم روان می کردند که جهیز بسیار موضوع اش...

لیدا: مهم بود.

سیما: وسیع است، بعضیها اینطور جهیزی می دادند که حتی موتر هم می آوردند.

لیدا: بلی خانه هم می دادند.

سیما: خانه هم می دادند مگر وضع اقتصاد مردم آنقدر زیاد نبود آنطور نفرها به فیصدی هم نمیاید که آنقدر می دادند. منتها حد اقل به همان سطح.

لیدا: فامیل شاه.

سیما: هان. منتها به همان سطح اقتصاد خود تا جایکه برایشان اجازه داده می شد آرزوی هر پدر و مادر بود که یک جهیز بسیار آبرومند برای دختر خود بدهد.

لیدا: بلی.

سیما: مثلاً جای خواب بسیار فوق العاده که بخمل، بخمل بسیار خوبش و یا ساتن بسیار خوبش می بود. یا جای خواب فوق العاده می دادند، ظرف های روزمره مثل از اینکه اگر عروس نَو به کار خود شروع کند و آشپزخانه داشته باشد و جای یعنی کل چیزهایش.
باید دستش پیش کسی دیگر دراز نشود که برای من یک کاسه بده یا قاشق بده یا گلاس بده یا غوری ندارم یا اینها. همه چیزها را پدر و مادر دختر بقسم جهیز برایش می آوردند.

لیدا: بلی هان.

سیما: دیگر آن هم از جزء رواجهای بسیار مهم ما بود که جزء عروسی و ازدواج بود.

لیدا: بلی هان.

سیما: و البته باز بعد ازاینکه این گپها تیر می شد دیگر پای وازی ها شروع می شد.

Sima: Very special food. Then actually, at the morning of the wedding day when there was breakfast, the bride's family would take breakfast and jaiz and other things to her husband's house.

In her young period of time or when she was 15 years old, a girl would save some house appliances, something that she had liked and bought. At least, if she didn't … she didn't do it herself…

Lida: They would give them to her as jaiz.

Sima: The parents usually plan ahead for jaiz for their daughter and would send the jaiz along with breakfast. Because the jaiz issue was…

Lida: It was important.

Sima: It is big. Some people would even give a car as jaiz.

Lida: They would give a house too.

Sima: They would give houses, but people's economical situation was not that good. There was not one percent among the people who would give that much. However, at least in that level.

Lida: The groom's family.

Sima: However in that level, at their financial level that they could afford. Parents would wish to give their daughter something very honorable.

Lida: Yes.

Sima: For example, a very extraordinary sleeping bed, it would be bakhmal, very good bakhmal and very good satin. Or they would give an extraordinary sleeping bed. And they would give kitchen utilities for daily use. For example, the bride would start new in her kitchen work, so she had to have everything.

She should not depend on others, so she should not ask anyone to give me a bowl, or give me a spoon, or give me a glass, or give me a tray, or something else. The parents would bring all these things for their daughter as jaiz.

Lida: Yes indeed.

Sima: Then, one of the most important parts of the wedding in our culture is the jaiz.

Lida: Yes indeed.

Sima: Obviously, after these things were over, then paiwazi would be started.

لیدا: مردم مهمانی می کردند.
سیما: کُل قومی و خویشها روی نماگی می دادند دختر را فرضاً...
لیدا: روی نماگی چیست؟
سیما: روی نماگی به این معنی که مخصوصاً فامیل داماد که دختر را برای دفعهٔ اول می دیدند باید یک چیزی برایش تحفه می دادند، فرضاً یا یک انگُشترِ طلاه می دادند، نظر به اقتصادشان بود یا بعضی ها سامان خانه می آوردند یا لباسهای خوب می آوردند، جاکت و کرتی و...
لیدا: تازه می آوردند.
سیما: هان چیزهایکه هر چیزیکه نظر به اینکه چی وسع شان می رسید دیگر روی نماگی هم می دادند عروس را و پای وازی هم می کردند.
هر کس مجلس بسیار فوق العاده کلان می گرفت و نان پخته می کردند و چندین فامیل دیگر را هم دعوت می کردند. اگر وضع اقتصاد شان خوب می بود حتی ساز هم می گرفتند در این پای وازی ها.
لیدا: بلی، ترتیبات صحیح می گرفتند.
سیما: ترتیبات بسیار صحیح می گرفتند تا که باز زن دیگر بسرحدی می رسید که دیگر اولاد دار می شد و باز مرحلهٔ زنده گی از اُو دیگر دیگر قسم شروع می شد.
لیدا: بلی.

Vocabulary

رسم *n* custom, culture *n* drawing, art
قروق *adj* داغ گرم hot, warm *v* heating up
چارتر reserve
نانای *colloquial* غذاهای *n* variety of food, different dishes *n* variety of bread
شَوِ خینه the night of henna (night of the wedding ceremony)
پیش خَوری *n* rehearsal dinner (a night before the wedding)
چندین دست *colloquial* چندین جوره *adv* sets, jewelry sets
دست *colloquial* جوره *adj* set *n* hand
خَو *colloquial* خواب *n* *sleep*
شَوِ نکاح *adj* night of the wedding ceremony
ناشَتائی *n* breakfast
ماغوت *n* dessert
پدر سلامی *n* groom visits his father the day after the wedding
دامات سلامی *adj* groom visits his father the day after the wedding

Lida: People would have invitations.

Sima: All the relatives would give the bride rooynamagee, for example.

Lida: What is rooynamagee?

Sima: Rooynamagee means that, when relatives would see the bride for the first time, they would have to give her a gift, especially the groom's family. For example they would give a golden ring. It depended on their financial situations. Some people would bring house furnishings, or would bring clothes, a sweater or jacket and…

Lida: Would they bring new?

Sima: Indeed, they would bring according to what they could afford, and also they would give the bride rooynamagee and would do paiwazi.

Everyone would throw an extraordinary and big party and would cook food and would invite many families. If their economical situation was good they would even have a music band at the paiwazi.

Lida: They would have a great preparation.

Sima: They would have a great preparation, until, and then the bride would reach her time to have children. Her life period would start differently.

Lida: Yes.

نانا *colloquial* غذاها *n* variety of food, different dishes
جیز *colloquial* جهیز *n* a bride's personal property, exclusive of her dowry
کچری قروت *colloquial* *n* thick and mushy rice with lentils and yogurt sauce
ایا *colloquial* اینها *pro* their *prep* these
امو *colloquial* همان *prep* that, that much
بخمل *adj* velvet
ساتن *English* *adj* satin
اوم *colloquial* آن هم *phrase* also that
میمانی *colloquial* مهمانی *n* dinner invitation
روی نماگی *colloquial* *n* gifts that the groom's family members present to the bride for the first time they see her after the wedding
تازه *colloquial Persian* جدید، نو *adj* new *adj* fresh
صیی *colloquial Arabic* صحیح *adj* correct, proper, right *adj* complete

کار در امریکا[73]

سیما: من (مارگج) خانه ام را میدهم تنها پنج شش ساعت شب خواب می کنم باز دیگر نیستم، کار استم.
لیدا: کار استید دیگر بیست و چهار ساعت.
سیما: دیگر از آن خاطر است، که هیچ من پشت دیگر چیز نگردم.
لیدا: من هم هفته ای هفت روز کار میکنم منتها...
سیما: حالی هم کارت در خانه ات است یا میروی واشنگتن؟
لیدا: دفتر دارم سیما جان، به داخل (جورج تَون).
سیما: در واشنتن خو خو.
لیدا: بلی هان.
سیما: خی اینجا نمی کنی کار هان؟
لیدا: نی، تقریباً از دسمبر تا حالی به واشنتن کار می کنم.
سیما: خو خو، مستقل خودت یا..؟
لیدا: دفتر است منتها (سی و چهار هفده) یک نصف آفیس است، منتها تقسیم کردند بر دو.
سیما: خو خو.
لیدا: دیگر آفیسش خوب است منتها تنها دلیلیکه من آنجا رفتم نزدیک یونیورستی است، نزدیک جورج تَون یونیورستی است، می خواهم تبلیغات بکنم که همین شاگردهای مکتب بیایند آنجا.
سیما: خو.
لیدا: تا حالی البته سه چهارتا آمدند یک چیز دیگر هم است (ترول ایجنسی) دیگر هم است. رفتند آنجا قیمت کردند تکتها هفت صد دالر،پیش من آمدند سه صد چهارصد دالر.
سیما: که (ترول) کنند یا...؟ خوخو.
لیدا: چندتا تکت تا حالی فروختم منتها هنوز تبلیغات به آن صورت وسیع نکردم.

---

[73] In this selection the speakers are Sima and Lida. Sima finished university in Afghanistan and speacks the Kabuli dialect of Dari, Lida was born in Herat Afghanistan and emigrated to Iran at a very young age and then she came to the U.S. and she is a high school graduate. Lida speaks the Herati dialect of Dari, which is influenced by the Iranian Farsi.

Work in America

Sima: I pay my house mortgage. I sleep only six hours at night, then I am not home, and I will be at work.

Lida: Then you are at work 24 hours.

Sima: Because of that, then I don't have to look for anything.

Lida: I also work seven days a week.

Sima: Do you still work at home, or do you go to Washington?

Lida: I have an office in Georgetown, dear Sima.

Sima: In Washington. OK, OK.

Lida: Yes indeed.

Sima: So you don't work here anymore?

Lida: No, approximately, since September until now I have been working in Washington.

Sima: OK, OK. You by yourself or...

Lida: It is an office, however 3417 (address number) it is half of an office. However, they divided it into two.

Sima: OK, OK.

Lida: Other than that, the office is good; the reason why I am there is because the university is there. It is near Georgetown University. I advertise so school students come there.

Sima: OK.

Lida: Three or four came up to now. There is one more thing, one more travel agency. They went there and checked the price of tickets, they were seven hundred dollars. They came to me; it was three or four hundred.

Sima: So they can travel or? OK, OK.

Lida: I have sold some tickets, but I have not advertised that widely.

سیما: نشده خو.

لیدا: دیگر می خواهم آن کار را بکنم یک خواهرخوانده ام آن شب زنگ زده میگوید برو به جورج تَون یک صنف هم بگیر.

سیما: خو خو.

لیدا: بچه های جورجتون کلگی ملیونرهاستند.

سیما: خو خوب است.

لیدا: که دیگر کار هم نکنی.

سیما: که دیگر کار هم نکنی.

لیدا: میگوید من شَوهر خود را از چیز آشنا شدم و اینها، تو هم باید بِروی صنف بگیری.

سیما: خو از یونیورستی؟

لیدا: گفتم اگر صنف هم بگیرم. هان میگوید برو آنجا شاگردهای آنجا کلگی پیسه دار استند. گفتم در گیر من حتماً یک گدا می افتد.

سیما: طالع و بخت ما خوب نیست.

لیدا: اگر ملیونر هم باشد گدای ملیونر.

سیما: هان.

لیدا: دیگر همین چیزها.

سیما: خو حتماً پدرهای شان ملیونر است که بچه های خود را آنجا روان کرده، مگر باز بچه اش ملیونر است یا نی؟ اُو که نَو کالج را می خواند فکر نکنم اُو کمبخت هیچ چیز نخواهد داشت.

لیدا: خو دارد نی بابا من به نَوَد و پنج هم همراه جان بیرون می رفتم،

سیما: هان.

لیدا: شاگرد هم بود منتها اینقدر پیسه که اُو خرج می کرد،

سیما: راستی؟

لیدا: هیچ کس دیگر تا حالی سرمن پیسه خرج نکرده.

Sima: You have not (lit. it has not happend,) OK.

Lida: Then I want to do that. A girlfriend of mine called me last night and told me to go and take a class at Georgetown University.

Sima: OK, OK.

Lida: Georgetown boys are all millionaires.

Sima: OK, it is good.

Lida: So you don't have to work anymore.

Sima: So you don't have to work anymore.

Lida: She said that she met her husband there, here. So I have to take a class too.

Sima: OK, from the university?

Lida: I said if I take a class also. Yes, she is saying, "Go there; everyone is rich." Then I said, "I am sure I will get a beggar."

Sima: We don't have good luck and good fortune.

Lida: Even if he were a millionaire, he would be a beggar of a millionaire.

Sima: Indeed.

Lida: Then these things.

Sima: Obviously their fathers are millionaires that they sent their sons there.

Then, is their son a millionaire or not? Now that he's going to school, I don't think that (he) unfortunate would have anything.

Lida: OK, they do have. not at all, I used to go out with John in 95.

Sima: Indeed.

Lida: Even though he was a student, still he would spend a lot of money.

Sima: Is that right?

Lida: Nobody ever spent that much money on me.

سیما: خو، خو دیگر خی جورج تَون چیز هم میروی... جورج واشنتن یونیورستی.

لیدا: جورج واشنتن هم است جورج تَون هم است.

سیما: خو...

لیدا: تبلیغاتش را باید بکنم دیگر.

سیما: اگر به یونیورستی بروی درس بخوانی، چه می خوانی؟

لیدا: اگر من بخوانم چیزیکه من می خواهم بخوانم به کارم نمی خواند، من می خواهم لتریچر بخوانم، ادبیات.

سیما: هان می فهمم هان.

لیدا: بخاطر از اینکه به شعر و اینها زیاد علاقه دارم.

سیما: هان می فهمم.

لیدا: منتها چیزیکه پیسه می سازد (مارکیتنگ) است اگر بخوانم باید مارکیتنگ بخوانم که به همین چیز رشتۀ خودم کارم باشد.

سیما: خو خیر است از هردوش بخوان می توانی (میجرت) را (بزنس) بِگِیر منتها باز می توانی (لیتریچر) هم بگیری. من خودم (میجر)...

لیدا: شما به افغانستان؟

سیما: به افغانستان، بلی من چی است فاکولتۀ تعلیم و تربیه را خواندم رشتۀ انگلیسی.

لیدا: بر همین انگلیسی تان اینقدر خوب است.

سیما: (انگلش لیتریچر) هم، من (میجرم) (انگلش لیتریچر) بود. من که از فاکولته فارغ شدم باید معلم انگلیسی می شدم که گریختم از دست روس برآمدم. آمدم اینجا و خوبی اش این بود که اینجا که آمدم بسیار چانس آوردم که آماده بودم از نگاه لسان.

لیدا: بلی هان.

سیما: به نیویورک آمدم پیش از اینکه یک اپارتمان پیدا کنم اول بَرایم کار پیدا شد. خودم به هوتل بودم راستی میگویم. خودم به هوتل بودم پشت اپارتمان می گشتیم منتها یک نفر چیز کرد، که (بلوکراس بلوشیلد) نفر کار دارد به ایچی بود، تیلفون (انترویور) که برای داکترها (کلیم) و اینهایشان را چیز می کردیم. تا آخر ماه من در (بلوکراس بلوشیلد) کار خود را شروع کردم. (آی بی ام) کمپیوتر را (یوز) می کردم.

Sima: OK, OK. So you go to Georgetown thing...Georgetown University.

Lida: There is George Washington and there is Georgetown.

Sima: OK...

Lida: Then, I have to advertise.

Sima: If you go to the university, what would you study?

Lida: If I study, what I want to study, it would not match my work. I want to study literature, literature.

Sima: Yes, I know.

Lida: Because I like poems and things like that.

Sima: Yes I know.

Lida: However, what makes money is marketing. If I study I should study marketing, which would be part of my career and my work.

Sima: It is OK, study both, you can major in business; however, you can take literature also. I myself majored in...

Lida: You in Afghanistan?

Sima: Yes, in Afghanistan. I studied the thing, at the school of education and my major was English.

Lida: That is why your English is so good.

Sima: Also English literature, my major was English literature. When I finished college I was supposed to be an English teacher, but I escaped because of the Russians. I came here, and the good thing about here is that I was lucky because of the language.

Lida: Yes, indeed.

Sima: I came to New York; before I could find an apartment I found a job. I stayed at a hotel; I am telling the truth. I was in a hotel looking for an apartment, however someone did a thing, that Blue Cross /Blue Shield has an opening, it was a telephone interview to do the claims for doctors. By the end of the month I started my job at Blue Cross /Blue Shield. I used an IBM computer.

لیدا: بلی.

سیما: من هیچ فکر نمی کردم که در افغانستان که یک دوسال بعد من در کمپیوتر کار می کنم و می فهمم و جای خوب بود.

لیدا: کار تان خوب بود.

سیما: هان بسیار کار خوب بود خوش بودم بسیار. باز تا که اوربل شد.

لیدا: هان دیگر اولاددار شدی.

سیما: اوربل که شد یک دوسال خانه نِشستم باز آمدم وریجینیا.

لیدا: نیویورکَ خوش دارید دیگر.

سیما: نیویورک شهر بسیار خوب است. من باید دوباره پس بروم نیویورک. برای از اینکه نیویورک بسیار شهر پُرجمع وجوش است. من بسیار خوش دارمش. من از خاطر اولادهایم وریجینیا آمدم چون یک شهر بسیار آرام و چُپ و اینهاست منتها یک دفعه که این همین اولاد خوردم ایمل بخیر رفت کالج. باز این همین پلانم این است که اگر افغانستان تا آن وقت شرایط نشد.

لیدا: افغانستان نروید، نیویورک می روید.

سیما: اگر افغانستان نرفتم پس نیویورک میروم. برای از اینکه نیویورک بسیار شهر پُر جمع وجوش است. بسیار جای خوب و شهر زنده است مرا خوشم میآید نیویورک.

لیدا: من می خواهم کلیفورنیا بروم شما نیویورک می روید.

سیما: کلیفورنیا خوب است من هیچ وقت نرفته ام.

لیدا: هیچ نرفته اید در بیست سال؟

سیما: هیچ وقت، در این همین بیست سال من امریکاستم، کلیفورنیا نرفتم هنوز تا وقتیکه تکتها راستی (ناینتیناین) دالر شود.

لیدا: یکصدو پنجا هم میشود، شما باید بروید یگان وقت.

سیما: (روندترپ) میشود هان. چیز، من می خواهم بروم منتها یک موضوع است کسهایکه کلیفورنیا رفته،

لیدا: بلی.

سیما: زود دلزده شدند بخاطریکه فصل ها هیچ نیست.

Lida: Yes.

Sima: When I was in Afghanistan, I never thought that I would be learning and working with a computer two years later. And it was a good place.

Lida: Was your job good?

Sima: Yes, it was very good, I was very happy. Then until Orbal was borne.

Lida: Indeed, then you had children.

Sima: When Orbal was borne, I stayed home for a two-year period, then I came to Virginia.

Lida: You like New York then.

Sima: New York is a very good city. I should go back to New York because New York is a very lively city and I like it. I came to Virginia because of my children, and it is quiet and comfortable and these things. However, as soon as my youngest child, Aimal, goes to college and if Afghanistan's situation would not suit me, that is my plan.

Lida: Don't go to Afghanistan, you go to New York.

Sima: If I don't go to Afghanistan I will go to New York, because New York is a very lively city; it is a live city. I like New York.

Lida: I want to go to California and you want to go to New York.

Sima: California is good. I have not been there.

Lida: Have you not been in 20 years?

Sima: Never, in twenty years that I have lived in America I have not been to California yet. Until tickets become $99.

Lida: It comes down to $150. You have to go sometimes.

Sima: It would be round trip oh... The thing, I want to go, however, there is an issue that people who went to California...

Lida: Yes.

Sima: They are sick and tired of it because there are no seasons there.

لیدا: سیما جان فصل را چی میکنید در این خونکی. من از خانه نمی توانم برآیم.همین خونکی نباشد بهتراست. برف را چی می کنید؟

سیما: نی سیل کنِید، سیل کنید برف... برف نمی شود. هان برف نمی بارد. فرضاً تابستان عَرَق ریزان ندارد. آنجا کسهایکه است میگوید که ده سال هم که تیر شود ما فکر می کنیم هنوز یک سال نشده، برای از اینکه فصلها تغیر نمی کند.

لیدا: خو همانطور خوب است.

سیما: هان خو خوب است هان. من چون هیچ وقت نرفتیم این حالی خودم نمی فهمم که اگر من بروم آنخا خوشم میآیه یا نی.

لیدا: بلی هان.

سیما: برای از اینکه از نگاه فصل برای من بسیار خسته کن میشود، که اگر تابستان نیاید. باز ... خزان را من بی حد خوش دارم هیچ وقت خزا ن را آنها نمی بینند.

لیدا: بلی هان.

سیما: یا بهار را هیچوقت نمی بینند برای از اینکه همیشه آن در یک حالت است آن سبزه می ریزد دیگرش پس شروع میشود.

Vocabulary

مارگج *colloquial English* قسط *n* mortgage
مام *colloquial* من هم *phrase* I also, me too
آم *colloquial* هم *prep* also
ترول ایجنسی *colloquial English n* travel agency
خوارخوانديم *colloquial* خواهرخوانديم *n* my girlfriend (female friend of a woman)
مليونر *colloquial English adj* millionaire
تام *colloquial* تو هم *prep* also you
برِی *colloquial* بروی *v* you go
با بچیش *colloquial* باز بچه اش *phrase* then his son, their sons
کمبخت *adj* unfortunate person, poor guy
نخاد *colloquial* نخواهد *adv* may not
لتریچر *colloquial English* ادبیات *n* literature
می فامم *colloquial* می فهمم *v* I know, I understand
پیسه *colloquial* پول *n* money

Lida: Dear Sima, what are you going to do with the season in this cold? In this cold weather I cannot get out of the house. It is better without the cold. What are you going to do with the snow?

Sima: No, look, look it doesn't snow there. Oh... it doesn't snow there. For example it doesn't have a sweaty summer. People who live there say, "Even if would pass 10 years, it seems like it is not even one. It is because the seasons do not change."

Lida: OK, it is good like that.

Sima: OK, it is good, oh... Since I have never been there, now if I go there I don't know if I would like it or not.

Lida: Yes, indeed.

Sima: Regarding the seasons, it will be boring for me there. If the summer doesn't come... I extremely like fall; they would never see fall.

Lida: Yes indeed.

Sima: Or they would not see spring because it is always one condition there. The grass dies out and another starts growing.

بخان *colloquial* بخوان *v* you should study
میجرته *colloquial English* مسلکت را *n* your major
بزنس *colloquial English* تجارت *n* business
خوبیش *colloquial* خوبی اش *phrase* the good thing about it, it's good side
کلیم *colloquial English* ادعا مطالبه *v* claim
یوز *colloquial English* استعمال *v* use
پر جموجوش *colloquial* مزدهم *adj* lively, crowded
نرین *colloquial* نروید *v* do not go, you should not go
تکتا *colloquial* تکتها *n* the tickets
روند ترپ *colloquial English* دو طرفه *n* round trip
موضوعس *colloquial* موضوع است *phrase* there is an issue, there is a matter
نیایه *colloquial* نه آید *phrase* would not come

آ... ای *colloquial hesitation form* hesitation form 6

آبِ یخ *colloquial* آب سرد *n* cold water 6

اباتیش *colloquial* اباته اش *n her/his shelter and clothing* 44

اجازی رسمی *colloquial* اجازۀ رسمی *n* official permission 43

اچی *colloquial* چیز *prep* thing 37A

آخرا *colloquial* اواخر *adv* lately 42

آدمه *colloquial* آدم را *n, sing* to a person, to one's self, human, Adam, someone

ارتفایش *colloquial* ارتفاع اش *n* Its height 4

اس *colloquial* است *v, pres* is, to be 1

آستا آستا *colloquial* آهسته آهسته *adv* slowly 32

استن *colloquial* استند *v, pl* they are 1

استی *colloquial* هستی *v, pres* you are *v* being 1

استین *colloquial* استتید *v, pl* you (pl) are 1

آشَک *n* Afghan dish prepared with dough, leeks, "quroot," and served with yogurt sauce, similar to a dumpling 36

اقتصادی شام *colloquial* اقتصادی اش هم *phrase* also it is economical 1

اُقَدَر *colloquial* آنقدر *adv* that much 5

اِقَه *colloquial* اینقدر *adv* this much, that much 38

آلی *colloquial* حالا، فعلاً *adv* right now, now 27

ام *colloquial hesitation form* hesitation form 3

آم *colloquial* هم *prep* also 47

آمدین *colloquial* آمدید *past, pl* you came 1

اَمطو *colloquial* همان طور *adv, phrase* like that, that way 17

اَموجه *colloquial* همان جای *adv there, that place* 2

اَمی *colloquial* همین *adv* this one 2

آن *colloquial* خوب، بلی *adv, n* good, yes, OK 6

اُنا *colloquial* آنها *pro* they 22

اِنالی *colloquial* الآن، حالا *adv* now, now that 27

انتقال بته *colloquial* انتقال بدهد *phrase* to transport, to carry 13

اندوکش *colloquial* هندوکش *n* Hindu Kush the famous mountain range of Afghanistan 4

انشورنس *colloquial English* بیمه *n* insurance 42

اِنکَم *colloquial* عایداد *n* income 41

انگریزا *colloquial* انگلیسها *n* the British 35

آنموره *colloquial* همان را *adv, phrase* that thing, that object 8

اَنی *colloquial* یا نه *conj* isn't it?, or not? 2

اه *colloquial hesitation form* hesitation form 5

اَو *colloquial* آب *n* water 3

اُو *colloquial* آن that, that thing 7

اُو ... وی *colloquial exclamations of surprise* exclamations of surprise 5

او وخت *colloquial* آن وقت *adv* back then, that time 2

اَوار *colloquial* هموار *n* flat, laying flat 9

اورام *colloquial* آنرا هم *prep* then that, also that 2

اوشتکا *colloquial* اطفال *n* children 1

اوشتوکا *n colloquial* طفلها ، اطفال *n, pl* *children* 7

اوم *colloquial hesitation form* hesitation form 1

اَوم *colloquial* آن هم *phrase* also that 46

اُووا *colloquial* آنها *pro* they 29

ای *colloquial* این *adj, pro* this 1

ایا *colloquial* اینها *pro* their *prep* these 46

ایاره *colloquial* اینها را *pro* these, these things 6

ایبک *n* the capital city of Samangan province 5

ایره *colloquial* اینرا *adv* this thing, this 3

ایشه *colloquial* اینش را *adv* this one 45

ایقدر *colloquial* اینقدر *adv* this much 6

اینجه *colloquial* اینجا *adv, n* here, this place 1

اینطو *adv colloquial* این قسم ، اینطور *adv* this way, like this 7

اییا *colloquial* اینها *pro* these 29

با بچیش *colloquial* باز بچه اش *phrase* then his son, their sons 47

بار *colloquial* زندگی *n, sing* life *n* cargo, luggage 1

باشه *colloquial* باشد *v, sing* to be, is 1

باشین *colloquial* باشید *v, pl* you stay, you are, may you be, may you remain 1

باضی *colloquial* بعضی *n* some, few, portion 36

بانه *colloquial* بهانه *n* false excuse 8

باورت *n* your beliefs 41

بتانه *colloquial* بتواند *v* to be able 43

بچای *colloquial* بچه های *n* sons of 3

بچه والا *colloquial* فامیل شاه، فامیل بچه، boy's family, groom's family 8

بخان *colloquial* بخوان *v* you should study 47

بخمل *adj* velvet 46

بخیلم *colloquial* به فکر م، فکر میکنم، به خیالم *v, phrase* I think, I assume 36

بد می بُرد *colloquial* نفرت داشت *v* hated, was against 35

برتان *colloquial* برای تان *prep* for you, to you 1

بِرَسَن *colloquial* برسند *v* to get to do something, to get somewhere 45

برش *colloquial* برایش *prep* for him/her 40

بَرِش *phrase colloquial* برایش، برای او، بَرای آن *phrase* 1- for him/her/it *n* 2- its width 8

برف جنگی *colloquial* *n* snowball fight 37B

بِرَن *colloquial* بروند *v* they go 45

بِره *colloquial* بِرود *v* to go 9

بِری *colloquial* بروی *v* you go 47

بزنس *colloquial English* تجارت *n* business 42

بزنس *colloquial English* تجارت *n* business 47

بسازه *colloquial* بسازد *v* to make, to create 39

بغلان *n* a province in northern

Afghanistan 5

بِفامه *colloquial* بفهمد *v* to understand, to know 18

بگره *colloquial* بگیرد *prep* to happen, to become *v* to take 24

بلَد *colloquial* آشنا، وارد *adj* knowledgeable *n* city, town 36

بودک *colloquial* بود *v* was 41

بودن *colloquial* بودند *v, pl* they were 1

بورسی *colloquial French* یک بورس *n* scholarship 45

بوریه *colloquial* بوریا *n* reed mat 2

بیارن *colloquial* بیاورند 22

بیخی *colloquial* بکُلی، تماماً *adv* totally, completely *n* with the root 20

بیدر *colloquial* برادر *n* brother, pal 2

بیدرزادایم *colloquial* برادرزاده هایم *n* my nephews (my brother's sons and daughters) 3

بیس *colloquial English* اساس *n* base 41

بیس بال *colloquial n* baseball 32

پارت *colloquial English* جزء *n* part 41

پارتی *colloquial English* میهمانی، مجلس *n* party 39

پالوی *colloquial* پهلوی *prep* next to, beside 2

پُت پُت *colloquial* مخفیانه، پنهان *adv* secretly, concealed n close, coverd 37B

پَتُو *colloquial n* coarse woolen cloth use by men as an outer garment 31

پدر سلامی *n* groom visits his father the day after the wedding

پر جموجوش *colloquial* مزدهم *adj* lively, crowded 47

پرابلم *colloquial* مشکل *n* problem 44

پرایمنستر *colloquial English* صدر اعظم *n* prime minister 41

پرسان *colloquial* جویان، سوال *adj* questioning, inquisitive *n* question, inquiry 8

پسانا *colloquial* اواخر *adv* lately, later on 42

پسمانده *colloquial* عقب مانده *adj* undeveloped, left behind 5

پَو *colloquial* پاو *n* 0.985 pound 6

پوستای *colloquial English* پوسته های، مرکزهای *n* military posts, military bases 30

پیسه *colloquial* پول *n* money 47

پیسه *colloquial* پول، افغانی *n* currency, Afghani currency 2

پیش *colloquial* نزد *adv* from 7

پیش خوری *n* rehearsal dinner (a night before the wedding) 46

قهر پیشانیشان تُرش میشه *colloquial* میشوند، نا راحت میشوند *phrase* (lit. their foreheads would become sour) they will be unhappy 36

تا و بالا *colloquial v* to take care of the children putting down and lifting up 42

تازه *colloquial Persian* جدید، نو *adj* new *adj* fresh 46

تاقن *colloquial* طاقین *n an embroidered cap with curved top (often worn under a turban)* 31

تال *colloquial Arabic* معطل *adj* delayed *adj* postponed 36

تالی *adv* تا الآن، تا الحال yet, until now

45

تام *colloquial* تو هم *prep* also you 47

تانستن *colloquial* توانستند *v* were able, had the ability 35

تراژید *colloquial* غمناک *n* tragedy 38

ترمز ترمز *n* the border between Afghanistan and Uzbekistan 5

ترول ایجنسی *colloquial English n* travel agency 47

تکتا *colloquial* تکتها *n* the tickets 47

تکسیران *n* taxi driver 42

تکلیف می تُم *colloquial phrase* please pardon the trouble *phrase* 36

تکی *colloquial* تکه ای *n* fabric 11

تنا *colloquial* تنها *adj, adv, conj* only, just, alone 1

تورغندی *n* the border checkpoint between Afghanistan and Turkmenistan 28

توی *n colloquial Turkic* عروسی *n* wedding, wedding cermony 8

تیر *colloquial pash* خوب گذشت *adj* good, fun *adv* the act of passing, the act of crossing *n* an arrow, a dart *n* the fourth month of the Persian solar year 37B

تیر *colloquial* گذشتاندن *adv, n* the act of passing, the act of crossing *v* staying 1

تیروزرم *colloquial* عمل تیرورستی *n* terrorism 1

جزبازی *n* a children's game similar to hopscotch played with a (potshard) 37B

جمعیت *Persian* نفوس *n population*

جُنحه *colloquial* جنایی *adj criminal* 27

جیب خرچی *n* pocket money 42

جیز *colloquial* جهیز *n* a bride's personal property, exclusive of her dowry 46

چار *colloquial* چهار *n* four 4

چارتر reserve 46

چاغ *colloquial* چاق *adj* fat, a heavy person or animal 32

چانس *colloquial English* فرصت *adj* chance 45

چشم پُتَکان *colloquial n* hide and seek 37B

چشمای ما *colloquial* چشمهای ما *n, pl* our eyes 1

چقه *phrase colloquial* چقدر، چه اندازه *adv, phrase* how much 8

چندین دست *colloquial* چندین جوره *adv* sets, jewelry sets 46

چوطو *adv colloquial* چطور condition, how

چون و چرا *colloquial* شک *n* doubt 42

چیزا *colloquial* چیزها *n* things 1

چیزایتان *colloquial* چیزهای تان *n* your things 3

چیستک *colloquial* چی اس *phrase* what is 41

چیسته *colloquial* چی هست *phrase* what is it 43

حولی *colloquial* حویلی *n* house, courtyard 37B

خالیتان *colloquial* خالهٔ تان *n* your aunt 37B

خانمه *colloquial* خانم، زن *n* woman 37A

خانه *colloquial* فامیل *n* family *n* home, house 1

خانه داری *colloquial* کار خانه *n* housework *n* having a house *n* getting in bed with a spouse 42

خبرا *colloquial* خبرها *n* the news 20

خَو *colloquial* خواب *n* sleep 46

خو *colloquial* خوب *adv* good, OK, well 1

خوارخوانديم *colloquial* خواهرخوانديم *n* *my girlfriend (female friend of a woman)* 47

خواهرزاداره *colloquial* خواهرزاده هارا *n* my sister's children (sons and daughters) 40

خوبش *colloquial* قشنگ، زيبا، خوب *adj* beautiful, nice 5

خوبيش *colloquial* خوبى اش *phrase* the good thing about it, it's good side 47

خودام *colloquial* خود را هم *phrase* also my 40

خودتام *colloquial* خودت هم *phrase* also you, and you also 30

خى *colloquial* خوب، خير *adj, adv* good, well *adv* wishing good luck 8

د *colloquial* در *prep* in, at 1

دَاشِ *colloquial* در آن *phrase* in it, with it 37B

داره *colloquial* دارد *v, sing* it is happening *v, sing* to have, he/she has 1

دامات سلامى *adj* groom visits his father the day after the wedding

دبل *colloquial English* ضخيم *adj* thick, double 25

دختر والا *n* *colloquial* فاميل دختر، فاميل عروس *n* girl's family, bride's family 8

در دادن *v* *colloquial* آتش زدند ، به آتش كشيدند *v, pl, past* they burned them 7

در صد *colloquial* فيصدى *adv* percentage 45

دست *colloquial* جوره *adj* set *n* hand 46

دستک *n* round beam, girder (used in roofing) 25

دستهاره ور ميزنيم *colloquial phrase* I will fold up my sleeves 36

دفه *colloquial* دفعه، مرتبه *adv* degree, grade, periods of time 8

دق *adj* sad, depressed 40

دكانا *n* *colloquial* دكانها *n, pl* stores, shops 7

دُگام *colloquial* ديكر هم *phrase* and also, in addition to that *adv* more 27

دگه *colloquial* ديگر *adj, adv* other, else *adv* then 1

دگى *colloquial* ديگر باقيمانده، *adv* other, the rest of 7

دگى *colloquial* ديگرى *adv* other, another, the rest of 2

ده بورى *n* name of a district in Kabul 37A

ده مسكين و رباط *n* name of two villages in northern Kabul 31

دوتايش *colloquial* دو نفر، ايشان، دونفر آنها *phrase* two of them 37B

دوستها *colloquial* دوستا *n* friends, relatives 1

ديدين *colloquial* ديده ايد *v, pl* you have seen 5

ديگيش *colloquial* ديگرش، ديگراش *adv* the other one 14

دیوال *colloquial* دیوار *n* wall 2

رائی *colloquial* روان *n* sending 30

رستورانت *colloquial English* رستوران *n* restaurant 42

رسم *n* custom, culture *n* drawing, art 46

رفتین *colloquial* رفته اید *v, pl* you have gone 5

رفیقا *colloquial* رفیقها *n,adj, pl* friends 1

ره *colloquial* را postposition used after definite direct object 20

روند ترپ *colloquial English* دو طرفه *n* round trip 47

روی نماگی *colloquial* *n* gifts that the groom's family members present to the bride for the first time they see her after the wedding 46

ریفوجیهای *colloquial English* مهاجرین *n* the refugees 45

زنگ نمی زدشه *colloquial* زنگ نمی زد آنرا *phrase* it would not rust 6

زیر *colloquial* تحت *prep* below, beneath, under 1

ژورنالست *colloquial English* خبرنگار *n* journalist 38

سات *colloquial* ساعت *adv* an hour *n* a watch 6

سات تیری *colloquial* ساعت تیری *n* playing, amusement, having a good time 3

ساتن *English adj* satin 46

ساتیری *colloquial* تفریح *n* entertainment, having a good time 32

سازای *colloquial* سازهای، موسیقیهای *n* music 32

سازه *colloquial* سازد *v, sing* to make, to turn into 1

سپین بولدک *pash n* a border checkpoint between Afghanistan and Pakistan 28

ستنگر *n* stinger missile 35

سخته *colloquial* سخت را *adj* the dificult one 3

سر *colloquial* توسط *adv* by, with *n* head 3

سر *colloquial* سقف *n* roof, top, ceiling 1

سرخ *colloquial* *v* sauté *n* red 36

سردستی *colloquial* کار آسان خانه *phrase* easy housework, light housework 3

سرش *colloquial* بالای آن *adv* over it, on top of it 25

سرم *colloquial* برایم *phrase* for me, to me, on me 40

سروی *English n* survey 23

سطح پایین *colloquial* طبقۀ پایین *n* low class 42

سلامالیکم *phrase religion colloquial* السلام علیکم *phrase* Islamic greeting (May peace be upon you) 1

سلَری *colloquial English* معاش *n* salary 41

سیستم *colloquial English* شیوه، منظومه *adj, n* system 28

سَیل کُو *colloquial* ببین *imperative v* look, see 38

سینما *English n* cinema 43

شاره *colloquial* شارد *v* worn away 25

شاگردا *colloquial* شاگردها *n* students 2

شان *colloquial* ایشان *pro* they 1

شش نفر، شش شخص *colloquial* ششتا *phrase* six siblings, six persons (تا used between number and countable nouns) 39

ششتن *colloquial* نشستن *v* sitting 12

ششتیم *colloquial* نشستیم *v* we used to sit 2

شف *English* آشپز *n* chief 42

شق *colloquial* رشته، مسلک *n* hobby *n* major 34

شمالی *colloquial* شمالی *n* a region five miles north of the capital Kabul 4

شَوِ خینه the night of henna (night of the wedding ceremony) 46

شَوِ نکاح *adj* night of the wedding ceremony 46

شینگرس *colloquial pashtoo* شی گرز *n* right turn (military term), right face 21

صبا *colloquial* فردا *n tomorrow n* morning 36

صحتتن *n colloquial* صحت تو، صحت شما *n+pron* your health 1

صیی *colloquial Arabic* صحیح *adj* correct, proper, right *adj* complete 46

ضیف *colloquial* ضعیف *adj* weak 1

ضیفی *colloquial* ضعیفی *adj*, *n* weakness 1

طفلا *colloquial* طفلها *n* children 3

عام مردم *n colloquial* مردم عام commn people, ordinary people, public 7

فیشنی *colloquial English adj* fashionable 39

فیننس *colloquial* تجدید قسط *n* finance 40

قدیفه *n* a kind of cloth sheet used by men in Afghanistan as and outer garment *n* bath towel 6

قروق *adj* گرم داغ hot, warm *v* heating up 46

قندار *colloquial* قندهار *n* Kandahar (one of Afghanistan's largest cities) 5

قندوز *colloquial* کُندُز *n* a province in northern Afghanistan 25

کارتی چار *colloquial* کارتهٔ چار *n* a small district in Kabul 45

کاریز *colloquial* کاریز *n* underground tunnels dug to transport water, over 10 miles. Collected from the base of wetter mountains and delivered to drier basins to provide water for irrigation and domestic use. These tunnels, called Karaze, have supplied a significant portion of consumptive water in Afghanistan for many centuries. The mounds result from numerous vertical shafts used by workers to keep the water flowing. 4

کَتِ *colloquial* همراه *adv* with 6

کَتِ *colloquial* همراه، با *adv* with 30

کتابای *colloquial* کتابهای *n* thier book, books 2

کَتیِش *colloquial* همرایش *adv* with it 36

کچری قروت *colloquial n* thick and mushy rice with lentils and yogurt sauce 46

کرمبول *n* carom 37B

کفرج *colloquial English* مورد بیمه n coverage 42

کلانا *n colloquial* بزرگان ، بزرگواران ، ریش سفیدان *n, pl* elders, great men, great women, well respected old people or adults 7

کلچر *colloquial English* کلتور، فرهنگ *n* culture 36

کلش *colloquial* کل ایشان *phrase* they all, all of them 1

کُلَش *colloquial* همه اش تمام اش *adv, phrase* all of them 10

کلک *colloquial* کلک *n* a game played with a short pice of wood (the size of a pen) and a bat 3

کلگی *colloquial* همه *prep* all, everyone 1

کُلّه *colloquial* همه *pro* everyone, all 37A

کلیم *colloquial English* ادعا مطالبه *v* claim 47

کمبخت *adj* unfortunate person, poor guy 47

کمرشکست *colloquial* کم پول *n* broke 43

کَمَکی واری *colloquial* کمی *n* like a little 36

کنترول *colloquial English* تداوی *n* treatment, control 1

کنترول *colloquial English* تسلط *n* control, supervision 24

کنده باشیش *v colloquial* کنده باشد اش، کنده باشد آنرا *past* he/she has picked it 7

کنسرت *English n* concert 43

کنگینه *n colloquial* کنگینه *n, sing* container made of clay to keep grapes fresh in the fall and winter 7

کوچ *colloquial n* coach 34

کونش *colloquial* زیر *n* bottom 37B

کونه *colloquial* کند *v, sing* do, to do 1

کینگرس *colloquial pashtoo* کینگرز *n* left turn (military term), left face 21

گپ تند *colloquial* سخن سخت، تند گفتن، سخن تند *adj, n* rough talk 8

گپ نرم *colloquial* سخن نرم *adj* nicely speaking 8

گپا *n colloquial* چیزها *n* things, stories *n* talks 7

گدوبدی *colloquial* برهم خوردن، نا آرامی *adj, n* unrest, instability 22

گُردآلو *colloquial* آلو *n* plum 10

گریلائی *colloquial English* چریکی، پارتیزان *adj, n* guerilla 22

گلَمشانه جمع کرد *colloquial* شکست داد *v, phrase* defeated them, V, *phrase* fold their carpet or rug 35

گنشیپ *colloquial n* gunship helicopter 35

گَو *colloquial* گاو *n* cow, bull, ox 26

گُوپیچه *colloquial n* warm pants with a lining filled with cotton (people wear then in northern Afghanistan) 31

گوشتشه *colloquial* گوشتشرا ، گوشت آنرا *possessive phrase* its meat 7

گوشی *colloquial* گوشهٔ *n* part, corner 1

لاله *colloquial n* a polite word used for a Hindu male in Afghanistan 39

لتریچر *colloquial English* ادبیات *n* literature 47

لشپی بازی *colloquial* لشپاک بازی، جزبازی *n* a children's game similar to hopscotch played with a (potter shard) 37B

لگن *colloquial* تشت *n* tub, tray 37B

مابینش *colloquial* در بینش *prep* inside(n, pron), in 2

مارگج *colloquial English* قسط *n* mortgage 47

ماس *colloquial* ماست *n* yogurt 26

ماغوت *n* dessert 46

مالوم *colloquial* معلوم *adj* known, visible, clear 3

مام *colloquial* من هم *phrase* I also, me too 47

ماند *colloquial* مانده *v* is left, remains 7

مِتَن *colloquial* میدهند *v* they would give 28

مچم *colloquial* مه چه میدانم *v, phrase* I don't know 2

مخصد *colloquial* مقصد *n* aim, goal, purpose 2

مکرونی *colloquial English* *n* macaroni 36

مگم *colloquial* مگر *conj* but, besides that 1

ملیونر *colloquial English adj* millionaire 47

منجه *colloquial* منبَع *n* source 17

منطقی *colloquial* منطقه ای *n* region, area 4

مه *colloquial* من *pro* I 3

مه *colloquial* من *pro* I, me 20

موّ *colloquial* همان *prep* that, that much 46

موضوعس *colloquial* موضوع است *phrase* there is an issue, there is a matter

می بَرَن *colloquial* انتقال می برند، میدهند *v* they would transport, they would carry 28

می پرتافتیم *colloquial* جمع می کردیم، می انداختیم *v* we used to collect *v* we used to throw 2

می خاند *colloquial* می خوانند *past, pl* they studied 1

می خورد (lit. used to eat) *colloquial* می دزدید *v* used to stell 2

می رُم *colloquial* می روم *v* I will go, I would go 30

می رَن *colloquial* می روند *v, fut* they go, they will go 1

می شِشت *colloquial* می نشست *v* would sit, used to sit 2

می ششتن *colloquial* می شستند 6

می شه *colloquial* می شود *v, fut* will become, will be done, will happen 1

می طلبیست *v colloquial* می طلبید طلب میکرد would ask for, was asking for 8

می فامم *colloquial* می فهمم *v* I know, I understand 47

می گرفتیم *colloquial* می خریدیم *past* we would buy *past* we would take 6

می گفتن *colloquial* می گفتند *past, pl* they would say, they said 1

می گِی *colloquial* میگوئی *v* you are talking about 20

می ماندن *colloquial* می گذاشتند *v, pl* they put, they would put 2

می مانیم *colloquial* می گذاریم *v* we will let, we will wait *v* we will lay, we will put, we will allow 36

می وَرداشتن *colloquial* میبرداشتند، جمع میکردند *v* they would harvest 32

میایم *colloquial* میآیم *v, pres, pl* we are coming, we will come 1

میتن *colloquial* میدهند *v* they would give 15

میجرته *colloquial English* مسلکت را *n* your major 47

میرم *colloquial* میروم *v, pres, pl* we are going, we will go 1

میری *colloquial* میروید، میروی *v, pres, sing* you (sing) are going, you will go 1

میزنن *colloquial* میزنند، میگویند *v* they would say, they would tell 13

میگُ *colloquial* میگوید *v* he/she would say 30

میگن *colloquial* میگویند *v, pl* it has been said, they say 5

میگه *colloquial* میگوید *v* he/she says 8

میگویمشه *colloquial* آنرا یاد میکنیم *phrase* we call it 3

میمانی *colloquial* مهمانی *n* dinner invitation 46

نائب آباد *n* a district in northern Afghanistan 5

ناشتائی *n* breakfast 46

نان *colloquial* غذا *n* food *n* bread 30

نانا *colloquial* غذاها *n* variety of food, different dishes

نانای *colloquial* غذاهای *n* variety of food, different dishes *n* variety of bread 46

نانه *colloquial* غذا را *n* food, dish, dinner or lunch 36

نباشه *colloquial* نباشد *v, sing* not to be 1

نتانست *colloquial* نتوانست *v, phrase* was not able to, could not 38

نخاد *colloquial* نخواهد *adv* may not 47

نخت *colloquial* نقد *n* cash 16

نداره *colloquial* ندارد *v, sing* does not have 1

نداره *colloquial* ندارد *v, sing* will not, does not have 1

نرفتی *colloquial* نرفته ای *past* didn't you go? you didn't go 5

نرفتیم *colloquial* نرفته ام *past* I have not gone 5

نرین *colloquial* نروید *v* do not go, you should not go 47

نشدین *colloquial* نشدید *past, pl* you did not become, you did not get 1

نَشَه *colloquial* نشود *v* would not happen *v* should not happen 30

نگه *colloquial* نگاه *v* keeping *v* looking 6

نمی تانن *colloquial* نمی توانند *v, phrase* they are not allowed *v, phrase* they are not able, they can't 38

نمی ره *colloquial* نمیرود *v, sing* would not go, will not go 1

نیایه *colloquial* نه آید *phrase* would not come 47

همشیرایتان *colloquial* همشیره هایتان *n* your sisters 37B

همه گی *colloquial* همه *prep* all, everyone 1

هَمو *colloquial* همان *adv* that, that very 5

هموطو *colloquial* همان طور *adj* like that, that way 5

همیالی *colloquial* الآن، حالا *adv* now, right now 36

همیجه *colloquial* همینجا، اینجا *prep*

here 37A

همیس *colloquial* همین است، این است *v* this is it, this is 28

هوار *colloquial* هموار *adj, n* flat, level 5

هوشار *colloquial* هوشیار *adj* smart, intelligent 21

وارخطا *colloquial pash adj* nervous, confused, hesitant 37B

واری *colloquial* مانند، مثل *prep* like, same as 5

واقس *colloquial* واقع است *v* is located 4

وخت *colloquial* وقت *adv, n* time, period, moment *adv* early 1

وختا *colloquial* وقتها *adv* recently *adv* times, sometimes 1

وختا *colloquial* وقتها *adv* periods, times 1

وختر *colloquial* وقتر, زوتر *adv* earlier 36

یاد نگره *colloquial* اگر یاد نگیرد *v, phrase* if he/she would not learn 38

یاف *colloquial* یافت، دریاب *n* finding, obtaining 30

یکچند روز *colloquial* یک مدت، برای چند روز *adv, phrase* a few days, for a while 1

یکچندروز *colloquial* یک مدت، برای چند روز *adv* a few days, for awhile 1

یکیش *colloquial* یکی، یکی ازآنها *adv* one of them 5

یَنَه *colloquial* اینک *adv* here it is. 8

یوز *colloquial English* استعمال *v* use 47